ACE Your Life

A clearly written, step by step, and research-based guide to life transformation. It simplifies without talking down; guides without being bossy. A fun and helpful ride that will stick with you. Definitely worth the read.

    Steven C. Hayes, Ph.D., Foundation Professor of Psychology, University of Nevada, Reno, Originator of *Acceptance and Commitment Therapy*, and Co-developer of *Process-Based Therapy*. Author of 47 books including *A Liberated Mind, Get Out of Your Mind and Into Your Life*, and nearly 670 scientific articles.

Dr. Maidenberg nailed it! She has distilled substantive personal change into three key ingredients—acceptance, compassion and empowerment. Her approach is scientifically-supported and it puts change on the foundation of self-understanding and self-kindness. Before you take on another self-improvement project, please read this book.

    Christopher Germer, Ph.D., Lecturer on Psychiatry, Harvard Medical School, author of *The Mindful Path to Self-Compassion*, and Co-developer, *Mindful Self-Compassion* program.

Dr. Michelle Maidenberg's book, *ACE Your Life*, is an inspiring and helpful guide that will help you accept yourself and others, have more compassion for your vulnerabilities, and empower you to accomplish valued goals. We often find that our own thinking and habits have become the major obstacles to getting what we want. This book will help you overcome obstacles within yourself and obstacles that you face in the real world. Sometimes we must go through it to get past it and the journey is challenging. This book is what you will need to get your life back.

    Robert L. Leahy, Ph.D., Director of the American Institute for Cognitive Therapy and Clinical Professor of Psychology in Psychiatry at Weill-Cornell University Medical School. Author of *If Only…Finding Freedom from Regret, Don't Believe Everything You Feel, The Jealousy Cure, Beat the Blues Before They Beat You, Anxiety-Free: Unravel Your Fears before They Unravel You, The Worry Cure: Seven Steps to Stop Worry from Stopping You.*

Recognizing that perfection is a figment of our overactive imagination, Dr. Michelle Maidenberg developed an ingenious method to identify ways of acceptance, compassion and empowerment (ACE). Actualizing the ACE method puts you in the driver's seat like never before. Exceptionally well written, *ACE Your Life*, will motivate and guide you to make fundamental changes in your life which will make you fulfilled and proud.

> **Ruth Gotian, EdD, MS**, Thinkers50 #1 emerging management thinker in the world and author of *The Success Factor*. Chief Learning Officer and Assistant Professor of Education in Anesthesiology at Weill Cornell Medicine.

If you want to change behavior and become the version of yourself you most wish to be, acting with self-compassion and commitment is the royal road to realization. Michelle's book beautifully illuminates this path.

> **Dennis Tirch, Ph.D.**, Founding Director, The Center for Compassion Focused Therapy and Associate Clinical Professor, Mt. Sinai Medical Center. Author of *Compassionate-Mind Guide to Overcoming Anxiety: Using Compassion-Focused Therapy to Calm Worry, Panic and Fear*, *The Compassionate Mind Approach to Overcoming Anxiety*.

Is acceptance a fall back strategy? No! In this book, Dr. Michelle Maidenberg serves as a thoughtful and encouraging guide to learning how to accept yourself, embrace your values, and be empowered to act toward what's most important to you. It's chock full of exercises, strategies, and stories that you can use to be your best self.

> **Jason B. Luoma, Ph.D.**, CEO, Portland Psychotherapy – Clinic, Research, and Training Center and Affiliate Faculty, Oregon Health and Science University Associate Scientist, Oregon Research Institute. Author of *Values in Therapy* and *Learning ACT*.

The pressures and uncertainties of everyday life make it is far too easy to lose touch with what keeps us resilient, happy and strong. Integrating valuable psychological research with practical and proven exercises (along with lots of engaging graphics), Michelle Maidenberg's *Ace Your Life* allows you to reconnect with your best intentions and live an easier and more empowered life.

> **Mark Bertin MD**, Developmental Pediatrician, Assistant
> Professor of Pediatrics at New York Medical College, and
> on the faculty of the Windward Teacher Training Institute.
> Author of *Mindful Parenting for ADHD, The Family ADHD
> Solution, Mindfulness and Self-Compassion for Teen ADHD,
> How Children Thrive.*

ACE Your Life is a gem. Dr. Michelle Maidenberg uses evidence-based research and her vast clinical knowledge to guide the reader through barriers and practical implementable strategies so they can truly ACE their life. Acceptance, compassion, and empowerment is the key, and understanding the barriers and how to overcome them unlocks the door to living the life we all want. *ACE Your Life* is an essential and inspirational read if you want to make progress, forge ahead, and cultivate a meaningful life.

> **Marci G. Fox, Ph.D.**, Licensed Psychologist and author of
> *Think Confident, Be Confident for Teens, The Think Confident,
> Be Confident Workbook for Teens.*

This is such an important book. With this clearly and beautifully written work, Dr. Maidenberg has captured the essence of how anyone can feel good in today's world. She has identified the elements that keep people stuck in the ruts that keep them unfulfilled and provides a clear roadmap to long-term substantiative change. With her warm, engaging style, she provides practical exercises that immediately change how one can see him or herself differently. She has created a new and unique system to feel good.

> **Robert S. Schachter, Ed.D.**, Licensed Psychologist and
> Assistant Clinical Professor, Department of Psychiatry Icahn
> School of Medicine at Mount Sinai. Author of *Mindfulness
> for Stress Management: 50 Ways to Improve Your Mood and
> Cultivate Calmness.*

Dr. Maidenberg takes a unique approach to self-help with her comprehensive guide to personal growth and self-fulfillment. With the world facing adversity and many searching for new ways to cope, *ACE Your Life* could not be more timely. Its emphasis on breaking the cycle of stuckness seems particularly salient now, in the midst of a pandemic—where boredom and fear of the future reign. Individuals and clinicians alike will find this guide useful. Having it on hand is like having a life coach nearby, whenever you need one.

> **Ann Goelitz, Ph.D., LCSW**, Psychotherapist and author of *From Trauma to Healing,* now in its second edition, and *Shared Mass Trauma in Social Work.*

If you are stuck, *ACE Your Life* is exactly what you need to figure out how to move forward to live our best lives. Dr. Maidenberg offers a three-pillared approach to build self-acceptance, compassion and empowerment. It isn't easy to take a hard look at our values, past trauma, coping mechanism and barriers. But with the help of *ACE Your Life*, Dr. Maidenberg takes the reader through the steps with a great deal of support. In the end, the reader is in a much healthier space to live life to the fullest.

> **Catherine Pearlman, Ph.D., LCSW**, is The Family Coach* and author of *Ignore It!* Assistant Professor at Brandman University and writes the nationally syndicated "Dear Family Coach" column.

With relatable stories, powerful exercises and state-of-the-art tools, Dr. Maidenberg's well-written book expertly provides both an inspiring and practical guide to living a more psychologically rich life. An essential boost of hope and a proven path for change in today's challenging times!

> **Michelle Brody, Ph.D.**, Licensed Psychologist and Executive Coach. Author of *Stop the Fight! An Illustrated Guide for Couples* and *Own Your Armor: Revolutionary Change for Workplace Culture.*

ACE
YOUR
LIFE

Unleash Your Best Self
and Live the Life You Want

MICHELLE P.
MAIDENBERG
PH.D., MPH, LCSW-R

NEW YORK

LONDON • NASHVILLE • MELBOURNE • VANCOUVER

ACE YOUR LIFE

Unleash Your Best Self and Live the Life You Want

Published in New York, New York, by Morgan James Publishing. Morgan James is a trademark of Morgan James, LLC. www.MorganJamesPublishing.com

Proudly distributed by Ingram Publisher Services.

Morgan James BOGO™

A **FREE** ebook edition is available for you or a friend with the purchase of this print book.

CLEARLY SIGN YOUR NAME ABOVE

Instructions to claim your free ebook edition:
1. Visit MorganJamesBOGO.com
2. Sign your name CLEARLY in the space above
3. Complete the form and submit a photo of this entire page
4. You or your friend can download the ebook to your preferred device

ISBN 9781631958540 paperback
ISBN 9781631958557 ebook
Library of Congress Control Number:
2021952396

Cover Design by:
Rachel Lopez
www.r2cdesign.com

Interior Design by:
Chris Treccani
www.3dogcreative.net

Morgan James is a proud partner of Habitat for Humanity Peninsula and Greater Williamsburg. Partners in building since 2006.

Get involved today! Visit MorganJamesPublishing.com/giving-back

This is dedicated to the women warriors in my life who have all passed on but whose presence is forever in my heart through all my life's journeys. They continue to inspire me by all they modeled to me. They embodied authenticity, being with what is, and never forgetting who they fundamentally were and where they came from. I miss and love you deeply—Irene Berger, Rose Farkas, Margaret Gibelman, Mrs. Krieger, Augusta Sentizer and Selma Turkel. I am so blessed to have known you and to have learned so much from you.

TABLE OF CONTENTS

FOREWORD

Have you ever been on a train or airplane and sat next to a person who was just incredibly exciting and informative? Time runs by in a heartbeat. It's as if the trip ends too early. So much to learn. So engaging.

You say to yourself, *I was lucky today.*

Enter Michelle Maidenberg, PHD. This book, **ACE Your Life** is, of course, a double entendre. The *ACE Method* is intelligent and can change your life. The author frames acceptance, compassion and empowerment in just the right way to help us truly think differently.

It's so well done that as I read this work—truth be told—my mind began to shift. We have here a gifted healer practicing her craft. *For me, the read was a gift.*

At a deeper level, Dr. Maidenberg speaks to us, in some ways showing rather than telling, that we all possess a power to ace our lives; a power to be tapped with a just slight change of thinking. Power over ourselves, over our perceptions of others, over injuries of the past—*and over what is to come.*

This is a competent person. A capable person. A person who has taken the best of what she's learned over the years and granulated it into a book that is so easy to read, that you'll wonder why you never quite thought this way before.

Dr. Maidenberg teaches self-awareness about core values; about a form of acceptance that's radically liberating. Who wants, for instance, to be bitter anymore? It only gives power to the person you're angry with—and leaves you diminished.

She teaches about compassion. First towards yourself and then widens it to others. How to set healthy limits. How to begin detoxifying past injuries that no longer serve. *As a psychiatrist I often suggest to patients that the next 10 years are infinitely more important than the last 10 years.* Yet many of us seem to be dragged back incessantly. Negative self-talk, cycles of procrastination, repeating bad patterns.

Dr. Maidenberg helps us move forward.

Then, there's empowerment, A methodology that allows you to cultivate a new way of being. Imagine once again you're on the train or plane with that special person. Not only have you had an important conversation. But you walk away with concrete steps about what you can do to change your life.

ACE Your Life is not really a book. It's a course in how to live a better, freer life with worksheets, good questions and a methodology for empowering and sustaining progress. Dr. Maidenberg helps us to reframe past hurts, confront tired habits, deal more constructively with disappointment and see into the future with optimism.

A breath of fresh air. An important contribution.

It's funny. While writing this Foreword I was struggling with a particular problem. After reading *ACE Your Life* the problem had repositioned to a much better perspective.

I felt lighter.

Step-by-step.

I think you'll feel lighter too.

Mark Banschick MD

Child, Adolescent and Adult Psychiatrist, New York & Connecticut

Psychology Today Blogger

Cofounder of the Katonah Study Group of Integrative Medicine

Cofounder of Alums for Campus Fairness

INTRODUCTION

Transforming Your Life

Are you truly being your best self and
living the life you want to be living?

t's safe to say most of us *want* to do this—we want to be intentional, pro-active, confident, successful, and present, so we can fully experience each moment. But if we're being honest, all too often we allow our thoughts and feelings to drive and constrain us. We become remiss, reactive, complacent, and trapped by our inner commentator, our habitual patterns of behavior, and what we've learned within our social-cultural structures throughout our lives. We're unable to break free from patterns and monotony, bogged down in the "stuckness."

We have regrets. Our relationships might be strained. Other parts of our life suffer. Our self-worth and our confidence take a nosedive. We wonder where we went wrong and wish we could have a do-over. Sometimes we're so anxious, overwhelmed and exasperated; we get stuck in our own head and can't see a way out. We may feel confused or lack the focus to strategize and plan. We may be left feeling hopeless and helpless, doubtful our circumstances can ever change.

As a psychotherapist, I work with individuals who face a wide variety of situations and challenges. Some want general coping strategies to deal with everyday issues that they face. This can include navigating relationships, strategizing business and career problems, improving behavior and developing new habits, enhancing health and well-being, reducing stress, and functioning better. Some patients struggle with their mental health, while others experience a wide range of traumas—lost relationships, death of a loved one, unexpected diagnoses, and the chaos and uncertainty of a global pandemic. I am honored to provide a safe space for people to be seen, heard, and validated, as I help them discover internal resources to put them in the driver's seat and make the changes they want.

I've developed the *ACE Method* for behavior change to facilitate being our best selves and living the life we want based on the pillars of *Acceptance*, *Compassion*, and *Empowerment*.

"ACE" DEFINED

ACCEPTANCE
Self-acceptance is embracing who we truly are without expectations, conditions, or qualifications. We are all good enough.

COMPASSION
Having compassion means noticing, feeling emotionally moved, and responding to our own suffering as well as others'.

ACCEPTANCE

COMPASSION

EMPOWERMENT

EMPOWERMENT
Empowerment is the ability to recognize we are in control of our own decisions, and ultimately our own lives, and we are taking direct action toward our values and goals.

I've seen incredible change happen—absolute miracles—as patients rediscover their own values, their own truths, their own intrinsic worth.

They work to create a new reality where they finally turn down the volume on their inner critic, take control of their lives, and truly are their best selves. One where they are excited to wake up and face the day. One where they see themselves making real progress toward their goals. They are healthier physically, mentally, and emotionally and they have learned to be more gracious and kinder to themselves and others.

I'm not advocating for perfection—there's no such thing. Our humanness doesn't allow for it, and in any case, mistakes and failures give us experience and pivotal life lessons. But there is always the opportunity for substantial enhancement and progress. *We want to strive for progress, not perfection, and inevitable permanence of value-driven behaviors.*

I believe each one of us deserves to live fully and authentically. The ACE Method entails walking myself, patients—and now readers—along the roadmap step-by-step, with inspiring stories, examples, and self-reflective exercises along the way. The beauty of ACE is that I'm not the one with the answers; I'm just the friendly guide providing direction and encouragement. The answers lie within your own heart and mind. They always have. And they always will. You will observe your inner commentator evolve into an inner coach, inner advocate, and inner nurturer.

I include *unleash* in the title purposefully. The capability and power are already within you. To use that power, you must reach into your internal reserve and unleash it. It gets repressed or suppressed for a reason, typically a very good one. Your inner power helped you survive; it was never fostered; or you were in circumstances that didn't allow you to acquire the skills to access your power. It's not your fault, but as an adult, if you want a better or different life, you have the capability to do so. You become responsible for your own growth and healing. It's empowering to know that the magic is within you, and you don't need to rely on other people or anything outside of yourself to enhance you. With openness, flexibility, and curiosity, you can unleash your self-belief, self-love, and self-compassion.

WHO CAN BENEFIT FROM THIS BOOK?

It is far more meaningful and sustaining when a person works toward personal growth and life enhancement and reaches "aha moments" on their own. The journey to a more fulfilling life begins with the willingness to look within, to uncover what we believe and why, to rediscover our core truths and values, and then to align our actions and mindset accordingly. Because we are all intrinsically worthy, we *all* deserve this chance.

ACE Your Life: Unleash Your Best Self and Live the Life You Want is my approach to creating a life and legacy of fulfillment and love for yourself and others. I have worked hard to convey the strategies so that they're relatable. My hope is that you find the content encouraging and easily actionable so that it inspires you to take action. This approach to transformation is far-reaching. It could apply to people who are experiencing slight "stuckness" or who simply want personal growth and enhancement. It's also highly effective for people whose "stuckness" is more profound because of a trauma, cumulative stress, or other significant challenges that cause pain and distress. Individuals who want to enhance their life in a significant way and become their best self through the work and wisdom of personal growth will benefit.

WHY I CAN HELP

I am a person who practices what she preaches. I know my methods work because I practice them every day, personally and professionally.

One reason I'm so passionate about my work is my own history. Throughout my formative years, circumstances put me in a vulnerable position. Each of my four grandparents survived the Holocaust, while most of their family members were tortured and murdered. There was obvious generational trauma.

My very young parents divorced when I was three and constant relocating resulted in my attending five elementary schools. There was familial drug and alcohol abuse, constant arguing, instability, and emotional neglect. I often felt overwhelmed and that my life was out of my control.

Drama defined my childhood, which I now know put me at risk for repeated reactivation of the sympathetic nervous system and the stress response and an overexposure to cortisol and other stress hormones. I rarely knew what to expect or when the next shoe would drop. Fortunately, I had the wherewithal to seek out people and resources to help me to develop healthy coping responses and ways of thinking about myself, my relationships, and the world around me. From early on, I knew I'd dedicate my life to helping others, and I'd work my way toward a future that isn't controlled by the effects of the intergenerational trauma that I was exposed to.

My decisions coalesced during college when I thought intently about my values and how I wanted to live my life. I developed a healthy lifestyle and lost thirty pounds and put myself in therapy. I later broke off an engagement that wouldn't serve my future well, and I took out student loans to put myself through my graduate studies. Nothing would stop me from fulfilling my life and career goals. Every day I continue to strive toward living a better life.

I have seen people suffer physically and emotionally as a result of giving up, acting and reacting from a subconscious or unconscious place, and being remote from their values. In my practice and personal life, I'm exposed to individuals who want to make positive change but simply do not know how due to *"stuckness."* Fundamental change only comes when we're able to be present, gain keen self-awareness, and choose to behave in accordance with our values.

The ACE Method has shifted my habits, philosophy, and behavior. I'm aware of my patterns of thinking, feeling, and behaving. I don't deny my impulses, hide from them, or avoid them. I lean into my feelings, observe them, and revel in my humanness. I consistently remind myself how important it is to be my authentic self and live a value-driven, meaningful life. Through practice, I have fully incorporated these skills into my daily life. Of course, I falter at times; I'm human. But I study myself, learn from those experiences, and apply self-love and self-compassion. I accept that growth is an ever-evolving process I'm willing to take on for the price of a fulfilling life. I love the sentiment: *You only have one life to live, and if you live it meaningfully, one life is enough.*

Many books speak to a specific aspect of life. But with my method, you will be equipped to make positive changes in all areas of your life. I'm trained in many types of modalities, which allows me a more global perspective of what a person might need in order to grow and heal. I am advanced-trained in a variety of psychological evidenced-based treatments such as Cognitive Behavioral Therapy (CBT), for which I am a certified member of the Academy of Cognitive Therapy, Acceptance and Commitment Therapy (ACT), which is a third-wave highly effective behavioral treatment, and Structural Family Therapy. Additionally, I am Level II trained in Eye Movement Desensitization Reprocessing (EMDR), traditionally a trauma-based treatment, but one that has expanded to helping people overcome inertia and achieve meaningful behavior change. I am also a Certified Group Therapist through the American Group Psychotherapy Association.

My experiences lend to my understanding of human and cognitive development, and behavior change. I teach a graduate course in Mindfulness Practice as adjunct faculty at New York University (NYU), I serve on the Board of Directors of the Westchester Trauma Network (WTN) in Westchester County, NY, and am on the Board of Directors of The Boys and Girls Club in Mount Vernon, NY.

I am the Founder and Clinical Director of *Thru My Eyes*,[1] a nonprofit 501c3 foundation offering clinically guided videotaping to chronically medically ill individuals who want to leave video legacies for their children and loved ones. When videotaping individuals, they often disclose regrets about not accomplishing all that they wished they had because of missed opportunities due to maladaptive thoughts and behaviors that stood in their way.

I enjoy writing and have authored another book titled *Free Your Child from Overeating: 52 Mind-Body Strategies for Lifelong Health.*[2] I contribute to newspaper and magazine articles on numerous topics, blog for *Psychol-*

ogy Today, and am dedicated and invested in health and mental health advocacy.

There is no prescribed way I treat individuals I work with. Depending on their challenges and needs, I utilize a combination of treatments and teach skills based on what would be most helpful. Because each of us has a unique anatomy, upbringing, and experiences, within these chapters I describe skills in general ways so you can apply them to yourself, based on who you are, what you need, and the life you want to continue developing for yourself.

HOW ACE YOUR LIFE WILL HELP

When you learn these skills, you will be able to use them in all areas that challenge you. The lessons will endure over your lifetime if you continually reset, reconnect, and reinvest. There's endless usage for this knowledge, and expansive opportunities for change, growth, and healing. The more curious you become about what you believe and why, the more you're able to continue peeling back layers and learn about yourself.

The ACE Method applies to—and benefits—anyone's life. No matter your race, your religion, your socioeconomic status, your country of origin or community, how you were socialized, or how you identify, it's accessible and comprehensible. The ACE Method is effective at creating change and healing because it's individualized and unique to YOU.

From a very young age, we learn to avoid discomfort of all kinds, and the evasion perpetuates as we grow into adulthood. As far back as we can remember, when we got hurt, our parents would just kiss our boo-boos to immediately make everything okay. When we argued with friends, we were told to apologize. "I'm sorry," and all would be forgotten. We participated on sports teams and received awards simply for showing up.

Social media inundates us with glorified messages that happiness is the ideal state. We think we need to be happy *no matter what*. If we're not, we need to *become* happy. Our culture is indoctrinated toward avoiding discomfort and finding any means by which to secure physical, emotional, or social comfort.

We expect a quick fix for anything that challenges us or evokes negative feelings. If we can't solve or repair what makes us feel bad, we've failed, and therefore, there's something fundamentally wrong with us. We avoid or try to get rid of all discomforts, and that inherent pressure to be content often leads to overwhelming emotions, distress, and suffering. We relentlessly pursue what feels good—what we instinctually and understandably want more of, and we perceive that to be what's best for us.

Don't believe me? Consider how often you avoid discomfort. Reflect on times you opted to feel less in order to avoid the complexity of self-reflection, sitting and being present with the discomfort. Reflect on when you turn from making challenging decisions that might intensify and prolong the discomfort.

When we choose to shut down, yell, overeat, or procrastinate, we act out of impulse in an attempt to diminish or rid ourselves of fear, sadness, shame, frustration, or disappointment. During these moments, our inner commentator overwhelms us and takes over. Our behavior is led by our fear or anger, rather than by our core values.

When we're willing to come close, welcome, and befriend negative emotions, validate ourselves, and engage in self-compassion, we "leave room" for growth. Then these feelings can direct and clue us into what's important to us. The feelings will provide guidance as to how we can behave in accordance with our values to be our best selves. That's where the real growth occurs. The power lies within *US* if *WE* are open and curious.

When we approach life with openness and curiosity, we make a statement about our level of commitment to our most important asset—*ourself.* We wouldn't dare invest in a car or phone unless we researched and studied what it's capable of. We owe it to ourselves to gain an understanding and appreciation for all we are and do, which we can achieve when we approach our lives with mindfulness, care, and value-driven behaviors.

Accepting our own humanness allows us to appreciate the humanness of others, inclusive of their thoughts, feelings, perceptions, and judgments.

Approaching the world with *curiosity and flexibility* opens us up to new experiences and opportunities to facilitate personal growth and self-satisfaction. Through acceptance, compassion, and empowerment, we find our strength, our fortitude, and the life we were meant to live.

STRUCTURE OF THE BOOK

ACE Your Life is divided into four parts: Our Thinking & Connecting to Our Values, Acceptance, Compassion, and Empowerment. Each section walks you through definitions, benefits, barriers, methods, and strategies to effectively cultivate and embody the skills. The end of each chapter includes curiosity-based questions and self-guided growth exercises to promote growth, healing, and a path toward personal fulfillment. I've also included links to applicable guided meditations where you can log on and participate.

Whether you are learning or refreshing the skills, or you are seeking a reminder, encouragement, and support, please keep in mind that you can easily go in and out of chapters based on your needs. *ACE Your Life: Unleash Your Best Self and Live the Life You Want* does not replace working with a mental health practitioner if warranted and you would benefit. This book can be used independently or with a therapist, coach, or another practitioner.

Also, please note that all the examples in the book are based on actual individuals I assist and support. Their names and minor details of their stories were changed to maintain their privacy and confidentiality.

THE ACE MODEL

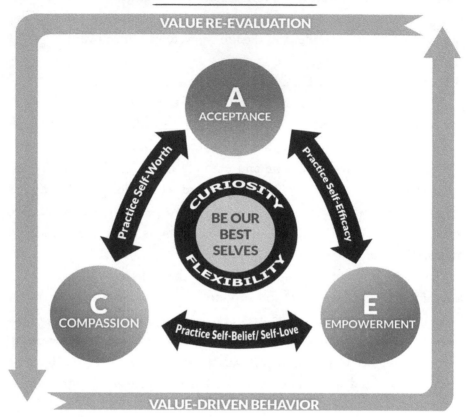

This figure represents how you can ACE your life. The outer circle represents a continual process of reviewing your values and behavior based on those actions. You begin the circular process with a Values Review and conclude by engaging in value driven actions. Throughout the ACE process, you're fostering your self-worth, self-love, and self-efficacy while exercising curiosity and flexibility. With each chapter, we build on this method of cultivating your best self and the life you want to be living.

Chapter-by-Chapter Synopses

PART I: OUR THINKING AND CONNECTING TO OUR VALUES

To get grounded in the ACE Method, you'll first gain self-awareness through understanding how your mind functions. You'll better recognize your inner commentator and how you beat yourself up. Following this, you'll identify and specifically define your core values. Value clarification will help you stipulate daily actions and behaviors to make more mindful decisions, enhance your self-confidence, be kinder to yourself, and lean into living your best and most meaningful life.

Chapter 1: Our Self-Protective Mind and Thinking

You'll learn the evolutionary and biological purposes of our thinking, and how it affects us psychologically, socially, and spiritually.

We can go from *autopilot* to *mindfulness* as we get to understand our thought processes and what drives us. Understanding how our mind works, our thought patterns, and gaining self-awareness regarding our behaviors will create space for processing thoughts and constructing a life where actions are underpinned in our core values. Transforming our inner commentator to an inner coach and inner nurturer leads to a fulfilling life of self-discovery, so we become our own self-advocate and behave in a manner that enhances us and instills personal pride.

Chapter 2: Discovering Our Values: What Are Core Values, and How Do We Select Them?

What does it mean to have values, and what are the benefits? Values help us understand what's meaningful. They guide our choices and decisions. They reflect the direction we'll take in order to adjust how we want to live. You'll learn ways to formulate a practice where your core values proactively guide you into the thriving life you want.

PART II: ACCEPTANCE (THE FIRST STEP IN THE ACE METHOD)

Self-acceptance lets us embrace who we truly are without expectations, conditions, or qualifications.[3] The concept of Acceptance champions being who you are, remaining present with where you are, and using energy and inspiration to work toward becoming that better version of yourself. Foundationally, we are all good enough, worthy, and deserving of love and respect.

Chapter 3: What Is Self-Acceptance & What Are the Barriers That Get in Our Way of Cultivating It?

You'll learn what self-acceptance and radical acceptance are and the benefits of practicing them. You'll learn several ways to practice overcoming barriers as you build self-acceptance. You'll embrace your shadow self, overcome negativity bias, let go of your need for control and forgive yourself for past mistakes and regrets. You can then be intentionally more accepting of yourself, others, and the world around you.

Chapter 4: Why We Resist Self-Acceptance and How to Embrace It

Societal influences, such as comparing ourselves to others, striving for positive and comfortable emotions, while refusing to acknowledge our full range of thoughts and feelings build barriers to self-acceptance. You'll learn to work through those barriers toward acceptance, gain self-awareness regarding self-acceptance, and assess your self-belief and self-efficacy. Lastly, you'll learn steps toward self-acceptance and how to cultivate a self-acceptance mindset.

PART III: COMPASSION (THE SECOND STEP IN THE ACE METHOD)

Having compassion means noticing: feeling emotionally moved by, and responding to your own and others' suffering. At its core, compassion means to "suffer with." Self-compassion entails acting in a warm and caring way toward yourself when you are having a difficult time, fail, or notice something you don't like about yourself.[4] Instead of harshly judging yourself or ignoring your pain, you acknowledge and validate it. You realize that suffering, failure, and imperfection are part of a shared human experience.

Chapter 5: What Is Compassion & What Are the Barriers That Get in Our Way of Cultivating It?

The best, most enduring, and most authentic source of validation comes from within. It is internal and intrinsic. We're more likely to receive it because we always have access to ourselves, not others. You'll learn what self-compassion is and its benefits, including how it increases our satisfaction and sense of self, and how it can have a positive influence on interpersonal relationships. Also, you'll learn to overcome the barriers that thwart it and the types of limiting thinking and rationalizations that inhibit it.

Chapter 6: Discovering and Practicing Compassion

The many barriers to compassion include our core beliefs, our shadow self, and regrets. Thankfully, there are just as many ways to practice overcoming the barriers and building self-compassion as there are barriers themselves.

It is challenging to fully face all facets of ourselves. There are parts we are proud of, revel in, and want more of. There are other parts we try to avoid, are ashamed of, or want to get rid of. Through several exercises you'll learn how to practice being more self-compassionate toward all parts of yourself.

PART IV: EMPOWERMENT (THE THIRD STEP IN THE ACE METHOD)

Changing how you look at yourself and continually shifting your narrative helps unleash your awareness of all the goodness that's already there within you. You have the ongoing task of accepting, showing compassion to, and empowering yourself. This is an ongoing process of development that will continue throughout your life. Your quest to be your best self and live the life you want to live is continual and everlasting.

Chapter 7: What Is Empowerment & What Are the Barriers That Get in Our Way of Cultivating It?

You'll learn the definitions and benefits of empowerment, as well as empowerment barriers such how language influences self-perception, your fixed mindset, and a lack of concrete values. But you'll also see how developing a strategy for maintaining and sustaining positive and value-driven behaviors can change everything.

You'll learn the importance of self-efficacy and psychological flexibility, the characteristics of individuals who lead empowering lives, and what it takes to attain self-empowerment. You will get clearer about your values and what it takes to engage in committed action so you can practice mindful daily living.

Chapter 8: Discovering and Practicing Empowerment

Constant reminders of how fragile and unpredictable life can be bombard us daily. Although we have limited control over the curve balls thrown our way, we do have control over what we *do* to ensure we're living our best life even when facing difficult situations.

You'll discover ways to work on habits to foster the empowerment process, how to recognize sabotaging cycles, and how to effectively handle setbacks, slips, and falls. Lastly, you'll explore facets of your confidence, behaviors of empowered people, and how to commit to the 3Rs—Reset, Reconnect, and Reinvest.

With this information, examples, and exercises, you'll be able to see a path ahead of you that is enhancing, uplifting, and full of hope. Your empowerment allows you to assume responsibility for the things in life you can control so you can take full ownership of your decisions, and ultimately, your life.

ON YOUR WAY

You took the first step and picked up this book! This promises to be an eye-opening exploration, one well worth embarking on. You'll take inventory and accept who you are with your full array of thoughts and feelings. You'll learn to be self-compassionate and how to engage in behaviors that further connect you to your values. Unlike temporary shifts you may have experienced in the past, you'll have the skills to promote long-term changes.

Thank you for your courage and willingness to commit and invest in *you*. You are well worth the time, effort, and investment. Think about how many times you've tried to make changes (just like everyone else—it's not just you!). Calculate how much money, time, and energy you've spent on Band-Aid methodologies. This time will hopefully be different. This book is written with warmth, care, and support for you. I appreciate and believe in you, wholeheartedly and unconditionally.

Part I:

Our Thinking & Connecting to Our Values

To get grounded in the ACE Method, you'll first gain self-awareness through understanding how your mind functions. You'll better recognize your inner commentator and how you may beat yourself up. Following this, you'll identify your core values and be able to specifically define them. Value clarification will help you to stipulate daily actions and behaviors to make more mindful decisions, enhance your self-confidence, and lean into living your best and most meaningful life.

CHAPTER 1

Our Inner Commentator and Thinking

Most humans are never fully present in the now, because unconsciously they believe that the next moment must be more important than this one. But then you miss your whole life, which is never not now.

–Eckhart Tolle

The comedian Emo Philips said, "I used to think my mind was the most important organ. Then I noticed what organ was telling me that." Psychologist Steven Hayes, one of the creators of Acceptance and Commitment Therapy (ACT) and the author of over 47 ACT books, referenced this quotation in an article. He went on to say, "The human mind is arrogant beyond belief. Because our minds can talk about anything, this organ between our ears thinks it knows everything. Our logical, analytical, predictive, problem-solving mind knows how to live, knows how to love, and knows how to be at peace. Not."[5]

We do not have control over our thoughts and feelings, only the way in which we choose to behave. Our mind incessantly tries to guide and protect us, so much so, that it often convinces us thoughts are facts and we have an indisputable reason to be sad, frustrated, anxious, angry, or any of the whole array of feelings that surface. It takes its role very seriously. To pro-

3

tect us, it often judges, overreacts, or becomes overprotective, hypervigilant, or defensive, even when not prompted or welcomed.

Our mind constantly buzzes and plays mind games, seemingly independent of us. This often puts us in a loop of struggling with our thoughts, while having thoughts about our thoughts, thoughts about our feelings, feelings about our thoughts, and feelings about our feelings. What a mouthful! Why does this matter? Your thoughts have a direct impact on your feelings and behavior.

Traditionally, you learn that if you want something, set your intention, and put forth some effort, you'll achieve whatever you're trying to accomplish. Simple as it sounds, the formula does not significantly take into account the impact our thinking and emotions have on our current or sustained behavior, and how it can often distract and derail us. You don't need to go outside of yourself to figure out how to manage your thoughts and emotions; the answer already lives within you. You can transform your inner commentator to inner coach and nurturer so that you not only think about your best life, but live it.

Integrating curiosity, acceptance, compassion, and empowerment creates space for you to pay attention to how thoughts and feelings impact healthy and adaptive behaviors. With awareness, you decide which behaviors are in line with your values and goals. You can make the changes that benefit and sustain you over the long term so you can be your best self and live the life you want.

The concepts and exercises in this book are grounded in Cognitive-Behavioral Therapy (CBT), Acceptance and Commitment Therapy (ACT), Eye Movement Desensitization Reprocessing (EMDR), and mindfulness practice. CBT was introduced in the middle 1960's, and mindfulness has been practiced for thousands of years by Buddhists and those who embrace other Eastern philosophies. However, it is only since the late 1980's that ACT and EMDR was developed. These methodologies have been applied to, researched, and studied in the context of behavioral modification and change.

HOW OUR MIND WORKS

Positive, negative, comfortable, and uncomfortable thoughts pass through our minds all day long. *New research suggests that most humans have an average of 6,200 thoughts each day.*[6] That's part of what makes us human. While amazing and wondrous, trying to break through the constant evaluations, judgments, buzz of ideas, and information running through our head day and night can also be frustrating. No wonder we gravitate toward thinking about our past and future and are rarely in the present—where our focus matters most.

Our thoughts are maps representing and corresponding to things our brains either perceive with our senses, feel with our emotions, or form as an action plan.[7] These can be based on our experiences, how we were socialized, and who we are. Thoughts may be fleeting, or they may consolidate as memories. For example, if someone has been traumatized (with a little t or big T), a trauma trigger can induce an involuntarily memory, which can be fragmented in time consisting of primary sensory information such as images, smells, and sounds, and linked to physiological or emotional symptoms.[8] Due to the lack of autobiographical context, the memory can be relived as happening in the present. This process can create barriers when we're attempting to align with our values and are working toward current needs and goals.

For example, long after the events of 9/11, individuals in the vicinity reported to me that hearing a plane overhead startled them. They tensed, feared imminent danger, and filled with the urge to flee. They shared that prior to this event, they never had this response. Intellectually, they knew they were safe and that the chances of a similar circumstance were extremely rare. Although they'd never questioned their safety prior to the attack, when hearing a plane overhead, the thoughts, feelings, and sensations were automatic and intense.

Throughout our lifetime, our mind consolidates memories and experiences. When an individual is triggered into high arousal and stress, the body releases the neurotransmitter norepinephrine, which strengthens the neural networks, challenging the ability to "see" future situations more broadly and flexibly.

Our brain forms new neural connections throughout life because of neuroplasticity. This allows our brain to continually grow, change, and adapt. The pre-frontal cortex, home of decision-making, attention, focus, and social self-control, controls executive functioning. Through awareness, mindfulness, and behavior change, we have the capacity to change our pre-programmed or over-learned automatic habitual responses.

Neuroimaging shows that sadness can activate up to thirty-five areas of the brain, while happiness tends to activate, on average, nine.[9] When challenges derail our lives, unproductive, overshadowing thinking processes skew our inner experiences. We swim upstream. Since our brain, our executive protector, is wired for survival, greater energy can too easily be spent dwelling on our problems rather than focusing on accomplishments and contentment.

We want to control our thoughts because they affect how we feel. We may beat ourselves up for having uncomfortable thoughts, and we try desperately to deny, avoid, disregard, or attempt to get rid of these thoughts and feelings.

At times, we all struggle with irrational and unwanted thoughts we wish we could control or never have to begin with. Those very thoughts often lead to negative feelings.

For example, it's just after dinner, and you're eyeing the leftover dessert on the counter. You know you just ate and think, "I really want that cookie. What's the big deal? I'll be more mindful tomorrow." You sigh. "Who are you kidding? You'll have that and more tomorrow," fills your head, and that's followed by, "I can't resist." Exasperation and hopelessness descend. "I'm such a loser. Why can't I get this right? Why can't my mind just be quiet?" Hopelessness intensifies. "At least I'll feel better if I eat it." You eat the cookie and are left feeling frustrated, ashamed, and helpless.

Who wants to admit to these negative thoughts and feelings? Who wants to carry them around? Everyone prefers to hold onto positive thoughts and avoid negative ones. Wouldn't it be nice if we could turn thoughts and feelings on and off like a light switch? Turn on the comfortable ones that make us feel good, and turn off those leaving us sad, disappointed, frustrated, or angry. Instead, we distract ourselves with activities or give into the thoughts to quiet down the chatter and avoid uncomfortable feelings. These avoidance strategies help in the short term, but in the long run they leave us even more intensely uncomfortable about the circumstances and ourselves.

ACCEPTING NOT CONTROLLING THOUGHTS

Dr. Robert Leahy, a distinguished leader in Cognitive-Behavioral Therapy, author and editor of 28 books, including *The Worry Cure*[10] expressed, "You feel more out of control as you desperately try to control your thoughts more and more. It's like slapping the water and drowning." He identified twelve strategies that don't work for trying to get rid of worry such as seeking reassurance, numbing with alcohols, drugs, and food, trying to stop our thoughts, etc.

Trying to make uncomfortable thoughts go away is exhausting and takes up a lot of brain space. No matter the effort, it doesn't work. Try this exercise. Pick a number from one to five. Repeat that number five times. You have three minutes to forget the number. Starting now, whatever you must do, forget the number. Try as hard as you can. Get it out of your mind. If you can't, try harder. Pull out all the stops and implement any strategy. Take three minutes to attempt to forget the number.

After three minutes, were you successful? Do you think you'll remember it tomorrow or the following day? Best of luck! Your number is here to stay. Your thoughts are your thoughts. As much as you'd like to, you can't control them. When they're important and emotionally evoking, they're that much harder to avoid or discard. When someone tells you to get thoughts out of your mind, or not have feelings about them, let them know it's only possible to control the behavior and actions you choose to take on behalf of your thoughts, feelings, or bodily sensations; you can't prevent the thoughts and feelings from entering your mind.

BEATING OURSELVES UP

We all fall victim to beating ourselves up. For some of us, it's merciless. For others, it may just be initial thoughts we notice and brush off, rather than buying into them. The chatter is not the issue, *per se,* rather, it's the accompanying distress and struggle that becomes problematic. Inevitably, *the goal is not necessarily to get rid of the chatter but to lower the volume. Our mind is persistent, and the necessary chatter becomes a direct portal to our values and better understanding of what is meaningful and important to us.*

The thoughts alert us to what we want and what we don't want, to what is meaningful and fundamentally important. Rather than berating your mind, think of it as a reliable barometer, providing you with invaluable insight into the way you think, feel, and want to behave. It means well but does not always have the best delivery. You can listen to your mind, but it is you who inevitably gets to choose your behavior and reaction to thoughts and feelings.

I had a patient whose boyfriend unexpectedly broke up with her. She beat herself up for thinking that she should be less emotionally impacted by his abruptness, as well as for his inconsiderate behavior throughout their relationship. I thanked her mind for reminding her that her values dictate that she be troubled by his behavior and that she would benefit from being more mindful in her future relationships. The chatter that caused her to repeatedly ask, "How can a person behave this way to another person?" gives direction to her own behavior. It is her mind's way of relentlessly reminding her of the lessons she learned from her former relationship and protecting her from future emotional pain.

15 Ways We Beat Ourselves up and Solutions to Thrive

Based on our inner commentator, there are (at least) fifteen ways we inadvertently beat ourselves up. While challenging at times, we can also consider that it's our mind's way of guiding, protecting, and reminding us of what we truly value. We:

1. Compare Ourselves to Others

Comparisons come naturally. Since childhood, it's been the way our mind helps gauge if we are okay. As there is always someone smarter, better looking, and/or more successful, we often berate ourselves for not being as good as or good enough.

Solution: Notice where your focus is, and redirect it to yourself without judgment. Ask, "How will I be *my* best self? What are *my* goals, *my* desires, and *my* needs?"

2. Focus on Everything That Is "Wrong" With Us

Even though we know as humans we are all imperfect, our mind leads us to believe we ought to be flawless. Our mind often defaults to tough-love tactics to motivate us. For some, that works well, but it can discourage others and lead to hopelessness.

Solution: When you notice you're focusing on your negative characteristics or attributes, expand by leaving room to recognize and appreciate your more favorable and positive attributes.

3. Dwell on the Past or Future

Our mind wants to prevent repeating past mistakes and making future ones. It naturally gravitates this way to ponder regrets and predict future experiences, flooding the mind with regret or anxiety so that we often lose sight of the present moment.

Solution: Commit to a mindful practice where you purposefully pay attention to the here and now. Evidence-based research studies have shown that mindfulness practices make a significant difference in our neurobiology, cognition, mental health, health, relationships, behavior, and wellbeing.[11] This can easily be practiced in daily life by slowing down and paying close attention to your day-to-day experiences or directly engaging in a gratitude or meditation practice. (I highly recommend the free *Insight Timer* app that has a combination of mindfully based guided meditations (over 100k), talks, music, etc. or utilizing a gratitude journal.)

4. Base Our Mood and Behavior on External Things We Often Cannot Control

Our thoughts get caught up and attach to feelings which impact our mood. For example, if someone acts unfriendly, behavior we can't necessarily control, we become hurt, disappointed, and angry. Our thoughts can be self-directed ("I'm such an idiot for letting her treat me that way") or externally directed ("She's so selfish; I'm never going to talk to her again").

Solution: Respect these thoughts and feelings. Notice them; acknowledge them, but ask yourself, *"How else can I see this?"* and, *"Is my prompted reaction/behavior leaning toward or away from building my confidence and a reflection of my best me and who I want to be?"* Recognize that an aggressive, angry thought or feeling does not mean you are an aggressive, angry person. You can have those thoughts and feelings and still choose to behave thoughtfully and mindfully.

5. Perseverate Over "Mistakes"

When we think we've made a mistake, we can dwell on it for days or longer—recounting what happened and how it could or should have been different.

Solution: Recognize that as humans, we are all imperfect. Mistakes are bound to happen. Mistakes are just that, mistakes. Rather than hoping things were different, be with what is. Make a point to identify what you learned that will help you to be the person you want to be to improve your future. Retrospection lets you recognize it as a regret. In the moment, you may have had different information, or at the time, it seemed like a good idea. Your insight comes from your direct experience. Going forward, you can make the choice to behave differently.

6. Do Not Differentiate Between Stress and Distress

Our minds often confuse normal and average *stress* with *distress*. For example, we expect that stress accompanies moving (transition, packing, unpacking, organizing, etc.). Distress comes when we struggle with and attempt to get rid of our stress. As Buddhist philosophy postulates,

Pain × Resistance = Suffering. Tara Brach reframes it as Pain × Presence = Freedom.[12] The resistance manifests itself in intense and uncomfortable thoughts, feelings, and reactions. We may think, "I shouldn't be stressed about this," or "If I'm stressed, it means that I can't handle things."

Solution: Identify the source and intensity of your stress. Acknowledge your vulnerabilities and how the stress impacts you. Seek out the support you need and deserve.

7. Place Stipulations on Our Actions

We think things must be organized a certain way or follow a certain schema in order for us to take direct action. For example, we may think, "I'll exercise when I'm feeling up to it," or "I'll look for a new job when there are several to apply to." Because things don't always align, we procrastinate and lack follow through. Consequently, we get down on ourselves.

Solution: Avoid attaching contingencies to behavior. Do things that attach to your values, without stipulations, even if it takes effort, is challenging, and you don't feel like it. We don't feel like doing many things unless it's fully pleasurable. Most things that we want badly, are important to us, and enhance us, take time, effort, and continued practice.

8. Negatively Label Ourselves and Neglect to Recognize and Accept the Different Parts of Ourselves

We may refer to ourselves as "not good enough," "thoughtless," "unsuccessful," "lazy," "impulsive," etc. When our other parts present themselves, we may not give them as much credence, because they do not fit into the schema of how we see ourselves. Labeling ourselves and not noticing our different and distinct parts thwarts progress toward self-acceptance, self-compassion, and self-love, and promotes thinking that the negative attributes are all of what we are (i.e., I am bad vs. I did something bad).

Solution: Recognize that even when we feel one-dimensional, in fact, we are not. We have different parts that make up our whole. It's our nature to notice and focus on our negative attributes and behaviors. Our mind wants to improve and be "good enough" or "as good as." It will naturally dwell on the negativity. To notice the more positive attributes and behaviors, often takes a concerted effort. Make that effort, and even when your mind continually (and inevitably) pulls you away, return to your goodness and wholeness, irrespective of your parts. If you are generally mindful about acting in accordance with your values, you will have much positivity to reflect on.

9. Avoid Discomfort, Shame and/or Uncomfortable Thoughts and Feelings

It's no wonder why we'd want to avoid discomfort and shame. Our mind tells us it's uncomfortable and to run for the hills! But doing that deprives us of seeing things differently, having a corrective experience, and the opportunity to build resilience and coping skills. We reinforce our negative thoughts, feelings, and experiences because that is all we know and believe to be true. Our past experiences do not let us believe otherwise.

Solution: If we are to see and experience things differently, we need to test our assumptions. Challenging ourselves requires us to experience and lean into uncomfortable thoughts and feelings. When they arise, notice them, label them (e.g., *uncomfortable, shameful,* etc.) and observe them. Notice when they tend to show up, how they specifically impact you, and whether they directly impact your behavior. Be mindful about how you want to behave, and consider your values when you are problem-solving. Remember, thoughts and feelings are fleeting. What often feels like a catastrophe in the moment usually dissipates with time, rational thinking, and the ability to process it more openly and expansively.

10. Don't Recognize That Our Disparaging Thoughts Often Show up as Self-Importance

Disparaging thoughts may manifest as, "it only happens to me," "everyone thinks this way of me," or "everyone notices my mistakes/flaws." For example, we wash our face in the morning and notice a pimple. We feel annoyed and self-conscious. Someone glances at us on the street, and we assume they're staring at the blemish. As if they have nothing more important to think about than your measly pimple! Even though these thoughts feel legitimate, they can also be self-focused and reflect self-absorption.

Solution: When you realize you are self-focused and it becomes all about you, expand your field of vision. Notice others and think what their experience may be. Ground yourself with the notion that your thoughts, feelings, and experiences are typical and universal. You are okay just as you are.

11. Equate Negative Thoughts and Feelings With Facts

Our mind sometimes makes the mistake of not reality-testing our negative thoughts and feelings. Because our mind relays it, it must be credible.

Solution: Remember thoughts are not facts and that they are often unpredictable, irrational, and fleeting. Give yourself permission to be curious. Be open to all possibilities. Reality-test thoughts and expand your thinking to consider a multitude of alternatives.

12. Have a Plethora of "Shoulds" and Expectations for Ourselves and Others

We have developed a script of our expectations, assumptions and rules for our lives and others'. If any of us behaves out of line with that script, we often get judgmental, frustrated, and angry. We've set ourselves up for disappointment because of life's guaranteed uncertainties. Things do not always go the way we want and expect them to, people don't always behave the way we want and expect them to, and often we might behave in unanticipated ways.

Solution: Understand what your "shoulds," "ought tos," and "musts" are. Recognize that your reaction is based on your own perspective. Others may not share these perspectives. It is their right not to. Consider other alternatives and ways of looking at yourself and others.

13. Expect That We Will Not Be Understood

We often expect others not to understand or meet our needs, thus we prematurely react based on that prediction. We may not bother trying, we avoid or cut off, and/or become frustrated. Because we feel hopeless and helpless, we negatively act out or just give up.

Solution: Notice the insecurities that get evoked when you approach and interact in your interpersonal relationships. Make the effort by being open to experiences, risking being vulnerable, and explaining yourself to others in an effort to be understood.

14. Expect People to Read Our Minds

There is an expectation that others, especially partners or those emotionally closest to us, should and can read our minds. We think, "If they know me well, they should know this about me," or "They should know what I want by now." When they can't, we get down on them for being "inadequate" and on ourselves for not effectively getting our needs met.

Solution: Because people are always experiencing growth and development, we are forever changing and in flux. Based on your mood or the circumstances, one day you may want to receive physical affection when you're feeling down, while other days, you may want space and time alone to gather your thoughts and regroup. Others most definitely cannot read our minds, just as we cannot read theirs. Express your desires and needs as they arise, or you run an even greater risk of being misunderstood and not attended to.

15. Perpetually Second-Guess Ourselves

We go through the motions of wondering why we did not make the "best" decision. Maybe there was another choice not considered. We lack self-confidence, self-assurance, and conviction in our thoughts, beliefs, and actions.

Solution: Decisions are typically not black and white. Most can have negative and positive consequences that may run contrary to values we hold in high regard making conviction difficult. Learn to effectively problem solve by recognizing all alternatives. Decide which values are a priority in the moment. (For more specific guidance with this, please see my Psychology Today blog *6 Tips for Making Difficult Decisions: Challenging Decisions Often Pit Our Core Values Against Each Other*).[13]

DON'T BEAT YOURSELF UP

IF YOU FIND YOU...	DO THIS INSTEAD
Compare yourself to others and decide you're "less than."	Redirect the focus to how you will be your best self.
Dwell on what's "wrong" with you.	Remember you're human and not flawless. Attune to your positive traits.
Dwell on the past or future.	Be in the present. Pay attention to the here and now.
Base your mood on external things.	Respect your thoughts and feelings, and behave mindfully.
Relive mistakes over and over.	Recognize you're human and not perfect. Examine what you learned.
Assume you're distressed instead of just stressed.	Identify the source of the stress. Seek the support you need.
Place stipulations on your actions. (ie: exercise when you feel up to it)	Don't wait until things line up to act. If you value the behavior, do it.
Negatively label yourself.	Notice positive attributes and behaviors.
Avoid discomfort, shame or uncomfortable thoughts/feelings.	Learn from those feelings. You must challenge yourself to grow.
Allow disparaging thoughts to become self-importance.	Notice others and their experiences. Disparaging thoughts are universal.
Equate negative thoughts with facts.	Allow yourself to think and feel. Be curious and expand your thinking.
Have too many "shoulds" and expectations for others.	Don't impose your perspective or expectations on others.
Expect to be misunderstood.	Notice your insecurity. Risk being vulnerable. Explain yourself.
Expect others to read your mind.	Realize they can't, and express your desires and needs.
Constantly second-guess yourself.	Decide which values are a priority, and make a mindful decision.

Our minds wonder, get distracted, and consumed by a multitude of thoughts. With thinking there naturally follows a surfacing of comfortable and uncomfortable feelings. Welcome all thoughts and feelings. They generously teach us about ourselves, what is important to us, and what we want out of life. Be compassionate and generous with yourself. With curiosity, notice your thoughts, observe them, and be open to learning from all of them.

LEARNING TO BE COMFORTABLE WITH BEING UNCOMFORTABLE

There's great power in learning to be comfortable with being uncomfortable. In David Burns's book *Feeling Great: The Revolutionary New Treatment for Depression and Anxiety*[14], he writes that there are positive ways to reframe negative feelings so that we can see the advantages of these feelings and understand how it connects to our core values. It's worth understanding this better so we're more readily open and accepting of our negative emotions.

Dr. John Forsyth, co-author of *The Mindfulness and Acceptance Workbook for Anxiety* explains:

WAFs [worries, anxieties, and fears], along with other emotional pain and hurt, are not your enemies. They are your teachers. Think about that for a moment. Without experiencing disappointment, you'd never learn patience. Without the hurt and frustration you receive from others, you'd never learn kindness and compassion. Without exposure to new information, you'd never learn anything new. Without fear, you'd never learn courage and how to be kind to yourself. Even getting sick once in a while has an important purpose—strengthening your immune system and helping you to appreciate good health.[15]

Studies have shown that the ability to embrace negative feelings can provide a plethora of benefits.[16] Those who accept all their emotions without judgment tend to be less likely to ruminate on negativity[17], less likely to try to suppress mental experiences[18], and are less likely to experience negative "meta-emotional reactions"[19] (i.e., feelings about the feelings and thoughts about the thoughts).

Being with all that shows up takes concerted commitment and practice. Our mind perpetually pulls at us to get rid of the discomfort. Our mind wants desperately to return us to a state of comfortability. Through learning to accept your thoughts, feelings, and sensations, to cultivate self-compassion, and to empower yourself to be your best self, you will gradually grow that part of you willing to be uncomfortable, vulnerable, and committed to valued actions.

Abby, a twenty-eight-year-old I'm working with, has decided to break up with her boyfriend of seven years. She loves him but recognizes that the long-term relationship doesn't meet her foundational needs. She's increasingly unhappy and resentful in the relationship. If she is not willing to explore, accept, prepare for, and work through the discomfort of what separating with her boyfriend will provoke, such as the inevitable loss, grief, and sadness, she won't follow through with breaking off the relationship.

Typically, when we do something that facilitates our growth, like ending a relationship, changing jobs, or improving our health, the process brings along a variety of complicated thoughts and feelings. It also requires us to do things we don't necessarily want to do because of the intensity of discomfort and the fear of pain and suffering we may endure. *We also feel more comfortable with familiarity than the frightening unknown, even if it's painful, distressing and less than ideal.* Our mind formatively worries about what will be and anticipates and fears the worst-case scenario.

Abby is leaving behind a relationship she's ascertained is not serving her well. She'll risk venturing into new relationships where, while she may get hurt, there's a chance for true connection and intimacy. That's a worthy tradeoff, she says, rather than just remaining "stuck and suffocated."

In order to make major changes, we can't expect to just *feel good*. If we did, we'd hover in a holding pattern most of the time and wouldn't proceed to living the life we want to be living.

INTENTIONALLY SHOWING UP & BEING PRESENT

We explored how our mind has "a mind of its own." As hard as we may try, we can't control incoming thoughts, but there's value in experiencing discomfort. Learning to be present through mindfulness activities helps to *tame the mind so there's space between the thinking and doing.* Pema Chodron, a Buddhist nun who wrote numerous books on mindfulness, describes it as creating space between the *craving* and *grabbing.* It alters our habitual responses by having us take a pause so we can think about the decisions we make. When we purposefully take the moment to tune in and expand our awareness, we get the chance to notice and pay attention to things we ordinarily might miss.

There tends to be confusion about what mindfulness is and why it's helpful. The most popular definition, expressed by Jon Kabat-Zinn, is "paying attention in a particular way: on purpose, in the present moment, and nonjudgmentally."[20] *In a nutshell, mindfulness is simply fully paying attention to what you are doing without judgment.* It's described as a state and not a trait.[21] People are not inherently mindful; they practice mindfulness.

Because life is so busy and we are inundated with tasks and responsibilities, we naturally go on autopilot. How many times do you enter a room only to forget what it is you set out to accomplish? Or you sit down for a meal and before you know it, your plate is clean, and you can't even remember eating? Or you are about to leave the shower but can't recall if you washed your face? All because you are not *fully* paying attention.

A plethora of scientific evidenced-based journal articles verify the effectiveness of mindfulness and meditative practices.[22] Research reports the benefits of mindfulness and meditation for cognition, anxiety, stress, reactivity, high blood pressure, chronic pain, and sleep. It also helps emotional regulation and emotional processing, decreases levels of the stress hormone cortisol, decreases depression, and assists with body awareness, self-awareness, self-acceptance, and acquiring self-compassion and compassion toward others.[23]

People can practice a variety of mindfulness-based activities, such as yoga, tai chi, guided imagery, mindfulness-based stress reduction, mindfulness-based cognitive therapy, and meditation. Mindfulness has been compared to strength training for the mind. Engaging in the practice equips your brain to better handle life's challenges.

You may report feeling relaxed after a mindfulness exercise. Although not the goal of mindfulness, calm can be a by-product[24] All thoughts and feelings are welcome; we don't aim them in any particular direction. Just be with whatever presents itself. The objective is to "just be" with it all— the comfortable, the uncomfortable, and the neutral.

A systematic, daily practice of mindfulness will help to train your brain to "focus your attention on what's actually going on around you and inside of you."[25] It will help you gain concentration as well as awareness of the full array of your thoughts, feelings, and sensations. This allows you to create space so you can make more mindful, value-based decisions. You will learn to step back and avoid making assumptions about the way you think and feel, to pay keen attention to all that is being presented.

CREATING SPACE: TAKE MEANINGFUL & PURPOSEFUL STEPS TOWARD GROWTH

Most individuals I work with report that when they're reactive or avoidant because of fear or some other feeling, they go from "zero to ten" automatically. They don't remember having any thoughts in between the thinking (e.g., I'll be rejected if I approach Myles which will make me feel awful) and doing (e.g., avoiding or neglecting to connect with Myles, despite wanting to and having the opportunity to).

During and after the incident, they typically feel disappointed and frustrated. They experience shame and self-loathing. From their perspective, they weren't able to manage or control their thoughts, feelings, and behavior. We have all been there. We all need to create space in order to thoughtfully process a situation and make mindful decisions on behalf of our best self.

Creating space between the thinking and doing requires that we pace ourselves, observe ourselves, and remain curious about ourselves. All thoughts and feelings that show up in the process are okay; what matters most is how we choose to act on behalf of them. That is inevitably our choice.

BETWEEN THINKING & DOING

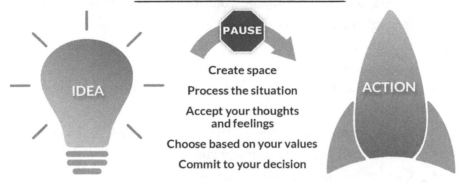

IDEA

PAUSE

Create space
Process the situation
Accept your thoughts
and feelings
Choose based on your values
Commit to your decision

ACTION

Acceptance is another element of creating space. It's in the willingness to accept your uncomfortable thoughts and feelings. The consideration is not the degree to which you like or dislike the thoughts and feelings, but rather your willingness to be with whatever shows up.

Part of acceptance is also your willingness to look deeply at yourself and evaluate who you are and how you function. This book includes steps to further learn about your thoughts, feelings, and behaviors in ways to help you live the life you want to be living.

Discovering Your Values, covered in Chapter Two, will compel you to pursue goals and objectives that directly link to your formative values.

Thoughts are just that and are not necessarily facts. Our minds tell that us we will fail, that we should give up, that meaningful effort and practice is too hard to sustain. We can recognize that these are merely thoughts. We don't have to fuse with them so that they become fact. We need to commit to direct action toward our values. Many individuals get caught up in "trying" to take action. There's a big difference between saying "I'll try to be on time in the future" and "I'll be on time in the future." Trying/attempting connotes a potential out with limited accountability. The actual *doing* facilitates change, not the *trying* to do.

To Facilitate Best-Self Behaviors, Be Aware That Your Mind:

- Actively and constantly processes information and consolidates memories,

- Tries to control in order to protect and avoid discomfort,
- Layers on thoughts about your thoughts, feelings about your feelings, thoughts about your feelings, and feelings about your thoughts,
- Can be slowed down,
- Has the ability to create space between thinking, feeling, and behaving,
- Can learn to be more comfortable with being uncomfortable,
- Has the ability to intentionally take notice,
- Can learn to defuse from the thoughts, and
- Has the ability to engage in self-refection and engage as a mindful observer.

7 Steps to Take When Disruptive Thoughts Arise

While our mind can sometimes sabotage us, it can also become more introspective, flexible, and mindful. It's helpful to know what steps to take when those disruptive thoughts arise.

Step 1: Identify the thought and the feeling associated with it. ("I'm having the thought…" "My mind is telling me…"). Make sure it's a thought (opinion or assumption) and not a feeling (experience of an emotion). Questions don't bring on as much feeling/affect, so be sure it's in a statement form ("she hates me"), rather than contemplating or questioning ("I wonder if she hates me").

Step 2: Label the quality of the thought and say it aloud. (i.e., judgment, worry, guilt, etc.).

Step 3: Keep to the original thought. Your mind may spiral to other thoughts and feelings based on that original thought. Keep returning to the original thought. Avoid responding to the thought because when you do, you give it credence, and you risk spiraling and having more thoughts that need responding to.

Step 4: Connect to what the thought is evoking. Consider whether the thought is connecting to or associating with a negative core belief, a worry, or an old narrative. It's likely it's a familiar and recurring thought you often think and tell yourself that's hurtful, disparaging, and negatively impacts your confidence and self-belief.

Step 5: Imagine it passing by gently and compassionately. You can imagine it passing by on a cloud, as a leaf in a stream of water, or anything else you want to imagine.

Step 6: Notice your bodily sensations and what it's bringing up for you. We often hold stress in our bodies, which we can also struggle with and have feelings about.

Step 7: Deactivate the mind and body. Use grounding exercises such as *Grounding: Create Personal Calm* by Winona University[26] to bring you back to the present moment (e.g., 5 things you see, 4 things you feel, 3 things you hear, 2 things you smell, 1 thing you taste); breathing exercises from *10 Breathing Techniques for Stress Relief and More* by Healthline [27] (e.g., Dr. Andrew Weil's 4-7-8 breathing) to help regulate your breathing and relax your body; affirmations and mantras (e.g., "I am enough" and "It's okay to be scared") to encourage and inspire you; words of compassion and validation (e.g., "It's understandable that I would feel disappointed" or "It's frightening to be in this situation") to comfort you, and a daily mindfulness practice so the mind learns how to take a pause, slow down, and re-regulate.

STEPS FOR
DISRUPTIVE THOUGHTS

1 **IDENTIFY:** Identify the thought and feeling associated with it.

2 **LABEL:** Label the quality of the thought and say it aloud. (ie: judgment, worry, guilt, etc.)

3 **RETURN TO ORIGINAL THOUGHT:** Keep returning to the original thought if you spiral to other thoughts and feelings.

4 **MAKE THE CONNECTION:** Consider whether it's connecting to a negative core belief, a worry, or an old narrative.

5 **LET IT GO:** Imagine it passing by gently and compassionately.

6 **FEEL:** Notice your bodily sensations and what it's bringing up.

7 **SETTLE AND GROUND:** Deactivate the body and mind and ground yourself.

CURIOSITY-BASED QUESTIONS AROUND YOUR THINKING

1. How does your mind protect? (e.g., overreacts, judges, overthinks, gets defensive, etc.)
2. How does your mind avoid discomfort? (e.g., distracts, discards, cuts off, minimizes, etc.)
3. What are some formative childhood experiences that have impacted the way your mind protects itself and avoids discomfort? (e.g., the way you were socialized as per your race, religion, identity; how your parents related to emotions and taught you about emotionality, etc.)
4. What are some typical thoughts that provoke self-defeating and self-demoralizing feelings?

5. Do these tend to be new or older thoughts? (Consistent, predictable thoughts may be based on past experiences or situations such as "I'm not good enough" or "I'm boring.") If older, how old? (Put a chronological age on the thought.)

6. When thoughts and feelings evoke discomfort, do you experience certain bodily sensations?

7. In what ways do you beat yourself up (refer to the 15 ways indicated above)?

8. What are some specific examples?

9. Are you willing to be uncomfortable and grow your discomfort and frustration in order to live the life you want to be living? How will you start doing that today?

10. Are you willing to integrate a mindfulness practice so that there's space between the thinking and doing? What kinds of actions will you take to make that possible?

SELF-GUIDED GROWTH EXERCISES: PAYING ATTENTION AND YOUR THOUGHTS

A. Being with Whatever Shows Up

Mix things up! During your typical morning or nightly routine, do tasks out of order, vary them in new ways. Let's say you floss, brush your teeth, and take a shower. Try switching the order. Floss, take a shower, then brush your teeth. Perhaps wear jewelry on the opposite hand for the day, wear two different length socks, etc. Of course, this is just a primer for bigger and more important tasks, the ones that really matter, such as working through inhibitions and anxiety, and acting on behalf of your values, despite uncomfortable thoughts and feelings appear.

1. *What was it like to do things differently? Did you experience willingness? Resistance? Anything else?*

_____

_____

_____

_____

_____

2. *Did you notice where your thoughts went as you switched things up? Did they shift? How?*

_____

_____

_____

_____

3. *Did you notice where your feelings went as you switched things up? Did they shift? How?*

_____

_____

_____

_____

4. *Did you feel sensations? Did they shift? How?*

_____

_____

_____

_____

5. *Were your reactions expected or were you surprised by them? In what particular way?*

_____

_____

_____

_____

B. Practice Mindfulness

Practice these behaviors below, first mindlessly and then mindfully, and record the differences. The tasks can be accomplished on the same or different days.

Mindlessly: Eat quickly through a meal.

Mindfully: Chew very slowly. Pay attention to savor each bite; notice aromas; textures, and flavors. Pay keen attention to what you're drinking, how the liquid tastes and feels as it enters your mouth and goes down your throat.

Mindlessly: Go outside and hurry down the block or around 200 feet and back.

Mindfully: Meander the same route, and stay aware of your senses and surroundings. Pay attention to what you see, hear, smell, etc.

Mindlessly: Take a quick shower.

Mindfully: Take a slower shower, paying attention to the full experience, including all the tasks accomplished and accompanying physical sensations. Notice as you wash your hair, scrub your neck, the experience of cascading water over your body, the temperature of your body, etc.

Mindlessly: Walk into a room in your house, glance around quickly, then exit.

Mindfully: Walk into the same room. Glance at the furniture, note the window treatments, items & their placements, shapes, sizes, and colors.

- Jot down some notes on when you mindfully engaged in the activity.
- How did it feel to take this approach?
- Did you notice anything different from accomplishing it mindlessly as opposed to mindfully?

- What specifically did you notice that you didn't necessarily pay attention to before?
- What were you missing out on by approaching it mindlessly?

C. Mind over Matter

Distance yourself from sabotaging thoughts by reframing them:

Instead of: "I can't express my needs to my partner."
Reframe to say: "I am having the thought that I can't express my needs to my partner."
Instead of: "I need to have the chocolate muffin now!"
Reframe to say: "I am having the thought that I need to have the chocolate muffin now."
Instead of: "My boss thinks I'm incompetent because of the mistake I made."
Reframe to say: "I am having the thought that my boss thinks I'm incompetent because of the mistake I made."

This exercise illustrates that by reframing your thought from a fact into simply an observation that has crossed your mind, you can create space in your thinking. This will allow you to process your thought and choose how you want to behave in response to it. Remembering "mind over matter" may result in your recognizing that it may be a thought rather than a fact. Furthermore, instead of being stymied by an absolute confining thought, you can process and work through the quandary intentionally and mindfully.

D. Write a Letter to Your Mind

This is an example of a letter to an anxious mind. Customize as you see fit. Writing a letter creates distance so you can observe your mind in a compassionate way rather than getting attached and hooked by its chattiness.

Dear Mind,

While you are a vital organ that helps me in fundamental ways, I realize I have a divisive relationship with you. I hope to improve the relationship, as I realize that if I work with you rather than against you, we can function synergistically, which will greatly benefit me.

You hold onto formative ways of thinking that become habit or an adaptation from your upbringing. You rely on older patterns of thinking and feelings because they're familiar, comfortable, and what you're used to. I get where you're coming from, but I also realize that what helped me in childhood doesn't always serve me well in adulthood.

While I appreciate how protective you strive to be, sometimes you become highly overprotective. You have good intentions to protect me from what you perceive as being dangerous, such as experiencing fear and rejection, but it's helpful for me to experience these things to build effective coping skills.

Everyday experiences and relationships are inclusive of challenges, and I need to be able to manage and work through my uncomfortable thoughts and feelings about them. If I avoid natural human emotions, I won't be engaging in day-to-day life experiences and living my best life. Also, cutting off negative or unpleasant thoughts and emotions puts me at risk for blocking out positive ones, too. This detrimentally impacts me and my relationships.

Your protective nature is also the impetus for your tough-love strategies. You compare me to others, criticize me, and try to convince me that if I think and feel something, it's representative of who I am. It sometimes makes it hard to believe I am good enough and don't need fixing, especially when you're so unrelenting.

Additionally, you try to prepare me for what may await. By bringing my attention to the worst-case scenarios and reviewing and ruminating over negative and catastrophic possibilities, you attempt to physically and mentally brace me for what may potentially come my way. While your intention is for my safety and to decrease my discomfort if something horrific were to genuinely happen, it scares and worries me, which makes me less functional if something were to truly occur.

I find that I may still get surprised, ashamed, frustrated, and disappointed when you think aggressively, impulsively, or irrationally. Although you have been influenced by so many factors—from your past experiences and societal pressures to your family of origin, age, race, religion—I expect more from you.

You are filled with rich perceptions, evaluations, judgments, and expectations. Sometimes that serves me well, while at other times, you can become extremely rigid, and it makes it difficult to open myself up to new and expansive ways of looking and feeling about things.

You also lead me to overthink, worry, catastrophize, have racing thoughts, or ruminate. Sometimes you are so insistent that you be noticed and heard that you come at me with all of those thought processes at once. When you do, I struggle. The discomfort from the "noise" compels me to want to avoid, get rid of, and have an internal wish that my thoughts and feelings can either just disappear or that I have the power to rid myself of them.

No matter how hard I try, I cannot get certain thoughts out of my head. It seems like the harder I try, the more difficult it is, and they just loop, spiral, and intensify. When I attempt this, I end up having thoughts about my thoughts, feelings about my feelings, thoughts about my feelings, and feelings about my thoughts. This mind loop can be exhausting, painful, and frustrating. Especially at night, when I attempt to fall asleep and there are no distractions or ways of avoiding my thoughts, they surface whether I welcome them or not.

I will give you permission to just be and let you know you are truly okay just as you are. All thoughts and feelings that surface are welcome, from the most comfortable to the most uncomfortable. I'm learning that it is vital that I experience and pay attention to my negative thoughts and feelings because they teach me about myself. They directly remind me of my values and what is important and meaningful, and they help me to identify what I want out of life.

From here on in, I'll choose how to behave, despite your input and banter. I will be driven by my values and best self rather than the thoughts and feelings you choose to highlight to me.

I will focus on being in the present moment and focus on *what is* rather than the *what ifs*. I do not know what tomorrow will bring. I only know what is before me in this moment. If I continue to look toward the past and future, I will continue to lose sight of and lack appreciation for what is afforded to me right now.

I won't believe everything I think, and I'll strive to be perpetually curious. I'll observe my thoughts and stay flexible to experiences, asking inquisitive questions such as "How else can I see this?" and "What are other possibilities?"

I commit to giving up my struggle with you. I realize it's not the chatter that is problematic, but rather the struggle that goes along with it. Inevitably, the goal is not necessarily to get rid of my thoughts, but rather to lower the volume.

It's challenging to have self-compassion when all of that "noise" surfaces, causing me to question, defend against, and desire to avoid myself. If I hate or admonish parts of myself, I cannot fully embrace myself and all that I am, which is essential for self-love and self-compassion. These are essential states for self-belief, self-efficacy, and living my life to the fullest.

I thank you for being associated with my brain, my most complex organ, and the physiological part of you. I know you will consistently consider my mental and emotional well-being and try to guide and protect me, no matter how hard I resist. I will work toward further learning to appreciate and align with you. I know I can't necessarily expect you to do the same, but nevertheless, I will accept you for all that you are because like me, you are truly enough.

Warmly,

Me

Please Listen to my TED Talk on Circumventing Emotional Avoidance[28] and Connecting to Our Body Guided Meditation:

Find all the ACE Your Life Guided Meditations at www.michellemaidenberg.com/ACEYourLife

SCAN HERE FOR
**CONNECTING
TO OUR BODY
GUIDED MEDITATION**

Congratulate yourself for taking another step toward ACE'ing Your Life.

Unleash your best self and live the life you want.

CHAPTER 2

Discovering Your CORE Values: What Are They and How Do You Select Them?

Our true nature is like a precious jewel: although it may be temporarily buried in mud, it remains completely brilliant and unaffected. We simply have to uncover it.

–Pema Chödrön

Values help us understand the choices we make and help us find a sense of purpose. They reflect driven actions whereby you are "living your truth."[29] They set the stage for how we want to live and the direction we'll take to do so. Values are emblematic of who we are, how we want to be, and what we choose to do every moment of every day in all our daily activities.

You'll explore what it means to have values and what the benefits are. You'll also learn to assess your values and understand what lies underneath them. You'll discover how values guide living a meaningful life and how they lead to effective decision making.

VALUES ARE A GUIDE TO ACTION

No matter how long you live, you want a meaningful life you're proud of. You want to tap into why what you seek to accomplish is meaningful, and how it will help you lean into what you need *to do* consistently to evolve and cultivate your best self.

Values affect what you want to *do*; not how you want to *feel*.[30] "I want to feel confident," only elicits an emotional response. To get to the value, ask yourself, "If I saw myself as confident, what would I be doing differently?" The relevant value may be connection with friends or more investment in your education. Underlining questions "How do I want to represent myself?" and "What do I want to be about?" transcend one distinct action but carry over to all you do, all day, every day.

It's essential to identify your core values. This is what you treasure in life and drives your behaviors. It is what you would be doing if nobody were watching.[31] *Our values are our guide to action.* Examples include family, self-respect, creativity, and integrity.

There are great benefits to recognizing and continually assessing your values. ACT creator Dr. Steven Hayes asserts, "Values are an inexhaustible source of motivation—inexhaustible because they are qualities to being and doing. They are visible only through enactments. They're adverbs, or adjectives, or verbs: 'I did something lovingly.' Because they are chosen qualities of actions, they can never be fully achieved, only embraced and shown. Nevertheless, they give life direction, help us persist through difficulties. They nudge us, invite us, and draw us forward. They provide constant soft encouragement."[32]

Additional benefits of identifying and acting on your values include reducing stress,[33] leading to better health habits,[34] helping with decision making and problem-solving skills,[35] increasing motivation,[36] [37] assisting with communicating more compassionately and enhancing interpersonal relationships,[38] [39] increasing personal assertiveness,[40] improving self-confidence,[41] and contributing to your vitality and feeling that life is to be truly lived.[42]

WHY ACT ON YOUR VALUES

→ Reduced stress
→ Better health
→ Better decision-making and problem-solving skills
→ Increased motivation
→ More compassionate communications
→ Enhanced interpersonal relationships
→ Improved self-confidence
→ Increased vitality
→ Feeling that life is to be truly lived

Values are derived from the ability to assign personal importance to aspects of our life through the art of valuation.[43] The word *valuation* implies worth, the ability to assess the meaning of our choices and desires. When you identify core values, prioritize them, and problem solve through them to formulate positive personal choices, you invest in a life with deep purpose and meaning you care about.

ASSESSING YOUR VALUES

With such benefits, it's worth the effort to go through the process of discovering your values. Dr. Steven Hayes suggests that we uncover our values by naming our heroes. They represent fundamental core values such as kindness, bravery, and justice.

Dr. Russ Harris, author of numerous books about ACT, provides a list in *The Confidence Gap*.[44] He suggests using one of these lists to select your top six to eight values: Financial Security, Compassion, Health/Fitness, Nature, Accomplishment, Creativity, Dependability, Loyalty, Beauty, Bravery, Gratitude, Love, Connection/Relationships, Learning, Leadership, Survival, Self-Preservation, Security, Adventure, Family, Work, Success, Calm, Freedom, Other _____.

You can do an online sorting and select nine to eleven core values from *James Clear's list of 57*[45] or *Scott Jeffrey's list of over 200 values*.[46] You can also use an online inventory such as the *Life Values Inventory*[47] or *Russ Harris's Acceptance and Commitment Therapy Values Card Sort*.[48] After selecting your nine to eleven values, **complete this exercise**:

- Take the time to put your values in hierarchical order in the shape of a pyramid. With this pyramid you can have more items per row (i.e., usually one up top, two in the next row, three in the next row, etc.). Here you can add more values in each row, as long as the values are in hierarchical order: most important up top to less important going downward.
- For each value, determine whether the value is:
  » Acquired (i.e., from your family, based on how you were socialized, your race, religion, etc. but you may or may not feel especially connected to, for example, wealth or traditions),
  » Aspired (i.e., you may have no acquisition, you may have some acquisition but may want more of it, etc., for example, patience or organization), and/or are
  » Circumstantial (i.e., based on a position or circumstance you currently find yourself in which may or may not be important

to you outside of the position or circumstance, for example, health or community).

- Define what each value means to you and specify what actions you need to take on behalf of each value.

WHAT LIES UNDERNEATH VALUES?

There are values we acquire, those we aspire to inhabit, and ones which are circumstantial. You can assess whether your values were ones you learned and acquired through your family of origin, from society, based on who you are characteristically (e.g., gender, race, religion), from your experiences, etc.

Because they are so often programmed and preached on, we can assume our values are learned or sometimes forced upon us. As children, we're rarely afforded the organic opportunity to unearth the sacred vitality of our values. We sometimes come to them as we mature and develop. Even then, we can get caught up in confusion and misunderstanding as to what our core values are and what we need to do to implicitly lean into them.

Evaluating whether your chosen values are ones you were taught and socialized with, and/or whether you personally hold them dear is part of the inquiry. For example, from a young age, you've observed your father work himself to the bone, constantly stressing the importance of "success," highly critical of mediocrity in others, you and himself. Despite observing your father disconnecting from his sense of accomplishment and joy, you fall into the pattern and micromanage during long workdays because of your intrinsic value of success.

You're often left spent and exhausted yet appreciate the accolades from your colleagues, and the financial rewards. You avoid rebukes from your father; you've earned his acceptance. Nevertheless, lack of sleep, proper nutrition, and exercise are affecting your health, and absence from your spouse and children, literally and emotionally, are dooming your relationships. You hit a roadblock. Your need for success is coming at a grave cost.

You realize that the value of success is an acquired one. The essence of it holds meaning for you, but the actions taken on behalf of it need to be reassessed and recalibrated to fit how you want to live your life as your best self. Future actions will balance other values of equal importance, from family to self-care, health, and self-compassion.

There are other values we aspire to, and some you act upon but want to improve. For example, your intrinsic value of consistency may fall short.

Because of your desire to do a good job, fear of losing clientele, and worry of being fired and replaced, you're conscientious and consistent at work. Yet when it comes to exercising, putting time into your relationships, or reading the pile of books on your side table, you fall short. You get in your own way. Despite intentions, you continually start and stop these and wind up frustrated and defeated.

Last are circumstantial values you're connected to because of a life event or experience. For example, if you experience hip pain necessitating an orthopedist appointment, anti-inflammatory medication, and physical therapy, your value of health will be formative, where ordinarily it may not be.

VALUES AND GOALS ARE DIFFERENT

Values are guides to actions ("I value my health, therefore I'll choose to participate in physical activity") or qualities of action that can be stated as adverbs ("eat healthily").[49] *Values drive our goals and the actions that we will inevitably take. Goals tend to be very specific, distinct steps we can attain.*[50] A person *can* check off goals when complete. For example, if we state, "I will limit snacking to one time per day" or "I will jog three miles three times per week." *We cannot check off values—they are ongoing and enduring.* Goals are steps toward our values. In truth, goals are more likely to be productive and achievable when guided by values. And instead of looking to others, a good sense of values will drive us to search inward for validation.

For example, if one of our values is learning, a goal might be to study something in our chosen field or field of interest. To achieve that, we can make an outline of how we'll approach the tasks, periodically assess how we're managing them, and apply the knowledge.

The value of learning will extend beyond that goal and lead us to a similar process (or one that may work better for us) of advancing our knowledge and career. If we didn't hold the value of learning, too easily we might check off that we're doing just fine, yet continue to be uninspired, disinterested, and avoid substantial advancement.

VALUES ARE PERSONAL

Jenna LeJeune and Jason B. Luoma, who wrote an ACT-based book about *Values in Therapy*, described values as behaviors which are ways of living, life directions freely chosen. Although they're immediately accessible, we could expect we'll never complete them.[51] If you think about values such as imagination, communication, adventure, community, and courage, they evolve throughout our life, and there's never an end point.

While discussing core values in a session with Jess, a thirty-three-year-old female, she specified perfection. When asked how she behaves based on that value, she explained she tries to do everything "perfectly" in her relationships so that she's liked and doesn't disappoint anyone. When I asked about specifics of the behaviors related to that value, she explained she's hypervigilant about almost everything she does and admitted that when she's interacting, she's left feeling anxious because she questions what other people think or feel about her despite how "perfect" she thought she was being.

Further probing revealed it was obvious to her that *perfection* isn't a value because it isn't possible to formulate goals to achieve perfection, since by nature, we're all imperfect. If, like Jess, one would attempt to take action to *be perfect,* it would compromise their underlying value, namely connection, and inevitably deter them from being their best self.

We discovered what was truly important and meaningful to her was her desire to connect with others. We talked about whether her actions contributed to connecting or detracted from it and at what cost. Jess recognized she was remote from her value of connection in her relationships because her attempt to be perfect had a negative impact on her spontaneity, on being her authentic self, and her inability to be in the present moment because of worry about whether she's liked and/or disappoints others.

To gauge whether a value is truly important, ask yourself, "If no one knew I were doing this, would it still be important to me?" For example, if you value showing compassion for your child, you would probably say even if no one knew, it would still be important to you.[52]

In your pain you find values, and in your values you find your pain.[53] Because values are personal choices that hold great meaning, you may experience pain associated with yours. For example, if you value connection and get into an argument with someone who matters, you will undoubtedly feel disappointed and sad by the current state of your relationship.

A failure to focus on a value doesn't cancel it out. If you were otherwise occupied all day and didn't have many learning moments, it doesn't mean you don't hold the value of learning. You've just chosen not to exercise that value in the moment. *Nothing can take away your core values. They are present even if they are not directly acted upon.*

Values have no contingencies. They're all about taking action and striving to reach goals that direct us toward the value. For example, showing empathy for your child. If you were to fully engage in that value, you would aim to be empathic *no matter what*. If you were seething because your angry child responded disrespectfully, you would be empathic and helpful if he fell and hurt himself. You may not feel especially connected to the action at that moment, but you'd show him empathy and not wait until he was respectful and likable.

There's no prescription for value selection. We are all special, unique, and different. We have varied upbringings, and spectrums of emotionality. We're socialized differently, in a world with wide-ranging social, economic, and political climates. You are wonderful just as you are. You can be you and do you and that is good enough! Your goal is simply to connect with your intrinsic values, create an action plan for how you want to show up, and continually practice being your best self.

COMPETING VALUES

Competing values often impinge on decision making and stir up internal conflict. Because you have a strong preference for one more than the other, deciding whether you want vanilla or chocolate ice cream is easy. If you must choose between a work event or your child's soccer playoff game, you're more than likely going to anguish over coming to a final decision. That makes sense because "*parenting*" and "*career*" are formative values for you. Would you want to *be okay* with missing out on either? Obviously, you'd rather walk away absent of negative or uncomfortable feelings. But because you're a conscientious parent and career driven, you're likely to get evoked emotionally. That reminder of how important both values are to you is something to take pride in.

I had a patient named Sarah, a forty-one-year-old female, who arrived at my office exasperated. She burst into tears, deeply disappointed in herself because she "allows" her ex-husband to "get underneath her skin even after all these years," a resurgence of feelings induced by disappointment for her nine-year-old child. Her ex-husband hadn't called their daughter to wish her a happy birthday until 9 p.m. "How can he have the nerve to call her at nine at night when kids wait all day to hear happy birthday from their parents?" was followed by expletives on her feelings and frustration.

I asked if she really wanted to be okay with him behaving that way and if she really cared to understand his behavior. She looked confused. I validated Sarah's reaction that she and her mind have every right to feel disappointed and angry because his action would justifiably bring up those feelings. I reminded her that *there is pain in values, and values in pain*. Her pain is indicative of her core parenting value being compromised. As an intrinsic value of hers, it's likely to bring up negative and distressing feelings. The behavior is so remote to how she would behave or think of behaving so she's likely never to understand it, nor does she want to, which she could be thankful for.

I reminded Sarah that every time she becomes frustrated with her ex's poor parenting behaviors, it directly connects her with her parenting value. It reminds her of how critically important parenting is to her and how she chooses and strives to be as a parent. Because it reminds her of how seriously she takes her love, care, and eternal devotion toward her daughter, her exasperation is to be celebrated. "Go ahead, let it all out," I added. "Your distress is a reminder of what an incredible mom you are. We sometimes don't feel appreciated as moms—we could all use the reminders!" Sarah giggled, thanked her mind for the reminder, which helped her let go of the layers of irritation, and happily ranted about her ex-husband and how she prefers to be as a mom.

Sometimes when we have competing higher order values, we recognize when we're compromising one value, we may inevitably be compromising the other as well. It's important to be cognizant that in the moment there may be a need to focus on one value over the other so that in the future both values can be attended to.

Violet, a sixty-two-year-old patient, came in voicing perpetual guilt regarding her divorce, which had been finalized years ago, because of a lack of emotional support and intimacy in the marriage. Even though she was happily remarried and had two additional children (four in total), she was saddened that she "selected her own needs over the needs of her family."

When parceling out her values, Violet feared that she acted "selfishly" because she decided to act on behalf of her self-preservation, mental health, and intimacy values, rather than on her family values. I brought to her attention that because she was in an unhappy and dissatisfying marriage, she was sullen and withdrawn, and therefore couldn't fully be the parent she wanted to be. By staying in the marriage, she was compromising both sets of values. By leaving the marriage, it undoubtedly evoked sadness and loss for the family, but it gave her the opportunity to lean into both sets of values, which she has successfully been able to do.

VALUES WILL GUIDE YOU INTO A MEANINGFUL LIFE

Your values are your guiding principles and represent who you are and what is meaningful to you. They guide your actions. There are deep emotions attached to these values and when they're compromised, you're bound to be uncomfortable. When you feel uncomfortable or distressed, you can map the pain back to a value it's rubbing up against. We saw this in the prior example with Sarah.

Ask yourself, would you truly want to be "okay" when these values get challenged?

What if you're waiting in line and someone cuts in? You may become enraged because it rubs against your values of fairness and justice. Of course, you wouldn't want to be *okay* with their unjust behavior. You also have the choice whether to curse and physically accost the person because of their behavior, or respectfully ask them to move to the end of the line. Or you could say nothing at all.

Assess on a daily basis whether you made concerted efforts to lean into your core values and identify what specific actions you took to carry them out. If you value respecting others, behaving compassionately and empathetically, you may openly and curiously consider a variety of reasons why the person may have cut the line (i.e., they have an urgency to get somewhere important; they didn't realize they cut the line, etc.), rather than concluding they're "inconsiderate" and "selfish."

You would decide to let the person know gently there's a line ahead of them which they may have inadvertently overlooked. Even though you were undoubtedly feeling agitated and frustrated, no matter how they chose to respond, you would re-align with your values of respecting others. Your values would lead you to continue to behave compassionately and empathetically toward them. The first line of order: *behave based on who you are and how you represent your best self. No matter what, it is irrespective of someone else's behavior.*

If I'm triggered with intense uncomfortable emotions, it's a clue to pause and consider what value is being rubbed up against and what feeling it's evoking. If it's prompting me to be reactive and respond to someone aggressively, I think "Is this going to help or hinder my self-confidence and keep me from sleeping at night?"

I know from experience if somebody is aggressive toward me, and I return the favor, my mood shifts. I sit with gnawing feelings and thoughts most of the day. I regret, perseverate, and replay how I might have behaved differently. "Why did I let that person get the best of me? I shouldn't have let them get under my skin. I shouldn't have said what I said. That's not how I wanted to be, and I wasn't my best self."

Being mindful and connected to my values in the moment allows me to process situations as they arise and respond in a calm and intentional way. I may walk away with frustration *about the circumstances* but absent of anger directed toward myself. I recognize that it most often takes confronting challenges in order for me to change, and I'm proactively committing to my growth by sitting in the discomfort. I reinforce that I'm grounded in my values and can choose to behave in a mindful, valued driven way. I'm proud of my progress.

IDENTIFYING WHY A VALUE IS IMPORTANT

We think we know what our values are. Often, however, we don't know their order of importance or what's essential to live them out.

If we say, "Health is important to me," but we don't understand what elements are critical for the need to live a healthy lifestyle, there may be a disconnect between our values and actions. It may require we dig and find some deeper meaning. As a parent, I believe if I'm not maintaining my health, I'm not fulfilling my parenting value. My health contributes to my longevity and connects to being physically present with my children. I'm active with them and model appropriate behaviors so they practice positive healthful habits themselves.

"Health is important," is not nearly as important as "Health is important because I want to be here for my children and live a longer life," That more specific statement moves me to a deeper level, fortifying direct action.

Pinpointing what's fundamentally important helps me redirect and recommit to more self-enhancing behaviors. It thrusts me toward identifying my value, recognizing why it is important, and what I need to do to effectively lean into it.

Do I think values evolve? Absolutely! If you're growing, they do.

Connection is another formative value and remains important to me, but how I define or act upon it will evolve based on my maturity and where I am in my journey.

For example, I used to think just seeing somebody was important for connection, but now, putting effort into getting to know them more deeply is what connection means to me. This value reminds me to follow up conversations, to note and acknowledge their milestones, and to ask about circumstances in their lives likely to evoke feelings. Now, I make even more of an effort to reach out or follow up. My values and my behavior evolved as my need for greater intimacy has increased.

THE VALUE OF DAILY ROUTINES

It's helpful to set intentions and actions for the day as a daily routine. My morning begins with meditation, then a weight training and cardiovascular workout. I have worked it into my daily schedule. Before I go to sleep for the night, I conduct a Values Review and think about which values I leaned into, in direct line with being my best self. I evaluate points where I digressed and chose behavior outside of being my best self. I combine curiosity, openness, and hopefulness when I ask, *"How will I do better tomorrow"* and *"What will I specifically commit to doing to make it happen?"* Curiosity and openness pave the way for growth. See the following figure to note the benefits of conducting a Values Review.

VALUES REVIEW

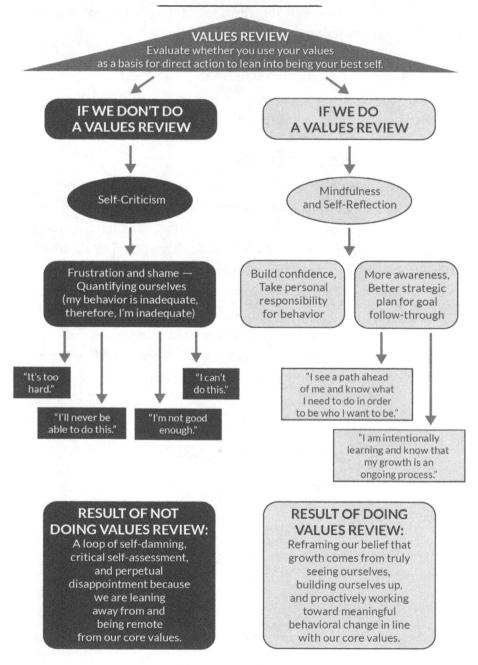

VALUES REVIEW
Evaluate whether you use your values
as a basis for direct action to lean into being your best self.

**IF WE DON'T DO
A VALUES REVIEW**

**IF WE DO
A VALUES REVIEW**

Self-Criticism

Mindfulness
and Self-Reflection

Frustration and shame —
Quantifying ourselves
(my behavior is inadequate,
therefore, I'm inadequate)

Build confidence,
Take personal
responsibility
for behavior

More awareness,
Better strategic
plan for goal
follow-through

"It's too
hard."

"I can't
do this."

"I'll never be
able to do this."

"I'm not good
enough."

"I see a path ahead
of me and know what
I need to do in order
to be who I want to be."

"I am intentionally
learning and know that
my growth is an
ongoing process."

**RESULT OF NOT
DOING VALUES REVIEW:**
A loop of self-damning,
critical self-assessment,
and perpetual
disappointment because
we are leaning
away from and
being remote
from our core values.

**RESULT OF DOING
VALUES REVIEW:**
Reframing our belief that
growth comes from truly
seeing ourselves,
building ourselves up,
and proactively working
toward meaningful
behavioral change in line
with our core values.

Our humanness dictates our imperfection. We're all evolving works in progress. Expect areas for improvement where you can focus more intentionally on living your life in alignment with your values. Berating yourself for what you didn't do results in diminished confidence, feeling poorly, decreased motivation, and another plunge going down the rabbit hole. Consider behavior you may need to focus more directly on the following day.

You may say, "I'm so lazy and useless because I decided to watch Netflix instead of doing laundry. I'm such a failure." Instead, review each of your values. "How did I lean into my value of organization today? Did I contribute to being and seeing myself as more organized? I could do better tomorrow by washing and drying the laundry and will fold it and put it away the following day. I will avoid getting distracted on my iPad and instead, I'll work on being more organized, which is important to me and builds my confidence. In order to lean into my values with my behavior, I will earmark specific times for when I'll dedicate myself to the work. I will limit my distractions, and I'll write down how I feel each day about the experience of being a more organized person.

A Values Review is an empowering evaluative process focusing on your values and behavior rather than a quantifying one which spirals into criticizing and judging yourself for what you should have done and how bad you are because you didn't successfully follow through the way you should have.

Over time, this spiral of criticizing and judging yourself will negatively impact your confidence and decrease your motivation. Change is thwarted further. Change requires you to believe you can do it, possess the internal will to do it, and have an effective plan to carry it out.

Take one day at a time. Day-to-day improvement can be made. You also get the opportunity to note each step and every effort along the way and notably see your progress. There's a boost to your will and motivation. You're the CEO of your value-driven life!

VALUES HELP US MAKE MINDFUL DECISIONS

In every circumstance, we have the opportunity to make mindful decisions. Even the most minute thoughtful decision can build your confidence, facilitate your personal growth, and help you to practice being your best self. Simultaneously, you can question yourself as to whether you are being led in the direction of your values or away from them.

Matt, a thirty-year-old male patient, was angered when his friends didn't behave the *right* way. People not communicating and behaving the way *he thought they should* constantly disappointed him. He was chronically frustrated by not being able to forge close-knit friendships.

I asked him how his *rightness* served him. Then I had him write *right* on a piece of paper, look at it, and describe how it made him feel. He said he felt strong, powerful, and in control.

Next, I had him put the paper with *right* on it up to his face and to continue to interact with me. He struggled to engage in the conversation, as he couldn't see me. Metaphorically, he understood that he couldn't see ahead of himself. His relationships were blocked because of the chronic divide between himself and others, so we worked on how he could expand, be curious, and be inclusive of friends' thoughts and opinions.

While there is no instruction booklet on how to foster meaningful relationships, he was able to shift his perspective, his behavior, and his expectations of others, which led to more fulfilling relationships. All because he was willing to look at his values and get curious about what *could be*.

When you purposefully take the moment to tune in, you get the chance to process, problem solve, and act on behalf of your intrinsic values. When you live aligned with your values, you are more likely to feel content and empowered. You take steps to contribute to your mental and physical health in a positive way and become your best self.

If you stay connected with your values, you behave based on who you are and how you want to be, no matter what. Despite being confronted by a challenging person, a difficult situation, or unforeseen circumstances, you face yourself and your actions being fully conscious and aligned with your values. In these moments, you give yourself the opportunity to build upon your self-identity, self-confidence, self-compassion, and resilience.

CURIOSITY-BASED QUESTIONS AROUND YOUR VALUES

1. From the exercise asking you to select your top nine to eleven values, how was the process of selecting your core values?
2. From the array of values you were selecting from, were some especially difficult to give up? Which ones? Why do you think that was the case?
3. Were you surprised by any values you selected? If yes, why?
4. Was there anything unexpected for you regarding the hierarchical order you selected?
5. Did anything surprise you about the values you acquired, aspired or were circumstantial?
6. How was your experience defining how you were going to act on behalf of your values? Where do you want to be in five years?
7. What may get in the way of where you want to be? What are you willing to do about it?
8. What meaningful thing(s) have you learned about yourself this past year?
9. What is your ideal self? What does it mean to be your best self?
10. What advice would you give to yourself three years ago?
11. Is there anything you're avoiding/running away from? Why?
12. Are you settling for less than what you are worth? In what areas of your life? Why?
13. What qualities do you want to embody?
14. What do you need to *do* in order to make your life more meaningful, starting today?

🏆 SELF-GUIDED GROWTH EXERCISE: PROCESS OF SELF-DISCOVERY

Below are six questions to guide you through this process of self-discovery:

1. Write the beliefs you learned about yourself when you were young from your...
   - Mother:
   - Father:
   - Siblings:
   - Friends:
   - Teachers:
   - Others:

2. Which of these messages continue to dominate your thoughts and behaviors today?

3. Which messages support and which messages detract from your confidence, contentment, and satisfaction?

4. Are there any messages that sabotage your leaning in and taking action on behalf of any of your values? If yes, which one and in which way?

5. When you're confronted with a situation that evokes pain/deep negative emotion(s), think about and identify which value it's rubbing up against and whether there's a value conflict.

6. Connect with the thoughts, feelings and bodily sensations that are surfacing. Before deciding on how you'll act or react to what you're thinking and feeling, connect with your values. Is your response in line with who you are and how you want to be? Will you sleep peacefully at night—without being disappointed/frustrated/sad about the situation and additionally with yourself?

Writing about values is shown to increase the ability to succeed.[54] [55] Take this time to write and continue to write, based on the questions provided, as it will give you a greater chance to succeed with the goals you set out to achieve. Use your answers to get to know your authentic self, identify areas of stuckness around your core values and behavior, and commit to participating in a daily evaluation of your values and behavior. The answers can guide you into being more insightful and mindful and help you to identify behaviors that assist you in leaning into value-based behavior and your best self.

Please Listen to A Value-Driven Guided Meditation:

Find all the ACE Your Life Guided Meditations at
www.michellemaidenberg.com/ACEYourLife

SCAN HERE FOR
VALUE-DRIVEN
GUIDED MEDITATION

Congratulate yourself for taking another
step toward ACE'ing Your Life.

Unleash your best self and live the life you want.

Part II:

Acceptance
(The First Step in the ACE Method)

Self-acceptance is embracing who we truly are without expectations, conditions, or qualifications.[56] The concept embraces being who you are, and present with where you are, with the energy and inspiration to make changes that lead you to work toward being a better version of yourself. Foundationally, we are all good enough, worthy, and deserving of love and respect.

CHAPTER 3

What Is Self-Acceptance & What Are the Barriers That Get in the Way of Us Cultivating It?

"In a society that says, 'Put yourself last,'
self-love and self-acceptance are revolutionary."
"Authenticity is the daily practice of letting go of
who we think we're supposed to be and embracing
who we are."
–Brené Brown

ACCEPTING OUR CIRCUMSTANCES

Our lives are full of painful experiences. Some unexpected, unfair, and out of our control which make it so challenging to be with what is, because of how negatively and intensely they impact us. Just three years ago, my nephew, a day shy of his sixteenth birthday and excited for the upcoming day to take his road test, tragically died in an accident. The day never came.

I get profoundly sad, but I continue to fight my urge to avoid thinking about him, because the intermittent moments I fully lean into my feelings, I feel deeper compassion for my brother and his family, and for myself. The pain signifies the love I can connect to and cherish.

The idea of acceptance traces back to Buddhism. The second of the Four Noble Truths of Buddhism stipulates that *desire* (or craving) is the root of all suffering. It is often our attachment to changing, manipulating, or reversing a challenge within ourselves or a situation that is the source of our pain, discomfort, and stress.

Acceptance, as it is known in the therapeutic, holistic, and psychological realm, is defined as one of the many aspects of mindfulness. It's being with *what is* without struggling to deny, dismiss, or disregard parts of it.[57] Within a stressful situation, we create undo suffering when we struggle with it. We go into the zone of thinking about how we, others, things, and circumstances should/ought to/must be. We either deny, resist, or ward off being with the thoughts and feelings evoked, which can be informative. Before we know it, we spiral into overwhelming anticipation, shame, fear, and dread.

Although your protective mind has a genuine wish to control all aspects of your life, you can find yourself in circumstances out of your control. You have limited control over how someone reacts to you, unexpected events like illness and death, and your innate physiology and genetics. Uncertainty and ambiguity are part of our humanness.

We can't avoid inevitable pain associated with these situations. It will naturally come with intense discomfort and negative thoughts and feelings because of the gravity of it. The more we disregard this pain, the more it morphs from pain to suffering. Pain will be there, but we can minimize and intentionally and mindfully work on the suffering. *We are not seeking to get rid of the thoughts and feelings. Even if we wanted to, we cannot, but we can lower the volume so that there's also room for awareness, contemplation, and sound value-based decision making.*

When we get hooked, we are stuck perseverating about why this happened, how it happened, and how to get rid of it, in order to avoid feeling uncomfortable and ineffectual. The spiraling multitude of thoughts creates stress, distress, and suffering, which negatively impacts our behavior and inevitably takes away from the life we want to be living.

Loosen your expectations. If you accept or weaken your attachments and engage in acceptance, objectively avoiding judging events or situations, you can often eliminate or mitigate suffering.[58] Sharon Salzberg, bestselling author and world-renowned teacher of Buddhist precepts and meditation practices in the West, wrote:

> Accepting suffering doesn't mean that it goes away, or even that it gets better. Too often, we conflate the idea of "being spiritual" or the idea of acceptance with the New Age-y cliché that we can simply say no to suffering. We can learn to feel discomfort in a far more pure and direct way, without the additional burden of distorted thinking. But I still maintain that some things just hurt.[59]

In her book *Letter to My Daughter* [60], Maya Angelou wrote, "You may not control all the events that happen to you, but you can decide not to be reduced by them." You may be thinking that it's easier said than done. Further, if a circumstance is out of your control and painful, how could you not let it negatively affect you? The impact will be there irrespective of whether you accept it or not. The difference is whether you are layering on the pain and further intensifying and exacerbating what already exists.

My forty-two-year-old patient Marnie's twelve-year-old daughter developed a rare spinal infection resulting in chronic urinary incontinence complications. Her attachment to why this had to happen to her daughter, why her daughter must suffer so much, and how much better off other kids are, kept her from being with *what was* and being in the present moment. Because of wishing and hoping things were different, and layering on her worries, she lost sight of ways she can empower herself and her daughter. She missed recognizing that within this unpredictable, challenging situation, there were prime opportunities to act on behalf of her values and strengthen her and her daughter's resilience and coping skills.

Marnie realized that she was far more able to be compassionate toward her daughter rather than to herself. She explained that she isn't special, because any good parent would be concerned and support their child. She gets frustrated for excessively worrying, getting hooked on catastrophizing thoughts about her daughter's future, and not accepting it all. She cannot control all these thoughts and feelings that get evoked, and due to the circumstances, they are typical and understandable.

If she were to notice thoughts and feelings arising, accept, observe, get curious about them, and react from a self-compassionate place, then she could reframe her position as hopeful and empowered. Even though Marnie's thoughts and feelings are bound to fluctuate as new concerns arise throughout her daughter's development, she can mindfully and intentionally work toward empowering herself and her daughter. She can hold conflicting feelings, such as frustration for her challenges and gratitude for the continual progress simultaneously. She'll be able to act on behalf of her best self, despite inherent challenges. It's okay to think how she thinks and feel how she feels.

RADICAL ACCEPTANCE

Marcia Linehan discusses the practice of radical acceptance and letting go of what isn't possible in her Dialectical Behavior Therapy (DBT). She stated, "Radical acceptance rest on letting go the illusion of control and a willingness to notice and accept things as they are right now, without judging."[61] She breaks it up into three parts: accepting the reality is what it is; accepting that the event or situation causing pain has a cause; accepting life can be worth living even with painful events.

RADICAL ACCEPTANCE

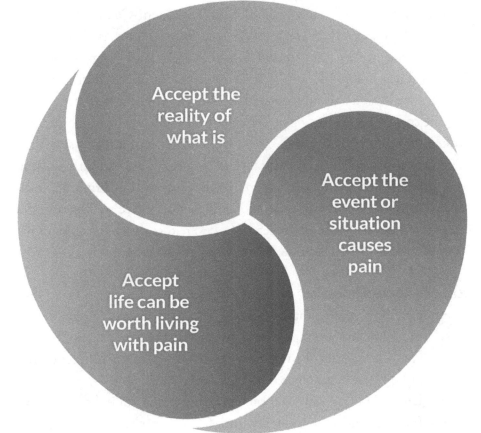

Accept the
reality of
what is

Accept the
event or
situation
causes
pain

Accept
life can be
worth living
with pain

From Marcia Linehan's *Dialectical Behavior Therapy*

Tara Brach popularized the notion of radical acceptance regarding mindfulness and Buddhist traditions and practices in her enlightening book *Radical Acceptance*. She defines radical acceptance as "clearly recognizing what we are feeling in the present moment and regarding that experience with compassion."[62] She sees the power of radical acceptance of all our human emotions which will bring greater peace, connection, and agency into our lives, our relationships, and communities. Her lessons focus on practicing mindfulness and compassion, befriending our self and offering forgiveness. She highlights "pain + non-acceptance = suffering" and the relationship of reality of what is and "recognizing" and "allowing."

Carl Rogers, the founder of Humanistic or Client-Centered approach to psychology astutely expressed, "The curious paradox is that when I accept myself just as I am, then I can change."[63] Carl Jung, founder of Analytical psychology, wrote, "What you resist not only persists, but will grow in size,"[64] generally abbreviated to "What you resist persists."

The common underlining precept is the idea that when an emotion gets evoked, fighting against it (i.e., non-acceptance) often leads to suffering. When a reality is painful, it's natural to try to push it away, fight against it, or numb out through unhealthy coping mechanisms (i.e., drinking, over-eating, engaging in unhealthy relationships, etc.). These strategies might cause a temporary sense of "relief." However, they bury the underlying issue and likely cause you to feel even worse in the long-term.

Radical Acceptance Is:

- Catching your "shoulds" "ought tos" and "musts" embedded in thoughts and feelings that counter acceptance such as "It's not fair," "It shouldn't be this way," and "I wish it were different." But rather, have acceptance of things as they are.
- Understanding what you can and cannot control in life.
- Internalizing that thoughts and feelings can't be controlled no matter how hard we try to change, modify, or adjust them. Even if they can be temporarily contained, they eventually return.
- Taking a non-judgmental stance. Notice your judgments, because we all have them based on who we fundamentally are (i.e., race, religion, identity, family of origin, etc.), Challenge them, and decide to act from a place of mindfulness and thoughtfulness.
- Avoiding labeling and quantifying people, situations, or emotions as "good," "bad," "right," "wrong," etc.
- Looking at "just the facts" of the situation (i.e., sifting out the add-ons derived from your thoughts, feelings, and experiences).

- Acknowledging your situation and the thoughts and feelings attached to them (for better or worse).
- Letting go, not fighting against reality (i.e., avoiding the struggle, resistance, and insistence).
- Willingness to be in the present moment, even if painful or uncomfortable.
- Having openness and space for all your emotions. Allowing yourself to lean into the discomfort of painful and uncomfortable ones, remembering no feeling lasts forever. If you sit with them, they'll eventually rise and fall, and come and go, much like a hill or ocean waves.
- Developing a keen awareness of your needs and what is important, then actively and consciously moving toward asserting your thoughts and feelings, meeting your needs, and living in accordance with your values and worth.

An Example of Radical Acceptance

Imagine you're driving to an important holiday dinner with your daughter, and you're stuck in bumper-to-bumper traffic. You can choose to get saturated in your anger and frustration: "This can only happen to me!" "I'm such a tool, I shouldn't have left so late," etc.

This spirals to judging your thoughts, feelings, and reaction to the situation, causing escalated stress and discomfort. "These things always happen to me," or "I knew better. I'm incredibly weak because I can't speak or stand up for myself and should have used my own judgment of when to leave." In a situation like this, you can work to "radically accept" the situation, to realize given the circumstances there is no way to change it. It's expected you would have frustrated thoughts and feelings because of how much you value independence, asserting your needs, punctuality, and your family's company.

You could choose to sit with the disappointment and frustration, accepting all that comes along with it. You reframe your situation to include acceptance and self-compassion. "I'm going to be late," "I'm disappointed at what is," and "I can't change it, so I might as well expand my thinking to include how I might make the best use of my time." You can decide to have a compelling conversation with your daughter in the car or listen to an inspiring podcast. Radical acceptance in this situation helps you to shift focus from unproductive ruminating to thinking about what a better use of your time and energy might be.

As the First Noble Truth of Buddhism points out, life is full of human suffering. But life is also full of joyful experiences. In your lifetime, there are bound to be experiences you want either more or less of. *Cutting off negative or uncomfortable feelings inadvertently also impacts your ability to connect with and feel joy and contentment.* You learn defense and coping skills throughout your life. Unfortunately, "your feelings" aren't progressive or sophisticated enough to decipher when to cut off or connect.

When you cut off any feeling, you teach yourself to numb out, disconnect, and avoid. This includes your full array of feelings, even positive ones you want more of. *What you put energy and effort into grows stronger over time. Every moment is an opportunity.* Would you rather strengthen your ability to connect with yourself or your ability to disconnect?

RADICAL ACCEPTANCE REQUIRES PRACTICE

Acquiring radical acceptance requires practice. When you accept, you experience *all* thoughts and feelings. Without judgment, you're allowing yourself to be frustrated, disappointed, sad, fearful, or whatever other feeling develops. Practicing acceptance every day, prepares you when life's most difficult experiences occur.

Acceptance means that you can begin to heal. Resisting reality delays healing and adds suffering to your pain. So accepting the heavy traffic and late arrival eases your suffering in that moment and being with what is, you'll become able to cope more effectively when difficult situations arise.

Radical acceptance is easier to understand than it is to practice. There are many obstacles to giving up suffering including resentments and anger toward yourself, others, or the world in general. If primary feelings underlining anger such as sadness or disappointment were shut down, ignored, and/or mocked from childhood to the present day, they may have become too threatening to express. Even the idea, let alone the act of expressing sadness or disappointment can leave you feeling vulnerable and exposed.

Anger or frustration may be formative feelings for you because of holding onto and asserting your anger makes you feel strong and powerful, and more in control. It's a way in which your mind seeks to protect you. Being met with discomfort, defensiveness, and dismissiveness from others taught you that displaying vulnerability is dangerous and unwelcome. You've concluded there is no upside for putting your feelings out there, and over time, you've built frustration and resentment, which you turn on yourself and others.

Radical acceptance can seem risky to emotionally sensitive people. Anger, withdrawal, and resentment act as armor to protect yourself. Maintaining anger and resentment and punishing whoever wronged you ensures they aren't "getting away" with being harmful, are receiving "justified" consequences, and you're protected from it happening again.

Your resentment may become unwieldy and difficult to manage. Your human instincts, directed toward being acknowledged, accepted, and validated, pulls you toward ensuring this, sometimes, at a negative cost to you or the other person. Whether or not they're realistic, feasible, or emotionally healthy, your mind will continue to strive toward these instincts.

For example, because of the insensitive thing she said, you may insist a friend understands why she hurt you. By getting caught up in your insistence, you may be judging her person rather than her behavior. You have a hard time understanding and processing her side of the story and avoid reconnecting because she is not sorry enough.

Radical acceptance does not mean you embrace yourself or the person who hurt you as if nothing happened. You go forward with new knowledge about yourself and the other person. The anger and resentment serve as a reminder of what your core values are, life lessons to take into your future interactions, and a better understanding of what's required to be a better version of yourself. You help release the handcuffs and cease the suffering by just compassionately accepting it.

Some people think that by accepting something or someone means they automatically also agree with it or them. You think, I will and can never agree with all they may have said or done. *Acceptance is not resignation. Radical acceptance does not mean you agree with a person, situation, or action. Rather, you're willing to let go of the past and things you cannot control. You focus on what you can control.* It means you acknowledge the event and its impact. The same is true if you don't accept your own behaviors. You did whatever you did. You don't have to approve or agree, but facts are facts. You agree to move forward.

We use language to avoid our reality. We say, "_____ shouldn't have happened," or I'll never accept or acknowledge it/him/her." Your refusal doesn't change the facts; it contributes to the suffering and emotional pain that accompanies the resistance.

It becomes a self-fulfilling prophecy. You seek to protect yourself from possible future suffering by doing something that creates suffering in the present. That requires finding a new way of moving forward. Through challenging yourself, the relief from suffering gained from practicing radical acceptance is worth the effort.

HOW THE CONCEPT OF RADICAL ACCEPTANCE CAN ACCELERATE OUR JOURNEY TOWARDS SELF-ACCEPTANCE

Sometimes, in order to gain control, we must let go of the need for wanting to control. This may seem counterintuitive, but this concept is what mental health and wellness experts such as Marsha Linehan and Tara Brach advocate and practice in order for individuals to feel more grounded. Rather than fight the negative thought or emotion, embrace it. Yes, most people may struggle, as embracing it may mean accepting bad behavior, forgetting about the challenge or situation, or dismissing responsibility of the self and others.[65]

Radical acceptance focuses on acknowledging and bringing awareness to the situation at hand, being objective and non-judgmental, recognizing what we can and cannot control, and being present with discomfort or "leaning into the discomfort" in order to take steps to make peace with it. When you radically accept your circumstances, you are concurrently working toward self-acceptance.[66]

Let's say you've spilled your coffee all over your shirt and the coffee shop floor. Rather than focusing on your wish you'd never dropped the cup, (i.e., "If I didn't rush, then this wouldn't have happened"), your embarrassment, and the response of others (i.e., "Everyone thinks I'm a klutz," "I can't do anything right" or "I always have bad luck"), focus on the humiliation without judgment. "I'm embarrassed and uncomfortable right now. But that doesn't mean I *am* an embarrassment. I've felt it before, and I'm bound to feel this way again. I'll clean up the floor and my shirt. After that, I'll get myself another cup of coffee."

The definition of embarrassment does not have your name included in it, and it does not mean failure or unworthiness. Radical acceptance normalizes not only this emotion but many emotions we deem as negative and then tie to our identity and feelings of self-worth. Self-acceptance is a skill we can nurture and practice so that there's better acquisition and utility in our lives.

As I write about acceptance, my closest friend is dying of lung cancer. Early in her illness, she shared that once the disease impacted her capacity to interact, she would cut off communication, wanting and needing to die with dignity. I unreservedly agreed to respect her wishes. Today was that day.

I feel helpless that I can't be in her physical presence. I yearn to hear her and share with her. My mind continually wants to dismiss and disconnect from the heart wrenching pain. "Was I a good enough friend?" "Did I say everything to her that I needed and wanted to?" "How will I be when she dies?" "Will I be included in her burial and memorial services as I'm only a friend and not a family member?" My mind has become an endless loop of questions.

I take moments to notice my concerns, worries, frustrations, disappointments, and sadness. I'm deliberately allowing myself to be, without judging my thoughts and feelings. I allow myself moments of tearfulness, exasperation, and the visceral pain of grief weighing on my chest.

I also expand my pain to include memories of our time together and recall her vulnerability as she shared her thoughts and feelings. Exploring what she meant to me and why we were so connected helps me realize the grief is emblematic of the love we shared. I hug myself to acknowledge the depths of my pain and remind myself that my thoughts and feelings are worthy of validation and nurturance.

ACCEPTING OURSELVES

Self-acceptance applies the principles and ideologies of acceptance, but the focus is directed inward. Self-acceptance is embracing who we truly are without any sort of expectations, conditions, or qualifications.[67] It is also our acceptance of all our attributes, whether positive or negative.

Where self-esteem is conditional and relates to how we feel about ourselves and our value, self-acceptance is considered unconditional and focuses on acknowledging who we are without attaching it to adjectives related to our value.[68] When I ask individuals if they consider all people to have worth and deserving of respect, they quickly respond yes. Yet, when I ask why they don't apply the same principle to themselves, they often smirk. It doesn't come naturally, because of all that we've said about how our mind functions Self-acceptance must be a consistent intentional practice.

THE OBSERVING MIND AND THE THINKING MIND

There is a distinction between the observing mind and the thinking mind.[69] With our observing mind, we are able to see ourselves just as we are, without adding judgments and criticisms. The thinking mind tends to get flooded with judgments and criticisms rather than simply seeing what is. These "add-ons" often impact how we perceive ourselves, our ability to be self-accepting, and inevitably, how we behave.

For example, "I have a blemish on my face," is an observation. "I look like a nasty freak," is a judgment. We most often make negative *judgments* rather than neutral *observations* about ourselves and in doing so, we perpetuate negative thoughts and feelings. This cycle erodes our self-acceptance and overall self-confidence.

To foster self-acceptance, make it a point to observe yourself just as you are without attaching anything to the observations. If you find the judgments filtering through, notice and label them "judgment" and return back to the observation. Remain attuned to and curious as to where your mind is trailing off to and how it feels to sit solely with the observation. Reframing can be utilized whenever judgments come up thwarting self-acceptance or acceptance of others, leading to negative myopic thinking.

THE BENEFITS OF SELF-ACCEPTANCE

Many will argue that self-acceptance may be one of life's most important skills to be put into practice, as it can lead to greater life satisfaction and a healthier relationship to oneself. Further, more and more research supports the mind-body connection, and that unnecessary stress and mental health challenges can even have physical ramifications such as headaches, backaches, hypertension, etc.[70]

Self-acceptance has been linked to an increase in positive emotions as it focuses us on our strengths and reframes our point of view. Kristen Neff, a premier researcher on self-compassion, shares that the practice of self-compassion can increase our well-being as well, by cultivating "greater emotional resilience, more accurate self-concepts, more caring relationship behavior, as well as less narcissism and reactive anger."[71] If instead of "I really messed up this time. I can't do anything right," when someone doesn't do well on a task, they practice self-acceptance, the monologue becomes, "I tried my best. I'm disappointed, but I'm also human. I know I'm smart and capable of doing well in the future regardless of this less-than-ideal performance."

The Impact on Our Relationships

Self-acceptance helps us connect with our common humanity and strengthens our compassion. Neff shares, "All humans suffer. The very definition of being 'human' means that one is mortal, vulnerable, and imperfect. Therefore, self-compassion involves recognizing that suffering and personal inadequacy is part of the shared human experience—something that we all go through rather than being something that happen to 'me' alone." *By being accepting and compassionate towards ourselves, we can more easily give others the same benefit of the doubt, as we are able to connect with what it feels like to be imperfect, and to suffer as well.*

Neff further stated, "People feel compassion for themselves, because all human beings deserve compassion and understanding, not because they possess some particular set of traits." It's the ability to accept things as they are for kindness' sake, to be gentle with the suffering of yourself and others.

For example, if someone is rejected in a relationship or a relationship did not work out in their favor, they may become overly self-critical and focus on what they may have done wrong, and what they should have done differently. They may say, "That relationship didn't work out because I'm unworthy of love and I'm not lovable. I hate them." A self-compassionate person may reflect, "I am lovable. Maybe they weren't the one for me, but I'm happy I put myself out there. I can learn from this relationship going forward. I wish them well."

Self-acceptance not only includes accepting what we like about ourselves or consider favorable attributes, but also imperfect or less favorable attributes. It's easy to fall into the self-criticism trap, to be hyper-focused, hung up on our "less-than-ideal" parts and previous mistakes, or blaming ourselves for misgivings. *Self-acceptance says we are born enough, and as part of being human and having human experiences, we are perfectly imperfect.*

Those who struggle with self-acceptance compare themselves to others, manipulate themselves into being who they are not, and unnecessarily criticize themselves rather than accept who they are. Individuals self-blame and shame themselves for not being "good enough" compared to others. Here, it is being attached to the idea of who *they think they should be, rather than who they are.* This encompasses all of us, including our thoughts and feelings, which we have limited control of. The only things we truly have control over are our actions and behaviors.

People fear accepting all aspects of themselves and others. They worry they'll get complacent, accept mediocrity, and lack the motivation to change and grow. From my experience, it has the opposite effect. Once individuals genuinely accept themselves, they can work toward building their confidence and focus on more self-love and self-compassion.

Seven years ago, thirty-two-year-old Raquel came to see me feeling depressed and hopeless. She'd failed the Bar Exam five times and left several short unhealthy relationships. She just wanted to focus on her depressive symptoms.

After some time, she retook the Bar Exam and passed. She's happily married, a parent, and planning for a second child and a job as an attorney that better suits her needs. This is all a result of her being proactive and intentional about fortifying acceptance of her situation, of who she is fundamentally, working toward being a better version of herself, and living the life she wants. She cultivates her best life daily as she leans toward her values and meaningful action (the skills to embody acceptance and empowerment will be reviewed in Chapters Four and Eight).

Through adversity and challenge, we can find our strength, our fortitude, and our sense of purpose. Research and literature on post-traumatic growth indicates there can be a shift from one's view of being "sick" or "weak" toward "strong" and "resilient." The conversation moves from "What's wrong with you?" to "What's happened to you?"[72]

There's no end point to improving ourselves and our circumstances. It's a lifelong process requiring effort to be made indefinitely. It is a state of mind and a state of being. We give up on anything we think of as having an end point once we reach our destination. But if you want to be engaged in a connected relationship, maintain good health, or continue learning, effort and commitment remain ongoing.

Our mindset impacts the way we approach our practice. Sharon Salzberg states that self-love is an adventure, not a destination.[73] Thinking about it as an adventure, rather than a chore or burden, affects the way we approach it. *Adventure* connotes exploration, curiosity, and intrigue. It opens us up to infinite wondrous possibilities.

OTHER BENEFITS OF SELF-ACCEPTANCE

Self-acceptance and self-forgiveness have been correlated with overall improved physical health and well-being.[74] Those who are more accepting of themselves may also have the clarity to engage in healthy habits, from nutritious eating and getting adequate sleep, to better stress management.

After they have engaged in some not-so-healthy behavior, those who engage in a self-acceptance practice may be able to have a gentler, more effective dialogue with themselves. You've binged on a supersized bag of gummy worms. Black and white thinking—"I'm useless; I'll never be able to successfully work on this"—is self-sabotaging and detrimental. Someone who embraces self-compassion will acknowledge that they've eaten the gummy worms, be prompted by openness and curiosity to seek to better understand their behavior, and thereafter, be able to move on and meet their goals. They recognize that there will continue to be bumps in the road as our humanism dictates we are imperfect and make mistakes from which to learn and grow.

Overcoming Procrastination

When people think of themselves or others who struggle with procrastination, they rarely think about how self-compassion may play a role. They may not consider whether kindness or lack of kindness towards oneself could be impacting their productivity or ability to tackle tasks head on. Practicing self-compassion is known to help mitigate procrastination and drive an individual to take action.[75] This makes sense, because they'll more readily recognize, be with, and work through their discomfort, and be proactive at following through.

Engaging in negative self-judgments related to obstacles or to-do lists isolates anyone ruminating on anxieties surrounding tasks, fears, and potential failure. Stress levels increase, and procrastination worsens. Self-compassion allows us to take a more global view regarding procrastination, helping us recognize we're not alone in suffering. An integral part of practicing self-compassion is the acceptance, awareness and understanding that we share a common humanity.

Common Humanity

Common humanity versus isolation is one of the core components of self-compassion. Criticisms or judgments about oneself easily creates loneliness and retreat towards isolation. Shame may exacerbate the situation. We assume no one will understand, or perhaps we've been rejected for expressing such feelings.

When practicing self-compassion, it's important to remember *common humanity.* As humans, we have commonalities and therefore, common suffering. The ability to connect with our common humanity can be especially powerful in strengthening relationships. Even if it feels like it, we're never truly alone in our hardships.

Higher levels of self-compassion are associated with having healthier interpersonal relationships.[76] We're better able to communicate needs effectively. We have a greater sense of connectedness, ability to perceive our behaviors from the viewpoint of others, and relate empathetically. Those able to utilize self-compassion and kindness may be more inclined to be kind to others. They accept their own limitations and imperfections, therefore recognize limitations within others in a less condemning and more positive light.

For example, if we feel particularly insecure about something, we may project our insecurities onto others, as we cannot accept that aspect in ourselves. Some people may judge others based on appearance. They cannot accept the other person because their ego is tied to the idea that appearance and fashion make them valuable as a person, ideas that often rely on external acceptance or validation.

At the root of the projection may be that the individual never felt good enough, was negatively evaluated, didn't want to venture into how those experiences were personally hurtful, and/or feared that they would be judged, criticized, and rejected. Obviously, there's nothing wrong with wanting to look fashionable. However, if it causes negative judgments and actions that deviate from your values, strengthening your self-acceptance and acceptance of others will enhance the relationship with yourself and others.

Childhood attachments also impact establishing self-compassion. Studies show those who report secure relationships growing up had higher levels of self-compassion.[77] If we have close compassionate figures in our early years who model the behavior, we develop it in ourselves. It's important to recognize that we have an ability to turn our past around. We get the opportunity to re-write our narrative and expand on our ability to be compassionate. We can learn, then strive toward a positive sense of attachment and be in loving, fulfilling, and healthy relationships.

Improved Well-Being

Those who have challenges with self-acceptance may also struggle with physical and psychological well-being, as well as feelings of unhappiness.[78] Low self-acceptance and self-esteem were linked to emotional distress and decreased grey brain matter,[79] responsible for self-control, emotional regulation, speech, and decision making. Those with decreased grey brain matter may struggle with anxiety and stress. They're feeling a loss of "control," which disrupts these areas and causes further deterioration and unhappiness.

Self-acceptance, one of the keys to life satisfaction levels, is the habit people implement the least. A University of Hertfordshire study on life satisfaction influences found those who practiced self-acceptance regularly reported higher levels of life satisfaction and well-being. Not surprisingly, researchers found that implementing self-acceptance was one of the biggest influencers that differentiated those who reported lower life satisfaction versus those who reported higher levels.[80]

Emotional and Physical Health

Self-acceptance and self-forgiveness have also been correlated with overall improved physical health and well-being.[81] High levels of self-acceptance can lead to less focus on negative aspects of oneself and a higher likelihood of engaging in acts of self-love.[82] Those acts vary individually from more keenly tuning into your needs and speaking more compassionately to yourself, to acting in accordance with your values and best self.

Mind and body are interconnected. Dysregulation of emotions, which includes feelings about the self and responses to stressors, increases cortisol within the body.[83] Increased cortisol has been shown to cause inflammation, which in turn has been linked to a multitude of health issues and diseases, including high blood pressure, rapid weight gain, muscle weakness, impaired brain function, diabetes, and even certain infections.

Those who practice self-acceptance have lower rates of anxiety and depression, despite external circumstances and stressors.[84] Low self-acceptance increases oxidative stress.[85] This increases free radicals in the body and possible imbalances regarding antioxidants, which in turn may cause cell or tissue damage which promotes disease and premature aging.

Practicing and implementing self-acceptance is critical to satisfaction and stress reduction, which reduces anxiety and depression and helps mitigate physical challenges related to psychological stress.

IMPACT OF SELF-ACCEPTANCE

CONSEQUENCES OF LOW SELF-ACCEPTANCE	BENEFITS OF HIGH SELF-ACCEPTANCE
Don't accept who they are, and make themselves be someone they're not	Improved physical health and well-being
Criticize themselves	Healthier eating and sleep habits
Compare themselves to others, and shame themselves for not being good enough	Better stress management
Think in terms of "I should be"	Healthier relationships
Black-and-white thinking (I'm either good or I'm bad)	More effective communication
Procrastination	Greater sense of connectedness to others
Increased cortisol leading to inflammation (results can be high blood pressure, muscle weakness, impaired brain function, diabetes, and certain infections)	Greater empathy and kinder behavior to others
	Greater satisfaction with life
Increased oxidative stress (increased free radicals in the body can lead to cell or tissue damage and premature aging)	Lower rates of anxiety and depression

It is evident why gaining self-acceptance is highly beneficial. We also need to understand what the barriers are to cultivating it and how to practice it.

BARRIERS TO SELF-ACCEPTANCE

How Negativity Bias Gets in the Way of Our Self-Acceptance

Negativity bias is the tendency to focus on the negative aspects of our environment or ourselves versus the positive aspects. In this society which expects positivity and perpetual happiness, individuals blame themselves for thinking so negatively.

There is an evolutionary explanation as to why we do this. We may actually want to feel the negativity or "dwell" as it activates our pain senses essential to survival, according to Timothy J. Bono, Ph.D.[86] *Our brain is hard-wired to focus on the negative by utilizing our amygdala, the structure that may take even short negative experiences or instances and convert them into long-term memories.* To prove this, take a moment to think of one of the most negative experiences you had and connect directly to the feelings you had during that experience. You can probably recall it deeply and readily. If I ask you to think of one of the most joyful experiences you had and connect directly to the feelings you had during that experience, you will have a much harder time connecting to the joy. *We can more easily recall memories of our pain than our joy, both cognitively and somatically.*

Disapproval and criticism we may have received from parents, siblings, other relatives, teachers, peers, etc., cause us to enter adulthood with a negative self-bias. We may see ourselves as inherently defective which can have enduring effects throughout our lives.

When trying to demonstrate the universality of personal self-criticism and lack of self-belief, I show my patients and students three powerful YouTube video clips: *Choose Beautiful,*[87] *Dove Real Beauty Sketches,*[88] and *Our Common Fate.*[89] Watch these and take in how you think and feel.

To various degrees, we all suffer from chronic self-doubt. Think about your relationship with your parents. Their positive regard was probably contingent on your actions. Through their overt and covert disapproval of behavior, you might have evaluated yourself as *inadequate, selfish, not good or motivated enough.* You learned there were contingencies to being accepted. It's hard not to beat yourself up when there are stipulations that affect *worth, acceptance, and lovability.*

Our Mind Is Wired to Survive and Protect

Our mind is always self-protective, always in survival mode. *Our reptilian brain thinks if we're hyperaware and hypervigilant, and we focus on the negative, the what-ifs, and what-could-inevitably-go-wrongs, then we're protecting ourselves from harm, failure, and discomfort.*

The need and desire to *always* predict and prevent can backfire into worry, anxiety, depression, and hopelessness. As hard as you try, you can't always protect yourself. Even trying your best doesn't guarantee successfully warding off harm or discomfort.

This is often the case in those who experience trauma or Post-Traumatic Stress Disorder (PTSD), but it can even occur in slightly traumatizing circumstances. For example, it may only take a moment for someone to be teased or insulted, but that impact can have lasting repercussions. As suggested, our memory holds onto those painful recollections.

Despite a person receiving a multitude of accolades, they may still focus on that one negative instance. Different brain hemispheres sort through negative and positive information, says co-author, Clifford Nass, Stanford University professor of communications, in *The Man Who Lied to His Laptop: What We Can Learn About Ourselves from Our Machines.*[90] In a *New York Times* interview,[91] Nass says,

> Negative emotions generally require more thinking, and the information is processed more thoroughly than positive ones. The extra brain power that's required to process negative emotions means we spend more time contemplating the negative and less time on the positive. This is a general tendency for everyone, some people do have a more positive outlook, but almost everyone remembers negative things more strongly and in more detail.

We all want to feel good, and our culture reinforces that "happy" and "feeling good" are the ideal. Susan David refers to this as "toxic positivity" in her book on *Emotional Agility*.[92] It presents a challenge when our minds are constantly inundated with negativity. With our automatic tendency to want to feel good but being inundated with negativity, we often don't know how to experience contentment, satisfaction, and joy, even when we have positive thoughts and experiences.

Personal Barriers to Self-Acceptance

Because they're too painful to face, you may avoid accepting aspects of yourself. You may fear that if you attempt to practice self-acceptance then there will be negative consequences. Perhaps you will need to take direct action, are concerned that you can't work with it or change it, don't know how to work with it or change it, or may feel paralyzed by not knowing where to start.

Too often, we get in our own way of living our best life because of negative self-talk and internalized criticism or rejection from others over the years, which we have now internalized. When we feel we should be a certain way, or we're not meeting personal criteria or the standards of others, we judge ourselves. In Robert Firestone's book *Overcoming the Destructive Inner Voice*[93], he describes negative "self-talk" or engaging in one's "critical self" as the concept of tying an individual's self-worth to their perceived failures or mistakes.

For example, if a perfectionist makes a "mistake," they may feel worthless and hopeless. Hyperfixation on perceived shortcomings, self-judgment, and condemnation of self-worth can compromise mental health and can lead to intense anxiety, depression, shame and self-destructive behaviors. It depends on the way we perceive mistakes and the significance they hold for us. Albert Einstein remarked, "A person who never made a mistake never tried anything new." Michael Jordan said:

I've missed more than 9,000 shots in my career. I've lost almost 300 games. 26 times, I've been trusted to take the game-winning shot and missed. I've failed over and over and over again in my life. And that is why I succeed.

Albert Einstein and Michael Jordan see the value of mistakes and failures as prime opportunities for growth, learning, and thriving. Pain and disappointment define those occurrences, but to their benefit, contemplation, gratitude, and progress follow. When we accept all of ourselves, we open ourselves to learning and significant personal growth.

CURIOSITY-BASED QUESTIONS AROUND ACCEPTANCE

1. List what you appreciate about yourself, including your talents, skills, and abilities.
2. How readily were you able to list these? Did you hesitate or struggle to decipher whether you should appreciate these characteristics about yourself?
3. How resistant are you to accepting less-than-favorable parts of yourself (i.e., angry, unmotivated, impulsive, etc.)?
4. When they show up, how do you feel and react to them?
5. Why do you think you're resisting?
6. If you were to accept those parts, what are you concerned about?
7. When you experience discomfort in your thoughts, feelings, or bodily sensations, how do you react to them?
8. When you experience unexpected or disappointing circumstances, how do you think, feel, and respond?
9. When you find yourself in painful situations, how do think, feel, and respond?
10. How judgmental towards yourself do you perceive yourself to be?
11. How judgmental towards others do you perceive yourself to be?
12. If you were to be fully accepting of yourself, what would be your concerns?
13. If you were fully accepting of others, what would be your concerns?

14. If you were fully accepting of your circumstances, what would be your concerns?

🏆 SELF-GUIDED GROWTH EXERCISE: A LETTER ENCOURAGING SELF-ACCEPTANCE

Write yourself a letter encouraging self-acceptance (A sample format can be found on the next page). Start by indicating what's getting in the way of your cultivating it. Start with your own barriers, then consider people around you. Who may be reinforcing your negative self-talk and negative self-belief? Indicate why you may be allowing it. Indicate how you'll reinforce your self-worth by setting boundaries, making your needs known, or other specific actions you may take.

Identify your regrets and lost dreams. Gift yourself with compassion and understanding for where you were at during that time, and acceptance for where you are currently. Visualize first, then write about what it means to fully accept yourself and your circumstances so you can strive to be your best self and live the life that you want to be living.

Write Yourself a Letter Encouraging Self-Acceptance

What's getting in the way of cultivating it?

What are my barriers? Which come from people around me?

Who reinforces negative self-talk or self-belief?

Why do I allow it?

How will I reinforce my self-worth?
　　Set boundaries, make my needs known, etc.

Identify my regrets and lost dreams.

Gift myself with compassion and understanding
　　for where I was then, and where I am now.

What does it mean to fully accept
　　myself and my circumstances
　　so I can be my best self and live my best life?

Please listen to I Am Enough Guided Meditation:

Find all the ACE Your Life Guided Meditations at
www.michellemaidenberg.com/ACEYourLife

SCAN HERE FOR
I AM ENOUGH
GUIDED MEDITATION

Congratulate yourself for taking another
step toward ACE'ing Your Life.

Unleash your best self and live the life you want.

CHAPTER 4

Why We Resist Self-Acceptance and How to Embrace It

There is something wonderfully bold and liberating about saying yes to our entire imperfect and messy life.
–Tara Brach

SOCIETAL BARRIERS IMPACTING ACCEPTANCE

We grow up in a western culture that perpetuates the belief that we must prove our worth, be competitive, and strive tirelessly. There are also distinct messages, overtly and subliminally, that the most sought-after state is one of "happiness," a "positive attitude," and eternal "gratitude." Our society supports these ideas and ideals. Take a look at social media posts that list five, ten, or twenty ways to happiness. Read those that depict individuals unsuccessful at achieving "happiness," as being depressed, stuck, and hopeless. It's enough to make anyone "unhappy"!

Numerous posts speak to how grateful we should all be. We should recognize how fortunate we are, keep gratitude journals and look in the mirror every day to affirm how worthy and terrific we are and relish the lives we lead. Easy to say, a lot harder to internalize and feel at the gut level.

Although there are certainly benefits to reminding ourselves of the positive elements in our lives and what we're grateful for, in order for these sentiments to be truly helpful and relevant, you must be willing to embrace them. However, thinking positively and holding onto gratitude runs directly counter to how we think and feel as human beings, therefore, at times it is hard to be grateful.

Individuals who assume there must be something fundamentally wrong with themselves suffer sadness, frustration, and disappointment. They can't rid themselves of interfering thoughts and feelings they perceive as getting in their way, no matter how hard they try to reach these "ideal" states. It's challenging to accept and have compassion for yourself if you consider yourself doomed because of being unsuccessful and flawed.

I am working with Tabitha, an eighteen-year-old who came to me extremely unhappy about leaving for college. She's frustrated at not being as happy as her peers with the transition and is convinced it is destined to be an all-around unhappy experience. Tabitha criticized herself for not being able to be grateful enough for her current life circumstances and being given this opportunity.

"Think positive thoughts," "be grateful you got into such an impressive school," and "be happy because you'll be independent and have your freedom," sounded great, but she wasn't connecting to any of it and felt even worse for not thinking and feeling the way her family and friends expected. Her basic level of disappointment (i.e., "unhappiness") was mingled with sadness, guilt and frustration over her and everyone else's *shoulds, ought tos, and musts.* Tabitha's disappointment was riddled with the expectations she has for herself and those that others have of her. Who could blame her?

CHALLENGING SOCIETAL INFLUENCES

Recognize that social influences cajole us into fixed ideas about how we should think and be. This makes it challenging for us to be truly accepting of our circumstances and who we are.

Striving Toward Positive and Comfortable Emotions

We're socialized to be perpetual optimists or to reframe our thinking to be ideally positive. This isn't realistic or helpful. Our thinking falls naturally on a continuum from the more or less "positive" to the more or less "negative." The more positive thinkers are referred to as optimists and more negative thinkers as pessimists. Some of us fall closer to the extremes, and some of us are somewhere in between. Because *our minds truly have a mind of their own*, some of us weave in and out of positive and negative thinking.

A multitude of factors influence the direction our thinking takes. It's ineffective to think unilaterally and always positively. Both positivity (i.e., hopefulness, anticipation, etc.) and negativity (i.e., fear, dislike, etc.) have a place. All our thinking is understandable and acceptable.

Societal notions strive toward positive emotions. As humans, we are afforded and entitled to an array of feelings. Our goal isn't to only experience the comfortable and positive but *to learn how to get comfortable with being uncomfortable*. We are not kids in a toy store, purchasing what we prefer and leaving the rest. Our emotional spectrum has a place and purpose. Inevitably, the uncomfortable will show up, whether we like it or not. Our humanness dictates that it's bound to happen. We don't have control over our thoughts or feelings, only over our actions and reactions.

Striving for Happiness

We're expected to feel happy no matter how unrealistic and unproductive that expectation. In reality, *all* feelings are necessary and to be welcomed. We can't strive for a singular feeling state because they naturally ebb and flow along a continuum from uncomfortable to comfortable. Our natural tendency and pull is toward rejecting, avoiding, and purging our uncomfortable feelings so we can reach and maintain a "happy" state. It's a typical human phenomenon to experience an array of thoughts and feelings. Thoughts and feelings are what they are.

Try the terms content and satisfied instead of happy. Attach an action taken on behalf of a value to assess your contentment. This varies from person to person. For example, if you aspire for improved health and have decided to exercise four days a week to contribute to your contentment, based on your plan, you can assess what you need to do or continue to do to support positive thoughts and feelings.

Striving to Have Gratitude

We're expected to inhabit gratitude, but we can't feel it just because we're told to. It doesn't show up innately. Numerous factors contribute to cultivating gratitude relative to personal experiences and circumstances, culture, socialization, etc. Some can live very modestly and feel gratitude and contentment, while others, discontent even in a life of wealth and luxury, consistently yearn for more.

Just because we want to feel gratitude doesn't mean we instinctually and automatically will. Integrating a state of gratitude is a process, not something that can be imposed. When we intentionally notice, rather than take for granted all we're afforded with, or when we're proactive and take direct action, we reach personal satisfaction and experience a true sense of gratitude. Cultivating gratitude is all in the noticing and doing. For example, if you and your family make efforts to support a cause close to your hearts, participation in a 5k run fundraiser can ignite gratitude for the organization, the event, and fellow participants. Contentment may result from recognition of your kindness and generosity. It's difficult not to feel gratitude when you see the powerful impact you can make directly.

HINDRANCE OF COMPARING OURSELVES TO OTHERS

Throughout our development, we're socialized to compare ourselves and our circumstances to others. In fact, our mind naturally generates comparison to assess that we're "okay." However, *constant comparison hinders our ability to connect to ourselves*. There's great value in remaining present with ourselves, evaluating our needs and focusing on personal aspirations.

KEEPING THE NEED FOR PERSONAL CHANGE IN PERSPECTIVE

While it's okay to initiate efforts for improvement, there needs to be more emphasis on us being fundamentally whole, worthy, and okay as we are. We don't need to aspire to any ideals or specific states of mind. It doesn't make us bad or wrong because we're not inherently happy or struggle with gratitude. We are who we are.

Tabitha and I explored why she was unhappy about going off to college by breaking down and identifying what she found important and what would enable her to better appreciate the process. She was able to pinpoint goals and how she'll assess her progress on campus. During our session she looked at me suddenly and said, "I just wanted to be happy, but I never knew what happiness was because I never knew how to get there or let it in." It clicked! Tabitha realized that she can be accepting of her feelings, validate progress and move towards creating the life she wants with whatever feelings happen to show up.

WORKING THROUGH RESISTANCE AND TOWARD ACCEPTANCE

There are ways in which we act out our resistance to self-acceptance and fail to be self-compassionate. As a result we wind up repeating detrimental behavior patterns, denying ourselves the ability to become our best self and who we strive to be.

How We Act Out Our Resistance

We:

- **Deny and avoid what is happening.** Denial and avoidance are classic defenses and resistances to confronting feelings, especially uncomfortable ones.
- **Try to minimize challenges.** If it's minimized, there's the perception that it's not all that important, it doesn't impact us that much, and there's less urgency and need to work on it.

- **Come up with rationalizations for the way you and things are.** These rationalizations tend to deflect personal responsibility and serve as defense against seeing parts of yourself as imperfect or off-putting.
- **Blame others**. Recognizing your roles and responsibilities in your circumstances is challenging. Facing yourself in your process toward self-acceptance may necessitate self-reflection, self-awareness, and proactive change. Blame is another way of avoiding the discomfort of proactively evaluating your self-perception, confronting yourself and others, and setting appropriate and healthful boundaries.

Dave, a twenty-one-year-old patient, has attention challenges and is highly disorganized. While reluctant to accept that part of himself, he readily judges others who exhibit these traits. His father's own lack of follow-through continues to leave Dave frustrated, angry, and disappointed. He fears that if he accepts that part of himself, he'll experience pain, have a bad self-image, and use it as an excuse for not accomplishing tasks as his father does.

While Dave expects he'll have to consider medication, he's resistant. In his mind, medication reinforces that he's "inadequate," "not good enough," and "a mess," making him feel even worse about himself. He fears if the medication doesn't work, he won't know where else to turn, and he'll be left feeling more helpless.

By denying his disorganization, he believes somehow things will change, that he'll either grow out of it or will be able to compensate. No one will notice how hard his challenge is so he can avoid feeling shame. Dave doesn't want to chance giving up this positivity and hopefulness.

He lacks role models. Dave saw his parents argue constantly because of his father's forgetfulness. His mother's anger and belligerence increased as his father's self-depreciation grew. Despite infrequent attempts to get organized, his father still couldn't remain consistent and inevitably returned to his typical behaviors. This cycle was met with his mother's resentment and aggression.

Dave feels stuck and riddled with shame, disappointment, and hopelessness. His attempts to deny, disregard, and cut off his feelings have led to self-sabotaging behaviors. He denies, lies, or gets defensive when he forgets something, then mercilessly beats himself up for the oversight.

He realizes fear of failure and predicting negative outcomes dominate him. He's triggered by his experience with his father and doesn't want to see himself as anything remotely like him. Dave also recognizes that when he's formally made efforts, he hadn't fully committed to the process. He gave up prematurely because of his fear and hopelessness. He rationalized not continuing, and justified why this can't and won't ever work for him.

GAINING SELF-AWARENESS REGARDING SELF-ACCEPTANCE

Unconditional Self-Acceptance Questionnaire (USAQ)

The Unconditional Self-Acceptance Questionnaire,[94] or USAQ, was a scale developed by researchers Chamberlain and Haaga to measure self-acceptance. It consists of twenty statements rated on a scale from 1 (almost always untrue) to 7 (almost always true). Scores on this measure were found to correlate negatively with depression and anxiety and positively with happiness and general well-being.

Sample items include:
- I avoid comparing myself to others to decide if I am a worthwhile person.
- I set goals for myself that I hope will prove my worth.
- Sometimes I find myself thinking about whether I am a good or bad person.
- When I am criticized or when I fail at something, I feel worse about myself as a person.

To gain insight into your self-acceptance, take the full questionnaire.[95]

SELF-AWARENESS REGARDING YOUR SELF-ACCEPTANCE

We often hold negative beliefs about ourselves that impede our ability to embrace a positive self-belief. Opening yourself toward assessing your judgments, defenses, fears, self-belief, and self-efficacy will facilitate self-acceptance.

Your Judgments

No one judges us more than we judge ourselves. We can be our own worst enemy. We often lack patience with ourselves and have a challenging time accepting our imperfections. Our perceived flaws are emphasized because we're with ourselves 24/7. We have plenty of time to notice and mull over them. They're often exaggerated, *not because of the imperfection, but the impact we think our imperfections will have on us.* We must let go of the "ideal." There isn't any. Let go of what you think perfection looks like. Life is perfection in all its imperfections.

For example, my twenty-nine-year-old patient Claudia worked as a fashion designer. As you can imagine, she worked surrounded by professional models, "one more beautiful and statuesque than the other." She desperately wanted to advance, but her frequent comparisons left her referring to herself as unattractive or ugly. Even worse, she feared others would feel the same and not take her or her work seriously. Even though she obviously can't read the minds of others, and others' evaluations of her were quite the contrary, she was mired in self-doubt. We worked to help her notice her judgments—of herself and others—and to develop goals based on what she can control, what's feasible, and what is in line with her values. Claudia expressed appreciation for the sign I had on my door, "Don't believe everything you think." She learned to act on behalf of her values, rather than on behalf of her thoughts and feelings.

Ask yourself these questions to assess your judgments:

What are your general negative judgments about yourself?

_____

_____

_____

_____

_____

How do they get in the way of self-acceptance and being your best self?

_____

_____

_____

_____

What are your general negative judgments about others?

_____

_____

_____

_____

How do they get in the way of self-acceptance and being your best self?

_____

_____

_____

_____

Your Defenses

We're all defensive; it's indicative of our humanness. Our defenses help us cope and have helped some of us survive through childhood. We often don't need those defenses during adulthood, but we maintain them throughout our development because they served us well—as they help us to feel safe and protected.

We also get defensive when we feel attacked or offended without stopping to ask why. It's easier to blame the other person because in our mind, they caused us to feel bad. Sometimes we act based on our perceptions and assumptions, before checking in with ourselves and the other person. *When we get evoked, it's a good indicator of how and when we're still triggered and what we need to further explore and personally work on.* We must own what it brings up in us, pause to elicit our conscious awareness, and make a mindful decision.

For example, sixty-eight-year-old Brady gets highly defensive when he suspects he's being disrespected. He's learned to recognize that this arises when he assumes he hasn't been heard or is misunderstood. This emotional trigger dates back to childhood where he felt perpetually ignored and misunderstood. Physical and verbal aggression sometimes escalated between his alcoholic father and his overtly angry, blaming, and preoccupied mother, forcing Brady to get in the middle.

He brings up many interactions where he feels offended, then gets defensive. Afterward his remorse, shame and exasperation make it dif-

DEFENSE MECHANISMS

DENIAL Refusing to accept something as true
REPRESSION Forgetting or burying an experience or memory
DISPLACEMENT Shifting emotions from the negative thing to other things or people
PROJECTION Assuming others feel what you are; blaming events and people
REACTION FORMATION Behaving the opposite of what you think or feel
REGRESSION Reverting to childish behavior
RATIONALIZATION Explaining bad behavior away with excuses or justification
SUBLIMATION Transferring emotions to something productive to avoid the issue
INTELLECTUALIZATION Focusing only on the intellectual component while avoiding the emotional
DISSOCIATION Escaping by mentally separating from your body or environment
AVOIDANCE Choosing to not deal with the issue, procrastination, changing the subject

ficult to acquire self-acceptance when he's disdaining the parts of himself that spur him into angry defensive reactions. He understands people don't intentionally mean to hurt him, even if it feels as though they do.

As a child, he never knew what to expect, always needed to be on alert, and had to protect himself from real harm. While no longer the case, Brady understands his perceptions may be based on his ingrained fears, and that he may not know how to effectively communicate his feelings because he was never taught how. Unfortunately, as a result, his true intentions sometimes get lost in translation during his interpersonal interactions.

Ask yourself these questions to assess your defenses:
What are some defense mechanisms[96] that tend to show up for you?

_____

_____

_____

_____

_____

How do they get in the way of your self-acceptance and you being your best self?

_____

_____

_____

_____

_____

Your Fears

General fear, uncertainty, and apprehension make us feel destabilized. *We're creatures of habit. We gravitate and become habituated to the familiar and what we know, even if it doesn't necessarily serve us well. We'd rather know what to expect than enter uncharted territory.* Worrying also gives us something to do and makes us feel like we're in control when we might otherwise feel helpless. Despite reluctance and discomfort, it's important to take small steps to build up your tolerance to uncomfortable emotions and inevitably create change. You can start by listing things that scare you, that you're inhibited by, or that you tend to avoid. Build from small changes; build yourself up incrementally from minor discomforts to the more substantial.

For example, nineteen-year-old Alyssa desires to expand her socialization. She's hesitant to interact in social settings, infrequently follows up on initiating plans, and sticks to high school friends she feels most comfortable with. She recognizes the superficiality of online communication keeps her from deeper more meaningful relationships, making it more difficult for her to believe she's likeable.

When Alyssa went to sleepaway camp at ten, she was bullied throughout the summer, leaving her feeling insecure and shameful. She never returned to camp and didn't share the incidences with her parents until years later. From that point forward, she entered new social relationships reluctantly and cautiously.

Alyssa wanted to widen her social circle, despite her anxiety. In session, she learned about her automatic thoughts, the somatic physiological responses she experiences based on those thoughts, what feelings surface when faced with new social situations, and the actions she's compelled to take that thwart her progress. By learning to challenge herself during fearful episodes, she increased her willingness to be uncomfortable in the service of her desire to be in connected relationships.

Ask yourself these questions to assess your fears:

What tends to evoke fears for you (e.g., health-related, social, uncertainty, etc.)?

_____

_____

_____

_____

_____

How do they get in the way of your self-acceptance and you being your best self?

_____

_____

_____

_____

_____

Your Self-Belief/Self-Efficacy

Self-efficacy is a person's belief in their capabilities to complete tasks and achieve their goals.[97] People with a strong sense of self-efficacy develop self-belief, which results in a deeper interest in their activities, a stronger sense of commitment to their interests, a quicker recovery from setbacks and disappointments, and an acceptance of challenging problems as tasks to be mastered.[98]

Acquiring self-efficacy can provide the foundation for motivation, well-being, and personal accomplishment. It makes sense. Judging yourself capable of success increases chances of actual success, as well as the reverse, judging yourself as incapable reduces the chances.

For example, Justine, a twenty-year-old patient, was a coxswain on her college's crew team, responsible for steering, rhythm and morale, the most challenging job on the water. She faced intense challenges every time she and her teammates entered their shell.

Justine recognized that her self-doubt and difficulty being in the present moment caused her to spiral into anxiety over her ability to be a contributing teammate and carry out her role successfully. When she was able to nurture her self-efficacy and focus on being with what is, rather than what she feared would be (what if's), she was able to concentrate and perform better.[99] She understood that her athletic skills qualified her as an accomplished coxswain, and she was capable of being proud of herself.

Ask yourself these questions to assess your self-efficacy/self-belief:

What are some defeating beliefs that keep you from embracing a positive self-belief (e.g., I'm not skilled enough, they are better than me, I can't, etc.)?

_____

_____

_____

_____

_____

How do they get in the way of your self-acceptance and being your best self?

_____

_____

_____

_____

Although barriers inhibit us from accepting all that is, self-awareness and proactively taking steps toward facilitating acceptance can help us thrive.

EMBODYING SELF-ACCEPTANCE

12 Steps Toward Self-Acceptance

There are productive steps to take to work toward self-acceptance.[100]

Step 1: Recognize Your Mind's Protective & Nurturing Nature. Acknowledge and observe that your mind is generally driven toward the negative. It's a highly protective mind that keeps you hypervigilant, prepared for anything and everything that's uncomfortable or dangerous. If it highlights the negative and is highly critical, then you'll take extra precautions and secure your safety.

Step 2: Identify When Your Mind Is Avoiding, Denying, and Cutting Off. Notice that your mind may be proactively working toward blocking you from seeing the potential upside or positive results to avoid possible negative outcomes. It doesn't want you to risk experiencing negative or uncomfortable emotions or self-perceptions. It makes strides to avoid disappointment, frustration, and sadness. It will also try to protect you from perceiving yourself as a failure, not good enough, and ineffective.

Step 3: Notice the Propensity to Keep Returning to the Negative. Observe that when you're willing to see things more flexibly and positively, your mind has a hard time holding onto it and draws you back to the negative, no matter how hard you try to stay open. That's why, although challenging, it would benefit you to make concerted efforts to reel your mind back to being more expansive and hopeful. It doesn't consciously mean to give you a hard time. It's self-protective, and it takes its job seriously.

Step 4: Be Aware That You Hold onto Patterns of Thinking and Behavior That Are Familiar and Comfortable. This doesn't mean they're helpful or healthy. Our thinking and behaviors get etched into our neural networks and become part of our mapping and the way we function. Over time, there also may be secondary gain from holding onto certain patterns which reinforce the behaviors. For example, if I react angrily/aggressively, people respond to me, and I feel stronger and more effective.

Step 5: Set an Intention of Being More Open and Curious About Yourself, Others, and the World Around You. Shift paradigms to reflect curiosity, openness, and acceptance, rather than doubt, blame, and a need to be defended. This becomes the lens you see through, inhabit, and behave from in your everyday life. For example, with curiosity, instead of expecting and predicting negativity, you may ask, "What did she mean by that," "How did she reach that conclusion," or "When he acted that way, what could have compelled his reaction?" By being open, you're prompted to question and explore rather than defend against, judge, and criticize.

Step 6: Be Present With All the Thoughts and Feelings That Show Up. All your thoughts and feelings have value and deserve a space to just be. Our humanness dictates that we have an array of emotions and experiences. That's what makes life unique and rich for each of us.

The more you struggle with your thoughts and feelings, the greater the chance it will transform from common stress to significant distress. Continual thoughts about the thoughts, feelings about the thoughts, and feelings about the feelings spiral toward pain and suffering. For example, when fearful thoughts or feelings show up, label them "fear" or "worry" and use imagery to imagine them floating by like leaves in a stream or clouds in the sky.

Step 7: Identify the Elements of Change. Opportunities for growth exist even within difficult and stressful situations. Perhaps not exactly how you want things to be, but you have no choice but to cope with *what is*, not what it should/ought to/must be or how you want it to be. Your mind will often paint a bleak picture, suggesting you're hopeless, helpless, and should just relent. *You, not your mind, get to decide the direction you want to take.*

Step 8: Notice and Celebrate You. We're quick to identify our "flaws" and all that is "wrong" with us. It becomes confusing when we're taught to not be too boastful or full of ourselves. We're also not directly taught how to acknowledge, appreciate, and accept ourselves. *It's uncanny, if you search up love songs, you'll find songs representing our love toward others. What about love songs directed toward loving ourselves?* We're just not conditioned to understand its importance.

There's a critical need to notice what's wonderful and wholesome about yourself. Pay attention and notice it *all.* Throughout your day, you perform acts of kindness (e.g., opening the door for someone, calling a sick friend, etc.), and expect it from yourself. Every single moment you lean into your best self is pertinent, noteworthy, and helps you get better at accepting and appreciating who you are.

Step 9: Forgive Yourself for Missed Dreams, Past Mistakes, and Failures. Part of self-acceptance is recognizing we grow on every level—physically, psychologically, socially, and emotionally through our development. We do the best we can with the information we have at the time we make those mistakes. We understand ourselves better by examining the conditions at that time—what was instinctive/automatic (i.e., our thoughts, feelings, and actions), what our needs were, and what we believed about ourselves (e.g., lazy, mean, selfish, etc.). Our past regrets can help us learn so that we have a greater understanding of ourselves, our needs, and what we want for our future.

Becoming more self-accepting necessitates recognizing who we are, and that our actions have been influenced by our background and biology. While we can take personal responsibility for ways we might have hurt or mistreated others, we also realize, given our internal programming, we behaved based on where we were at during that time. It's our task to construct a more fulfilling life going forward.

For example, you may often be left saying, what was I thinking when I did ____. You were thinking with your current mind experience and social/emotional maturity at the time. You can remind yourself by saying, "Back then, I made the best decision with the information I had at the time. I perceive things differently now because of my *present* wisdom and insight based on new experiences. If it were today, I would have made different choices because of all I've learned. I'll be mindful and make choices in line with my values and my best self."

Our inability to reconcile who we are, rather than who we would rather be or expected to be, often impedes our self-acceptance. It's okay to grieve over lost dreams or goals, but moving forward requires letting go of hope that past events can and will be different.

Step 10: Cultivate a Nurturing Life and Relationships. If you're surrounded by perpetually pessimistic others who put you down or don't support your ambitions, you're likely to feel discouraged and not be your best self. Willingness to accept this behavior is a clue to your mindset.

If you're around self-confident others, practice healthful behaviors, and live a valued life, then those are the meaningful characteristics you appreciate. Their positive influence promotes your personal growth and development. It brings out your best self and supports your healthful behaviors and aspirations. Create a support system based on the premise that you're worthy, valuable, and deserving. An individual able and willing to interact with you from that premise is likely to enhance you and be a better influence.

Step 11: Speak and Behave on Behalf of Your Best Self. You are your most important ally. I always tell my patients, "*The longest relationship you'll have is with yourself, and it's one you should take the most seriously.*" We need to nurture ourselves the way we want to be supported throughout our lives, the way we'd love and encourage our children or loved ones.

Use encouragement. Be self-encouraging in your self-talk and behaviors. Act as if you were speaking and behaving toward someone you love. If you accept that you're human, you'll recognize you're imperfect, that you're going to make mistakes. We all do. Our goal is to try our very best.

Step 12: Commit to Practicing and Not Giving Up No Matter What. You deserve unconditional love. Recognize the need to *demonstrate* actions on behalf of your best self for your own sake. Because you're fundamentally whole and worthy, despite your imperfections and humanness, commit to striving, to never giving up, no matter what.

Commit to consistently questioning yourself as to whether you're being led toward your values or away from them, and by the actions you're taking, are you increasing or taking away from your confidence? In every circumstance, you can make mindful decisions, facilitate your personal growth, and be more self-accepting.

Invest in practicing self-acceptance by bringing up thoughts, memories, or anything else that evokes uncomfortable emotions and incrementally learn to sit with it all. You want to work on acceptance all the time, even when you're not particularly sad, anxious, angry, or stressed. This will benefit you, so that you can apply it when you do feel any or all of those things.

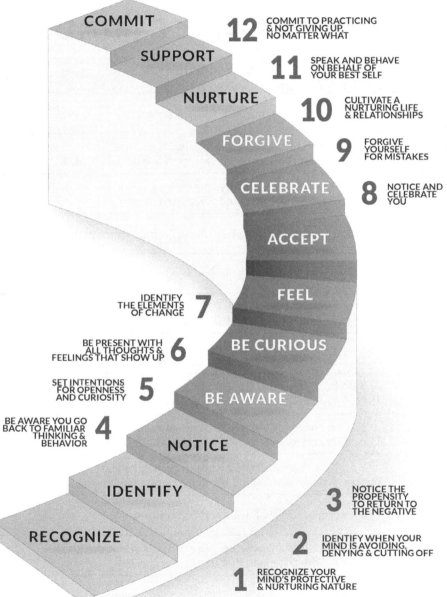

STEPS TOWARD
SELF-ACCEPTANCE

COMMIT — **12** COMMIT TO PRACTICING & NOT GIVING UP, NO MATTER WHAT

SUPPORT — **11** SPEAK AND BEHAVE ON BEHALF OF YOUR BEST SELF

NURTURE — **10** CULTIVATE A NURTURING LIFE & RELATIONSHIPS

FORGIVE — **9** FORGIVE YOURSELF FOR MISTAKES

CELEBRATE — **8** NOTICE AND CELEBRATE YOU

ACCEPT

FEEL — **7** IDENTIFY THE ELEMENTS OF CHANGE

BE CURIOUS — **6** BE PRESENT WITH ALL THOUGHTS & FEELINGS THAT SHOW UP

BE AWARE — **5** SET INTENTIONS FOR OPENNESS AND CURIOSITY

NOTICE — **4** BE AWARE YOU GO BACK TO FAMILIAR THINKING & BEHAVIOR

IDENTIFY — **3** NOTICE THE PROPENSITY TO RETURN TO THE NEGATIVE

RECOGNIZE — **2** IDENTIFY WHEN YOUR MIND IS AVOIDING, DENYING & CUTTING OFF

1 RECOGNIZE YOUR MIND'S PROTECTIVE & NURTURING NATURE

A SELF-ACCEPTANCE MINDSET

A shift in mindset reflects how you see yourself and the world around you. Remind yourself daily:

SELF-ACCEPTANCE MINDSET

REMIND YOURSELF DAILY
I am not my past; I am my present.
I will open myself up to looking at all aspects of myself and the world with an open and curious lens.
My humanness dictates me making mistakes. They're inevitable, and I will learn from them.
I will focus on me, because I can only compare me to myself.
I have great value, as all human beings intrinsically do.
I will reserve judgment of myself and others, because not everything is what it seems.
I'm not a bad, mean, etc. person; I am a person who has acted badly, mean, etc.
When I act badly, I'm not a bad person. I am a person who behaved badly in that moment and can improve upon my behavior in the future.
I don't have to continue to prove myself to others. My actions are connected to my values and what's meaningful to me.
I can work on myself without damaging and counter-productive blaming, shaming, or condemning myself.
I can reprimand my behavior without reprimanding myself.
Just because I think and feel a certain way about myself, doesn't mean that it's valid and true.
I am not my thoughts, feelings, or circumstances.
I can change; my narrative can change because life is forever in flux.

Self-acceptance can look different for each of us, depending on what we've struggled with and which parts of ourselves we'd rather not think about and acknowledge. The less favorable parts are the ones requiring the most compassion and nurturing.

There's a reason why we're angry, jealous, anxious, etc. If those emotions showed up in someone you love, would you deny, ignore, or berate them? If so, that person would likely feel worse and act out even more. You have value, and you deserve to be accepted for *all* that you are. You're here taking the time and effort to be courageous and brutally honest with yourself. You can move toward unconditional acceptance and acting on your own behalf to cultivate a life you're proud of.

CURIOSITY-BASED QUESTIONS AROUND ACCEPTANCE

1. What societal barriers get in the way of your self-acceptance (e.g., striving toward positive and comfortable emotions, comparing yourself to others, etc.)?
2. Do you find yourself in the happiness trap and striving toward achieving these ideals? How does it impact you?
3. In what way do you act out your resistance toward self-acceptance (e.g., deny or avoid, come up with rationalizations, etc.)?
4. What does this keep you from accepting about yourself?
5. Are there patterns of thinking that your mind tends to hold onto because they're familiar and comfortable, even if not helpful and/or healthy?
6. Are there patterns of behavior that are automatic and habitual because they're familiar and comfortable, even if not helpful and/or healthy?
7. What thoughts and feelings are most comfortable?
8. What thoughts and feelings are most uncomfortable?
9. Do you notice most, if not all, your accomplishments, even the smaller ones?
10. How do you acknowledge yourself for these accomplishments?

11. What past regrets, mistakes or failures challenge your acceptance? Why?
12. Are there relationships that don't promote your personal growth and self-acceptance? In what ways? Who are they with? What are you willing to do about it to enhance your self-acceptance?
13. Does your self-talk promote your self-acceptance? How?
14. What behaviors are you willing to shift in order to reinforce your self-acceptance?

SELF-GUIDED GROWTH EXERCISES: POSITIVE SELF-TALK AND NON-JUDGMENTAL CHALLENGES

A. Take the Positive Self-Talk Challenge

For twenty-one days, be keenly aware when you say something negative about *yourself* (e.g., I look awful, I'm not good enough, I can't do anything right, etc.). Take account daily. Note it in your phone or on paper. Label it *self-critical.* Say to yourself, "In this moment, I'm accepting myself as I am as it will help me to be my best self." Make sure not to respond to the thought. If you can't avoid spiraling into more self-belittling messages, follow them gently and non-judgmentally. In what ways? Bring yourself back to the present compassionately. Repeat these steps as often as you need to.

B. Take the Non-Judgmental Challenge

For the same twenty-one days or subsequently, be keenly aware when you say something negative about *someone else* (e.g., they're so stupid; they're a mess; they look ugly, etc.). Take account daily. Make note and label it *judgmental.* Say to yourself, "In this moment I'm accepting them as they are as it will help me to be my best self." As with **A,** make sure not to respond to the thought or let it spiral into more judgmental sentiments. If it attempts to go down that route, non-judgmentally, gently, compassionately bring yourself back to the present. Repeat these steps as often as you need to. It takes *at least* twenty-one days for the brain to reset habits and patterns. If you're not satisfied by then, you could return to your familiar, self-critical ways. Hopefully not! Because you'll realize there's power and progress in practice.

After the challenges assess what it was like to be so self-aware of your judgments.

What was the process of noticing your thoughts and feelings like for you? How readily were you able to come back to the present moment?

_____

_____

_____

_____

What surprised you about what you discovered?

_____

_____

_____

_____

Did anything change over time as you became more self-aware?

_____

_____

_____

_____

Please Listen to Praising Our Accomplishments Guided Meditation:

Find all the ACE Your Life Guided Meditations at
www.michellemaidenberg.com/ACEYourLife

SCAN HERE FOR
PRAISING OUR
ACCOMPLISHMENTS
GUIDED MEDITATION

Congratulate yourself for taking another
step toward ACE'ing Your Life.

Unleash your best self and
live the life you want.

Part III:

Compassion
(The Second Step in the ACE Method)

Having compassion means noticing, feeling emotionally moved, and responding to your own suffering as well as others'. In its core, compassion means to "suffer with." Self-compassion entails acting in a warm caring way toward yourself when having a difficult time, fail, or notice something you don't like about yourself.[101] Instead of harsh judgment or ignoring your pain, you acknowledge and validate it. You realize suffering, failure, and imperfection are part of a shared human experience.

CHAPTER 5

What Is Compassion & What Are the Barriers That Get in Our Way of Cultivating It?

Our self-criticism tends to undermine self-confidence and leads to fear of failure. If we're self-compassionate, we will still be motivated to reach our goals—not because we're inadequate as we are, but because we care about ourselves and want to reach our full potential. Self-compassionate people have high personal standards; They just don't beat themselves up when they fail.
—Kristin Neff and Christopher K. Germer

Practicing compassion increases our satisfaction and sense of self and can positively influence interpersonal relationships. Self-compassion needs to come from within. But how should we practice it so that we're connecting and integrating it into the actions we take toward ourselves and others?

Self-compassion does not mean accepting mediocrity and rationalizing our negative or unhelpful behavior, but rather empathizing and supporting our real experiences so we curiously and willingly venture into a journey of personal growth.

You will learn the details of self-compassion and its numerous benefits. You'll also understand the barriers that impact our ability to be self-compassionate and explore how to integrate it as a daily practice.

WHAT IS SELF-COMPASSION AND HOW WILL IT BENEFIT YOU?

Dr. Dennis Tirch, author of six books, including *The Compassionate Mind Guide to Overcoming Anxiety*[102] and the founder of The Center for Compassion Focused Therapy stated, "Self-compassion is not a feeling, it is more like a pattern of behaviors that are based on a deep and fundamental acceptance of and kindness to ourselves–the good, the bad, and the ugly."

The concept of self-compassion differs from self-esteem and self-acceptance, but it can be used as a vehicle towards self-acceptance and ultimately, a healthier sense of self. Formative researcher Kristin Neff differentiates between self-esteem and self-compassion. She writes:

> Self-esteem refers to the degree to which we evaluate ourselves positively. It represents how much we like or value ourselves and is often based on comparisons with others. In contrast, self-compassion is not based on positive judgments or evaluations, it is a way of relating to ourselves. People feel self-compassion because they are human beings, not because they are special and above average. It emphasizes interconnection rather than separateness. This means that with self-compassion, you don't have to feel better than others to feel good about yourself. It also offers more emotional stability than self-esteem because it is always there for you—when you're on top of the world and when you fall flat on your face.

I define self-compassion as a means to proactively take steps to validate, support, and nurture ourselves. *We go from having an inner critic to an inner advocate and nurturer*. It entails paying attention, grounding yourself, identifying your needs, and providing *yourself* with what you need emotionally from your most coveted caretaker (who may or may have not provided it). We can't always rely on the support and care of others because that depends on their awareness, knowledge, and capacity to do so. *We always have ourselves, all the time, without fail.*

Kristin Neff designed the Self-Compassion Scale (SCS),[103] and asserts that self-compassion can be broken down into three parts to be practiced: self-kindness, [understanding] a sense of common humanity, and mindfulness. You can take the scale online which self-scores.[104]

Self-kindness involves being gentle with ourselves and what we are currently experiencing.

Understanding a common sense of humanity is to understand *all beings suffer* to some capacity, which helps us understand we are not alone in our suffering.

Mindfulness, in this context, is described as inquisitiveness about what is happening in the moment, rather than being judgmental.[105] In an emotional and physical sense, Neff[106] and Germer[107] who co-developed the Mindful Self-Compassion (MSC) program recommend in order to be self-compassionate, *you let yourself be.*

As of 2018, over 1,840 evidence-based journal articles reported on the benefits of having or acquiring self-compassion. Higher levels of self-compassion have been associated with greater life satisfaction, emotional intelligence, social connectedness, motivation[108], learning and performance goals, wisdom, personal initiative, curiosity[109], happiness, gratitude, optimism, and positive affect. Self-compassion is also associated with less self-criticism[110], depression[111], anxiety, fear of failure, thought suppression, perfectionism[112], rumination, shame, suicidality, and disordered eating behaviors.[113]

Applying self-compassion has been shown to be effective in those who engaged in exercises to gain skills in how to be more compassionate to oneself in times of distress.[114] They found that working on self-compassion helps increase one's satisfaction and sense of self, even if practiced over a brief period of time. These exercises can be useful to one's journey in self-acceptance.[115]

But the key to self-compassion is "to understand that weakness and frailty are part of the human experience,"[116] according to Deborah Serani, PsyD, psychologist and author of *Living with Depression.* "Coming to accept who you are involves loving yourself *because* of your flaws, not in spite of them."[117] Only when we understand and pardon ourselves for things we earlier assumed must be all our fault can we secure the relationship to self that, until now, has eluded us.

WHAT WILL SELF-COMPASSION DO FOR YOU?

We all share the need to be attuned to, connected to, validated, and comforted. We have taken on the idea that it should or must come from others and be facilitated by certain people in a specific way. We become attached to fixed ideas about how we are to receive support and encouragement. Because we're so focused externally, we often lose sight of *our* ability to self-soothe, strengthen, and empower *ourselves.*

YOU are the only one who deeply knows and gets you. You're with yourself 24/7. You feel, experience, and venture out together for all the days of your life. *You will never leave you.* You are consistent, reliable, and accessible to yourself. Who is better equipped to provide nurturance to you than you? You can learn and work toward being your biggest fan and greatest asset.

Everyone deserves validation and nurturing, but we can't always leave that responsibility to others. Our thoughts, feelings, and needs can be fleeting and variable. As much as we want others to be accessible when we need support, no one can be reliable all the time.

Undertaking such a heartfelt exploration and expression of self-love inevitably generates increased self-compassion. We approach ourselves and take action based on the fundamental belief that we deserve to be noticed, attended to, and supported. We can notice our self-judgments and condemnations, and work to become softer, more thoughtful, and substantially kinder to ourselves.

We are quicker to recognize our common humanity and act empathetically when interacting with others. Cultivating this in our relationship with ourselves facilitates the way we approach ourselves, others, and life in general. Approach self-compassion with a keen sense of inquisitiveness, ("What am I thinking and feeling?"), curiosity, ("Why might I be thinking or feeling this way?"), and responsiveness, ("What do I need now, based on how I'm thinking and feeling?").

Adopting a more loving stance toward ourselves is the *key* prerequisite for self-compassion. We must realize that since childhood, in order to get noticed and accepted, we've felt obliged to demonstrate our worth to others, a concept reinforced as we've grown and matured. *Here and now, we revolutionize our belief and behavior, aligning with the mindset that power lies within to notice, accept, and react to ourselves. We become our portable ally.* By developing greater self-compassion and focusing on *how* we are and *what* we need, we gain a broader perspective and appreciation for who we are, how we process things, and how "human" we are.

Showing Compassion to Ourselves Is Transformative

Showing compassion to ourselves for our fallible and human imperfections is not a mechanism to minimize, rationalize, or relent to our negative or unhelpful behaviors.

Self-compassion is the change agent leading our transformation. It allows us to develop self-worth and self-belief which ignites our desire and willingness to achieve our goals. Strengthening our confidence helps facilitate the conviction that we are worth the effort, because we have the innate ability to transform and be our best selves.

I see vast change and progress when patients become more self-compassionate. Camille, a fifty-one-year-old female patient has been in treatment with me for more than a decade. I've supported her through the deaths of her mother, father, sister, and father-in-law. After a short hiatus, she reached out again. Her intense look of despair made it obvious something profound had happened. She shared that she'd recently lost her twenty-one-year-old daughter in a car accident. She didn't know that a month earlier, I had experienced the traumatic accidental death of my teenage nephew.

Due to our mutual loss and listening to her tell her story, it naturally evoked an intense sense of helplessness and grief in me. My reaction necessitated that I share my experience. I made a clinical judgment that the best thing I could do for her in that moment was to model humanism and authenticity. While remaining cognizant of staying with her and *her* experience, I validated our mutual disbelief, sadness, and inability to comprehend such senseless tragedies. She appreciated me sharing my story.

"I sometimes forget that you're human too," she said. Camille was comforted that I showed my vulnerability and could cry for the both of us without apologizing for my reaction or holding it back. She connected with me through our mutual suffering, for which I was able to provide a holding environment. This reinforced that she can just be, and however she showed up with me would be accepted, welcomed, and supported. Camille shared her feelings, from sadness, disappointment, anger, fear, to guilt and shame.

After the mutually painful session, I intentionally took a moment for self-compassion. I gave myself additional time to sob and process my feelings. I was in touch with deep compassion—for Camille, for myself, and all the others suffering through these unimaginable tragedies. I gently and lovingly closed my eyes and imagined being cradled by my grandmothers, one on each side of me, reiterating validation of my feelings. It was okay and understandable for me to be in pain, a wonderful reminder, illuminating how deeply I feel and how deeply I love others. The ability to be self-compassionate has helped me cultivate compassion for others. I strive to show up with self-awareness, authenticity, and a compassionate heart.

Because of the degree of intimacy it requires of her, Camille's lifetime experiences with grief and loss inhibit her ability to show and express that vulnerability and compassion. My display of compassion and care for her modeled how she can behave with herself and in her outside relationships with others.

We can be transparent with our imperfections, face them, and lean into our discomfort. It's a consistent message among scholars who understand human nature and the mind.

- Carl Jung: "What you resist not only persists, but will grow in size."
- Eckhart Tolle: "Whatever you fight, you strengthen, and what you resist, persists."
- Kristin Neff: "What we resist, persists," and "What we can feel, we can heal."

We can give ourselves the opportunity to heal mindfully when we consciously take the time to focus on it. There is a need to integrate self-compassion throughout the process of healing. Working on ourselves internally gives us the strength to move through the adversity and pain. One would mindfully ask, *"What am I experiencing right now?"* and *"How am I thinking and feeling about it?"* *"What do I need right now?"* and *"How will I be kind to myself when I suffer?"*

There is often no choice but to accept that things are and will continue to be painful. *If we can be kind to ourselves in the midst of suffering, rather than avoiding, distracting, warding off, or beating ourselves up because of the suffering, we can be with our anguish and sorrow with greater ease.*

We tend to fight ourselves (self-criticism), we flee from others (isolation), or we freeze (rumination).[118] When we practice self-compassion, we deactivate the threat-defense system and activate the care system. Oxytocin, a hormone and neurotransmitter produced in the hypothalamus and released by our pituitary gland causes feelings of love and closeness, and endorphins, the "feel good" chemicals produced naturally by the nervous system that acts as a pain reliever and happiness booster are released. These help to reduce stress and increase feelings of safety and security.

Pain in life—loss, worry, heartbreak, hardship—is inevitable, but when we resist, the pain usually intensifies. This add-on pain equates with suffering. We suffer not only because it is painful in the moment, but because we bang our head against the wall of reality, getting frustrated and hopeless because we think things *should be* other than they are.

Self-Compassion Enhances Our Relationship With Others

We don't often contemplate how we approach our relationships. Is it with openness and enthusiasm, reluctance and anticipatory anxiety, or in some other way? How we approach our relationships impacts our behavior while in the relationship, and the perception we give to the person we're relating to. Practicing self-compassion can increase our well-being by cultivating greater emotional resilience and more caring relationship behavior. Self-compassion helps us better meet our own needs, which, in turn, allows us to dedicate more emotional resources to meeting the needs of friends, family, and relationship partners.[119]

My thirty-four-year-old patient Emily became intensely emotional as she described witnessing her mother's seizure while at home with her family. Emily felt powerless not knowing how to help, and fearful her mother could have died. Emily repeated several times that she didn't know what she would have done if she'd lost her. She considers her mother her best friend, someone she highly relies on. She spoke passionately about how much her mother means to her and her deep love for her.

Her endearing sentiments touched me, and I asked whether she'd expressed them directly to her mother. She responded that she expressed fear of losing her, but not why. I wasn't surprised, as I'd been working with her on social anxiety and challenges she has with emotionally connecting to others due to fear of intimacy and being vulnerable. To avoid disapproval or rejection she thought inevitable in her relationships, she didn't openly share her intimate feelings.

Her inability to connect with her self-compassion kept her from connecting to others in relationships in the way that she wanted to. Difficulty recognizing, accepting, and acknowledging her own worth challenged her ability to believe others could find her likable and lovable.

I asked her to role play with me as to how she might express her feelings to her mother and address why it was so frightening to imagine life without her. As she tearfully and thoughtfully followed through, I interjected that if something more catastrophic had happened, her mother would have missed those loving messages. She understood holding back not only prevents her from deepening their mother-daughter relationship, but also from connecting directly with her values of family and love.

I then had her express gratitude, kindness, and love toward herself for being as caring and as loving as she was in a time of great need. And now we could add her willingness to go home and have this conversation directly with her mother, as well as her commitment toward enhancing her relationship with herself and others.

Intentionally and proactively engaging in self-compassion helped Emily reframe that instead of being inadequate, which was the way in which she saw herself and the narrative she told herself, she is a thoughtful, warm, and caring daughter and person in general and has much to offer in her relationships. It made it more seamless for her to approach her mother, express herself in an emotional and relational way, and carry over these behaviors when interacting with others.

I strive for all of my patients to have a keen sense of self-awareness, to be accepting of who they are fundamentally including *all* parts of themselves, to assert compassion toward themselves and others, and lean proactively into their values.

BARRIERS THAT THWART SELF-COMPASSION

Early in life, many barriers can get in the way of integrating self-compassion. You may have grown up around demeaning or hypercritical caretakers; had negative social experiences in which you were mistreated or rejected; had a characteristic or challenge you felt unsure about or loathed; or had an especially disapproving or protective mind. Societal influences and expectations, such as standards of beauty and perfectionism, also impact us.

Our objective should be to counteract the barriers with direct action to integrate self-compassion as a daily practice. If we believe everything we think, we'll inevitably come upon situations in which we perceive things differently from how they actually are. These perceptions—which Dr. Aaron Beck, founder of Cognitive-Behavioral Therapy (CBT), terms "cognitive distortions" or "thinking errors"—can get in the way of achieving goals and acting on behalf of personal values.[120] I call them "self-limiting thoughts."

Self-limiting thoughts set in motion the way you experience a situation or circumstance, the way you think and feel about it, and then the way you act. For example, if a high school student participates in, but loses his championship baseball game, he may understandably feel disappointed and frustrated. He might have a hard time getting past the feeling. He may think, "What was the point of playing the whole season? We lost the championship game to a lower caliber team." He may tell himself, "The coach is disappointed in us and thinks we suck." Since this thinking makes him feel profoundly sad and ashamed, he may neglect to thank his coach for his guidance throughout the season. He may even want to skip his awards dinner, throw his trophy in the garbage, and conclude he doesn't want to try out for next season.

This thinking *minimizes* the effort he and his team put in. While parts of the season were weak, his team made the finals because they won games and played well. And his guessing about his coach's opinion of him—mind reading—is another kind of self-limiting thinking.

Self-limiting thinking takes many forms. In this situation, it led the teen to want to quit the team after one bad game. Instead of seeing it as just one bad game, employing self-limiting thinking led him to criticize his abilities, undermining his self-compassion. Self-limiting thinking can affect self-compassionate behaviors, sabotaging this teen's motivation, making it less likely he will stick with the sport. Because of the significant impact self-limited thinking can have on our actions and behaviors, it is essential to understand when these self-limiting beliefs arise and how to work through them.

The Most Common Types of Self-Limiting Thinking[121]

1. All-or-Nothing: *Black-and-white thinking with nothing in the middle*

In line with her goals to manage her sugar intake, Tate has eaten healthily all week. Saturday at lunch with her family, she eats a healthy sub and feels content. Soon afterward, her family wants to go out for ice cream. She has a three-scoop hot fudge sundae. Guilt creeps in after she finishes. She tells herself, "I'm such a loser. I've blown my healthy eating plan. I'll never succeed at this. I might as well go off it for the rest of the weekend and start fresh next Monday."

Tate's all-or-nothing thinking keeps her from recognizing that one sundae is not the end of the world, and that giving up for an entire weekend is not in line with her goals. If anything, it will only pull her away from accomplishing even short-term goals and make it harder for her to start up again. Instead, she could consider being self-compassionate, acknowledging that having the sundae doesn't mean that she's failed. It's okay to account for it in her overall plan, *and* she could elect to immediately get back on track.

2. Catastrophizing: *Negative fortune-telling*

Nathaniel starts a new job and is learning new tasks. After reviewing a spreadsheet he completed the day prior, he notices an error. His concern produces looping thoughts about his ineffectiveness. He thinks, "I'll never learn this stuff. My boss will be very disappointed and fire me." He neglects to tell his boss about the error and sits with the information for the rest of the week.

If he's self-compassionate, he might contemplate that when learning a new task, there's likely to be mistakes made which bosses usually expect. He would recognize that because his job performance and competency is important to him, it's understandable to be disappointed in himself. He'd also accept that in the long run, holding onto the information can do more harm than good, so he'd empower himself to tell his boss immediately.

3. Emotional Reasoning: *Thinking your ideas must be true even though evidence says otherwise*

Kelly's a straight A student who's convinced that she'll fail every test despite evidence to the contrary; every time she prepares for a test, she does well.

To reconsider her fear, Kelly can reality test, consciously reminding herself that she has succeeded in the past, and given preparation, there is no reason why it should be different this time.

4. Magnification/Minimization: *Making the negative bigger and the positive smaller*

Darren gave a presentation at work showing senior leadership a new way of making more efficient use of company marketing funds. After the presentation was over, his boss told him he did a great job and that he developed a major breakthrough for the business. He also gave Darren a few pointers on how he could tighten up the presentation next time he needs to share it. Although Darren had hit the ball out of the park and had every reason to be proud, he brushed aside the praise and instead focused on the opportunities for improvement, beating himself up for not being flawless.

If Darren was not engaged in minimized thinking, he would cheer his success, taking pride in himself instead of brushing off the praise he received. And if he wasn't experiencing magnified thinking, instead of feeling disappointed that he wasn't perfect, Darren would simply feel appreciative that his boss was invested enough to give him helpful feedback.

5. Mental Filter: *Paying undue attention to one negative detail of the situation instead of seeing the whole picture*

Hannah stayed up late to finish an assignment needed before the next workday. In the morning, she didn't hear her alarm that would have allowed her to go for a run before heading to the office. She thinks, "I blew it. There's no other time. There goes exercising for today."

If she expanded her thinking, she'd reconsider and recognize that while she's proud she typically gets up early to run, it's not the only way to exercise. She could climb up and down the five flights of stairs at work and walk the dog when she gets home.

6. Mind Reading: *Believing you know what others are thinking*

Penelope sometimes struggles in her relationship with her parents. She hesitates to assert herself and make her needs known, especially when her parents make unannounced weekend visits that often take her kids away from participating in hockey practice. If she were to set boundaries around the visits, she's afraid they'll disapprove of her or become insulted. This has become a point of irritability and contention between her and her partner.

If Penelope reconsidered trying to read her parents' minds, she wouldn't assume they would have a negative reaction to her desire to schedule visits in advance. This would free her up to have an open dialogue with her parents who might turn out to be perfectly open to Penelope's request.

Irrespective of her parents' reaction, she can feel proud she asserted her needs and acted on behalf of her self-worth and her relationship.

7. Self-Deluding Thinking: *Rationalizing by telling yourself things you do not really believe*

Within Henry's industry, he gets wind of risky investments. He shares finances with his wife but has made several investments without consulting her. "What she doesn't know won't hurt her," he tells himself.

If Henry were not engaged in self-deluding thinking, he'd consider that even though she's unaware, his behavior still counts. Keeping it from her also doesn't reflect his integrity or support his goals of forming trust within their marriage. He'd recognize and accept the challenge to be fully transparent and commit to directly work on this because it better aligns with his family values.

8. Unhelpful Rules: *Making decisions without taking circumstances into consideration*

Emelia has a short fuse and can become exasperated and yells. Her kids complain about her being out of control, and she sees how destructive this behavior can be. She recognizes it's not good role modeling and not how she wants to behave, but she decides she cannot ask for help from a professional or her family. Emelia is following the "rule" that "I should be able to figure this out by myself. It's not their problem, so why should they have to help me." Because of this rule, she remains silent, continues to struggle with her anger, and continues to yell.

If Emelia were not obeying this unhelpful rule, she might consider that she needs more help than she's able to provide herself. Asking is brave. Also, her family wants to be supportive and do whatever it takes to assist her. Their help would come with care and make her feel comforted as she works toward her goals. She might also consider that they'd appreciate her change because it would benefit them.

9. Justification: *Avoiding responsibility for your behavior and finding reasons or explanations which hampers responsibility and change*

Aimee is trying to cut down on her overspending and shopping sprees. Even though she has several black dresses appropriate for her friend's fiftieth birthday party, she wants just the right one. She decides to shop for another. And she definitely doesn't need another pair of jeans but picks up a few. She justifies the purchases with, "It's only one more dress. I'll be able to wear this one to another occasion and the new jeans will be ready and waiting in my closet, saving me another trip."

If Aimee weren't justifying her behavior, she might reconsider. She has enough suitable black dresses. Even if she wanted another one, she'd already committed to saving. She could admit that the shopping for the black dress prompted her unnecessary secondary purchases of jeans. Rather than deny it, Aimee could face her challenge and act more mindfully in the future.

10. "Should," "Ought to," and "Must" Statements: *Insistence that things should, ought to, and must be as you like*

Kenny strongly believes maintaining relationships ought to be easy. It should take little or no effort. He decides if frustration or disappointments get in the way, it's okay for him to quickly give up and call it quits.

If his thinking were more flexible, Kenny would reconsider and acknowledge that most things he wants to do well in life require effort and that relationships always include some disappointments and frustrations.

The key is the ability to work through them in a healthy, helpful way. He'd recognize that better days and challenging days are a natural part of the ebb and flow in a relationship, and for the most part, better days outnumber challenging ones. Equally important, he'd have compassion for where he stands in his relationships, and when those hopeless feelings arise, he'd have patience with himself and his attempt to work through them.

Understanding what self-limited thinking is and how it gets in the way of self-compassion helps you identify and work through specific thought patterns for a more favorable outcome. Insight into these patterns provides awareness into why you have difficulty accepting your situation, how it contributes to negative thoughts and feelings about yourself, and how it impacts the way you choose to act.

To effectively work through the self-limited thinking, you can answer these questions:

Which self-limited thinking patterns pertain to you?

_____

_____

_____

_____

Can you relate to the examples provided? If so, what aspects of them pertained to you? If not, give a personal example that relates directly to you.

_____

_____

_____

_____

What do you notice about the particular self-limiting thought(s) that gives you insight into why you have difficulty accepting where you're at?

_____

_____

_____
_____

How does self-limiting thinking contribute to your negative thoughts and feelings about yourself?

_____
_____
_____
_____

How does it impact the way you choose to act?

_____
_____
_____
_____

COMMON RATIONALIZATIONS/EXCUSES

Our common rationalizations and excuses also get in the way of being self-compassionate. We use these to justify why we do things, to get ourselves off the hook for taking responsibility, and to avoid holding ourselves accountable for our behavior. It often leads us to feel helpless, hopeless, and disempowered.

Check off as many rationalizations/excuses that generally apply to you.
- ☐ It's too hard.
- ☐ I don't care.
- ☐ I'll do better next time.
- ☐ It's okay for me to do this.
- ☐ I want it.
- ☐ I need it.
- ☐ It's not fair.
- ☐ Everyone else is doing it.

- ☐ I'm going to do what I want to do.
- ☐ I don't want to disappoint or inconvenience _____.
- ☐ I deserve this.
- ☐ I am anxious.
- ☐ I am tired.
- ☐ I am sad/upset.
- ☐ I am bored.
- ☐ I'll just do it this one time.
- ☐ This isn't a problem. I could stop any time I want to.
- ☐ It is a special occasion.
- ☐ I can't do better.
- ☐ I am treating myself.
- ☐ I'll do it/start tomorrow.
- ☐ I will never stick with this practice anyway.
- ☐ No one will know.
- ☐ I have no willpower.
- ☐ I have no motivation.
- ☐ Nothing will ever change.
- ☐ I will end up doing it eventually.
- ☐ I won't do this again for a long time.
- ☐ I don't usually do this.
- ☐ I'm impulsive, lazy, not smart enough, etc.
- ☐ It's genetic—I'm just born this way.
- ☐ It won't/doesn't matter.
- ☐ I never learned any better.
- ☐ It's in the past. I don't have to deal with it now.
- ☐ Other _____

You have greater awareness of your checked-off excuses. When you experience a rationalization, you can remind yourself to consider alternative behaviors. Over time, it's possible to make positive changes once you face your rationalizations and habits. Being aware of and understanding your excuses allows you to catch yourself when these issues show up and to hold yourself accountable. You're able to focus on how you really want to behave based on your values, who you want to be, and how to be your very best self.

CURIOSITY-BASED QUESTIONS AROUND COMPASSION

1. What are your strengths and best qualities? How does it feel to point these out?
2. Do you find that it is easier to identify your best qualities than to note what your limitations are?
3. When you reflect on the level of intensity of your emotions, on a scale from 0-5 (from lowest to highest), how strongly do you feel compassion toward yourself? Compassion toward others?
4. When was the last time you told yourself that you love and appreciate yourself?
5. What is your level of comfort in doing so? Why?
6. Do you tend to be more self-critical or more self-compassionate? Why do you think so?
7. Do you tend to be more critical or more compassionate toward others? Why do you think so?
8. How willing have you been in the past to lean into your discomfort? What got in the way of fully doing so?
9. How willing are you currently to lean into your discomfort? What are barriers that can block your willingness?
10. When you were growing up and expressed feeling negative about yourself, how did each of your parents/caretakers react to you? Was their reaction what you needed or not?
11. Would a different response or reaction have been more helpful? If yes, what type of response or reaction?
12. How readily can you identify how you're feeling and why?
13. When you're experiencing discomfort or feel stuck, do you ask yourself "What do I need?" and "How will I be kind to myself when I'm distressed or suffer?"
14. How might you answer those questions?

15. What are you willing to do right now to expand your self-compassion and be a better version of yourself?

SELF-GUIDED GROWTH EXERCISE: CREATE COMPASSION CARDS

Now that you know more about self-limiting thoughts, you're able to examine and challenge your thinking. "Compassion cards" help you identify and document a self-limiting thought and rationalization thwarting self-compassion. Compassion cards can be created using three-by-five-inch index cards or by jotting notes in a smartphone, computer, or tablet. You can make as many as you find helpful toward your personal growth.

I recommend laminating index cards to carry with you. They'll hold up and keep you prepared when thoughts impeding your self-compassion surface.

Read the examples below, then write a few for yourself using the template.

COMPASSION CARD #1

SELF- LIMITING THOUGHT: I always procrastinate and have a hard time finishing what I start.
RATIONALIZATION: I'll do it tomorrow, and it won't matter.
HELPFUL REPLIES:
1. I choose to understand what's uncomfortable for me and what feeling I'm avoiding.
2. I could feel _____. That doesn't mean I have to avoid _____.
3. Convincing myself I can do it later is an excuse for why I'm not doing it now.
4. It does matter because I matter. I can stay on course, but when I procrastinate instead, it takes away from my self-belief and self-compassion.
5. When I'm successful at carrying tasks out, I'm proud of myself. I know the more I do it, the more I want to do it.
6. The challenges will come and will pass.

COMPASSION CARD #2

SELF- LIMITING THOUGHT: This change of eating and lifestyle will never work for me.

RATIONALIZATION: It's too hard, and I can't do better.

HELPFUL REPLIES:

1. I've never really made the commitment or followed a plan the way I need to. It's possible that if I stick to it, this experience will be different because of all I put into it.

2. In the past, that thought led me to give up, not to follow through, and not to achieve my goals. This time I'm all in!

3. A negative attitude will impact my mood. It's important that I stay curious, flexible, and see things openly and fully.

4. I know that when I've put in effort to accomplish things, I'm successful. There's no reason I can't be successful at this.

5. I have as good of a chance as anyone to succeed.

6. This is challenging for me. That's okay. Not everything comes easily and readily. I will have some better moments and some more challenging ones. That's what life's all about.

COMPASSION CARD #3

SELF-LIMITING THOUGHT: It's not fair that I generally struggle with anxiety.

RATIONALIZATION: It's not fair, and nothing will ever change.

HELPFUL REPLIES:

1. I could focus on how fair or unfair it is, but how does this lead me to work on what's coming up and getting in the way of me being my best self?

2. Life isn't fair. We each have individual challenges. This is mine, and it may be something different for someone else. This can feel really hard, and I'm okay just as I am.

3. People with anxiety have to work on self-regulation, manage their anxious symptoms, and find healthy, helpful coping skills. Putting work into this is in my best interest and will be helpful for me. I'm deserving of my time and effort.

4. This negative thinking leads me to give in to my unhelpful thoughts and make excuses for my behavior. I need to be mindful of my choices and be open and self-aware.

5. I have the power and ability to make choices, so I'm reminded to reframe for myself that I'm not my anxiety ("I'm anxious"), rather, I'm a person with anxiety. The challenges will come and will pass.

Please Listen to A Self-Compassion Guided Meditation

Find all the ACE Your Life Guided Meditations at
www.michellemaidenberg.com/ACEYourLife

SCAN HERE FOR
SELF-COMPASSION
GUIDED MEDITATION

Congratulate yourself for taking another
step toward ACE'ing Your Life.

Unleash your best self and live the life you want.

CHAPTER 6

Discovering and Practicing Compassion

Do not doubt your own basic goodness.
In spite of all confusion and fear,
you are born with a heart that knows
what is just, loving, and beautiful.
—Jack Kornfield

CORE BELIEFS ABOUT OURSELVES

We carry negative core beliefs about ourselves that make it challenging for us to truly embody self-compassion. In his research and work in Cognitive Behavioral Therapy, Aaron Beck identified: (a) helplessness/inferiority, (b) helplessness/vulnerability, (c) unlovability, and (d) worthlessness as our negative core beliefs.[122] When I speak about these, I refer to our core beliefs of ineffectiveness, unlovability, and hopelessness. These often surface over responsibility (e.g., "It's my fault"), safety and vulnerability (e.g., "I can't trust"), control and choice (e.g., "I'm trapped"), and connection and belonging (e.g., "I'm alone"). Past experiences and traumas, our intellectual ability, emotionality, and socio-cultural factors, are some key influences as to the cognitions that get formed for us.

Indie, a twenty-three-year-old who identifies as non-binary, came to see me to work exclusively on the trauma resulting from sexual abuse they experienced from ages nine to eleven at the hands of their tennis coach. They were very young, and the perpetrator was a beloved family friend who never experienced repercussions for his violations, exacerbating the circumstances. Indie's negative cognitions included "I should have done something," "I am permanently damaged," "My body is hateful," "I can't protect myself," and "I am not in control." Understandably, those formative experiences carried over into their adult relationships. They became increasingly anxious and cut off, withdrew, and held beliefs that negatively impacted their confidence and intimacy in their relationships.

Indie felt unlovable and hopeless, which resulted in somatic symptoms including headaches, backaches, and general numbness. In my work with them, we explored details of their experiences, how it impacted them in those moments, what negative beliefs they connected to, and how it gets evoked in their present-day experiences.

Deep in their subconscious, there were *blocking beliefs* keeping Indie from shifting their core beliefs about themself. For example, "I should have done something," resulted in shame, feeling they'd done something wrong and are not deserving of love. We went through their negative cognitions and blocking beliefs strategically, and were able to reframe their thinking about themself, about the experiences, and about the narrative they carry with them.

Through our work, Indie recognized that they reflect on the events based on who they are now, as an adult. However, the abuse happened in childhood, when they had limited control and were dependent on adults to ensure their safety. They were at a substantially different place intellectually and emotionally then, and the perpetrator's actions were heavily manipulative and calculated. After reframing their thinking, Indie's somatic symptoms decreased, and they stopped feeling triggered and disturbed by the formative experiences. Ultimately, they were able to function as more of their best self in their relationships.

EMBRACING OUR SHADOW SELF

Self-acceptance also involves our willingness to recognize and integrate parts of the self that until now may have been denied, disdained, or shunned. Carl Jung, the father of Analytical Psychology, coined the *shadow self* as what exists as part of the unconscious mind and is composed of repressed ideas, weaknesses, desires, instincts, and shortcomings. Our shadow self is made up of parts of us that may have sabotaged us in the past. Jung wrote:

> Unfortunately there can be no doubt that man is, on the whole, less good than he imagines himself or wants to be. Everyone carries a shadow, and the less it is embodied in the individual's conscious life, the blacker and denser it is. If an inferiority is conscious, one always has a chance to correct it. Furthermore, it is constantly in contact with other interests, so that it is continually subjected to modifications. But if it is repressed and isolated from consciousness, it never gets corrected.[123]

Jung further states, "Taking it in its deepest sense, the shadow is the invisible saurian tail that man still drags behind him. Carefully amputated, it becomes the healing serpent of the mysteries."[124] He stipulates that it's part of our nature to have a dark shadow. It must be brought to our consciousness and should be accepted and integrated so we become whole and functional. If we avoid, detest, or segment off parts of ourselves, full and unconditional self-acceptance and self-compassion remains out of reach.

I tell my patients if they're disdaining parts of themselves, they're disdaining all of themselves, because each of those parts make up who they are and every part of themselves is important and worthy. Even the darker sides are deserving and are in need of acceptance, compassion, and love.

We must openly and sympathetically understand the origin and elements of these darker sides, so we become less phobic of, and more accepting and compassionate toward them. They're often manifesting hurts, or deprivations we experienced in the past, which we can pay homage to by respecting them so they can progressively heal.

Before you get to know your shadow, it is helpful to cultivate a sense of unconditional kindness or friendliness toward yourself. In Buddhism, it's called a *Maitri* or *Loving Kindness* practice. Without openness and self-compassion, it is difficult to look at our darker parts. Start by accepting your own humanness, remembering we all have a shadow. *Everyone* is in the soup together, as Jung used to say.

The beauty of the healing process and being kinder to yourself is that you get to recognize you can empower yourself and have control over how those darker shadows are expressed and acted out. It will allow you to connect to your true and best self and compel you to lean into your values as a guide to your actions.

INTEGRATING YOUR SHADOW EXERCISES

As we tend to project our disowned/rejected parts onto other people, especially those we feel the safest with, our behaviors toward them may reflect the parts of ourselves we regret, are ashamed of, and would prefer not to act on. This can negatively impact the way we see ourselves because of the way we behaved, and our interpersonal relationships may suffer in the process.

For example, we have a strong visceral reaction to others who we perceive as "lazy" and "unproductive." We may chastise them and treat them unkindly because of the judgment we're making about these behaviors and shame we hold about those rejected parts of ourselves.

By integrating your shadow, you can increase your self-compassion, thereby improving your relationship with yourself and others.

We're going to take a deep look into our interpersonal interactions. Jung states, "*Everything that irritates us about others can lead us to an understanding of ourselves.*"

In this exercise you will:
- Evaluate your emotional reactions,
- Talk to and get to know the shadow part, and
- Empathize with and express compassion to that part.

For at least a week, after each day, assess what interactions were challenging. Then answer the following questions.

Evaluate Your Emotional Reactions

What thoughts and feelings got evoked during the dialogue/interaction?

_____

_____

_____

_____

What part(s) of me had a strong emotional charge (e.g., judgment, jealousy, anger, etc.)? Be sure to focus on yourself not the others' behavior.

_____

_____

_____

_____

How did I act based on that charge? Would I have preferred to act differently? If yes, in what way?

_____

_____

_____

_____

Talk to & Get to Know the Part(s)

Why are you showing up now?

_____

_____

_____

_____

What do you want me to know about you (i.e., the way you think, feel, react, etc.)?

_____
_____
_____
_____

When you get incited or provoked, how can I notice and validate you? What do you need from me?

_____
_____
_____
_____

Empathize & Express Compassion to the Part(s)
Write down the positive aspects of your shadow part(s) as though you are talking to a friend (e.g., when you show me your anxiety, it lets me know that you're scared of getting too close).

_____
_____
_____
_____

Acknowledge the positive part(s) and validate its position (e.g., I know your fear was meant to alert you to dangerous situations and so I can understand being scared based on your upbringing and that you never felt you had anyone who could understand and listen to you).

_____
_____
_____
_____

Thank your part(s) for showing up, and give them a word of encouragement (e.g., instead of rejecting you because of the difficulty of facing my own anxi-

ety, I'm going to make more of an effort to be patient and caring toward you because you are part of me and deserve my attention).

_____

_____

_____

_____

PERMISSION TO LOVE OURSELVES

When I ask patients to comment on their personal attributes, all too often they point out and complain about their "negative" ones, paying a lot less attention to or only briefly describing their positive ones. "I'm too sensitive and even the littlest things affect me," they say, or "I worry about the most ridiculous things." "I'm overly angry and frustrated." "I'm always so negative." "I have a horribly jealous and envious side."

We often make broad generalizations about who we are, how we function, and how we think, feel, and behave (i.e., I'm angry, I'm mean, I'm selfish, I'm anxious, etc.). And we all have thoughts and feelings that cause distress, impose self-doubt, and make us feel generally uncomfortable, that we want to get rid of. But this perpetuates the desire to get rid of the aspects of ourselves that we would prefer not having, because our perception is that we would be better off not having "it" or being "that way."

Try saying "I love myself," or "I am worthy of love," aloud.

How does it feel to express that? Most people report feeling awkward and having difficulty with connecting at the gut level. It says something about the way our mind works naturally, which was covered in Chapter One, how we were socialized (e.g., use criticism to motivate ourselves and others), the way in which we personally view ourselves, and how we may not have ever been taught to express appreciation and self-love.

As I expanded upon in Acceptance in Part II, when we berate ourselves as kids, we choose not to share our thoughts, or if we do, we're often told we shouldn't be thinking this way, that it isn't true, and to just stop it. Very few of us were taught how to personally respond to those sentiments. Who could blame our parents or caretakers? They worried about why we were saying those things, and they felt uncomfortable hearing it because it was so negative. They may not have had a helpful answer and probably wanted to get the thought out of our head as quickly as it got in.

We all know intuitively that parental figures can't be there to soothe us every time we have a self-loathing thought or feeling, and there's no uniform or prescribed way we need to be validated and attended to that cuts across all situations. When these negative assessments we make about ourselves aren't adequately addressed, the same pattern gets repeated, and is often replicated with our own children. Ideally, it would be healthier for us to learn effective ways to self-soothe and be self-compassionate.

As I write, I think of my dear friend from Chapter Three who was battling lung cancer. She has died, and I feel deep sadness and tremendous grief. She was one of the most warm, caring, and thoughtful people I've ever known. I feel fortunate, as I was able to support her through her end of life. I visited her bi-monthly, then weekly, three to four hours at a time. Our deep and meaningful conversations always left me with incredible insight about her, myself, and the world.

She was troubled knowing she'd die never having felt deeply loved. During our last unforgettable conversation, she explained she'd never felt it on the gut level. I was stricken by her comment given what a large supportive family she had, and how many friends and others cared and supported her. She wanted that to be the topic of our discussion, as she worried that she would die not fully embracing love in her life.

I replied that in some ways I wasn't surprised due to our innate inability to acquire and integrate self-love and self-compassion. I reviewed incidences with her from her childhood and beyond where she persistently questioned whether she was good enough or was worthy of love, and how that contributed to how she felt. Last, I proclaimed that feelings were overrated, and that often our thoughts and feelings aren't accurate or rational. It's more important to pay attention to what we can observe and what is in the present moment. I asked her to just be in the here and now, non-judgmentally, and to observe and take in the warmth, love, and nurturance shown to her. She said that she never thought about it that way, and that she felt relieved.

It's sad and astounding how many individuals I speak to whose internal self-criticism keeps them from seeing how truly special they are. It becomes our internal compass from which we perceive and encounter our world. This can change if we strive to be present, noticing ourselves, and proactively learning to be more self-compassionate.

LEARNING TO BE SELF-COMPASSIONATE

First Steps to Learning How to Be More Self-Compassionate

When I ask individuals what's the best way to treat a child throwing a tantrum, they inevitably reply with compassion and care. They recognize that going head-to-head with them would escalate the exasperated child's behavior. When I ask why they don't approach themselves in the same way when they feel sad, angry, disappointed, etc., and instead judge, loathe, and berate their thoughts and feelings, they invariably tell me it's where their mind goes, they can't help it, and they don't know how to direct it otherwise.

For as long as they can remember, some people have been frustrated, disappointed, or angry at themselves for having lost their desire and will to be patient, caring, and compassionate toward themselves. *Tough love has never been a strategy that worked, yet we still gravitate toward it and impose it on ourselves in the hope that we'll finally be able to force out our unwanted parts, thoughts, and feelings.*

I use a mindfulness exercise with my patients based on an analogy that reinforces how to be compassionate to ourselves and others in the midst of being evoked by intense discomfort. It is simply to relate to our mind as a child throwing a tantrum.

Use the Example of a Child Throwing a Tantrum Who Deserves Compassion

Consider: Understand that a child's basic human nature is good, even though they are having a blowup, meltdown moment.

Self-reflect with compassion: Your thoughts are simply something you have. They are not indicative of who you are. Having "mean" thoughts doesn't make you a "mean" person. An "off" moment is a prime opportunity to be inquisitive, to seek to understand yourself better, and to think about how you could lovingly nurture yourself.

Consider: During a tantrum, you cannot take what a child screams at face value. They are acting out of impulsivity, anger, frustration, etc., at an extreme level of a heightened emotional state.

Self-reflect with compassion: As adults, when we experience extreme levels of emotional states such as worry, anger, hopelessness, etc., we can't fully rely on what our mind is conveying to us about the way in which we're thinking and feeling. Our mind usually utilizes primitive and regressive coping mechanisms (as discussed in Chapter One) and resorts to thinking that it must save us from threat and danger. Exaggerated and disparaging thoughts and feelings usually come from a place of irrationality, inflexibility, and exasperation. It's best to wait on problem-solving and decision-making until you're able to come to a place of mindfulness and thoughtfulness, otherwise you risk gravitating toward unproductive safety behaviors such as avoidance.

Consider: When a child is in the midst of a tantrum, it's best not to react angrily toward them, berate them, or join in the chaos. You risk prolonging the tantrum as the child becomes more incensed.

Self-reflect with compassion: When you're at a fully heightened emotional state, it's counterproductive to dismiss, berate, or shame yourself. Your lack of compassion contributes to further negative thoughts and feelings about yourself, and a deeper state of hopelessness. Lack of compassion also prolongs and inhibits personal healing and working through your challenges.

Consider: During the tantrum, it's best not to react to the direct emotions of the child. Rather, get to the context of their feelings underlying their reaction, so you can work through it with them.

Self-reflect with compassion: As humans we all act and react based on emotions that get evoked. For example, anger is usually couched in underlying disappointment, frustration, sadness, and/or hurt. Avoid taking what's displayed at face value. Instead, so you can actively and healthfully work through it, get *underneath* the primary feeling to what may be compelling the reaction. If it's challenging to identify, go through the array of emotions to get to the underlying feeling.

Consider: You wouldn't try to talk to a child throwing a tantrum out of their feelings or invalidate them. This response would provoke them, instead of making them feel supported and comforted. You would recognize their value and not "kiss it away." You would want to talk it through and lead them to experience the feelings, but not necessarily to speak and act on behalf of them.

Self-reflect with compassion: When you're having difficult or uncomfortable thoughts and feelings, growth happens by leaving your comfort zone and fully experiencing whatever shows up. Your nervous system gets accustomed to fear, hurt, and other uncomfortable feelings. No matter how hard the attempt to push them away, it gradually copes and becomes less inclined to reject, disregard, and try to get rid of those that show up. There's great value in learning how to tolerate frustration and just be with all feelings, especially the difficult and uncomfortable ones. This leads you to self-empowerment, self-growth, and personal development.

Consider: Showing empathy, compassion, and love during a tantrum helps soothe the child. We need to carry out those actions, adhering to our parenting values of connectedness, even if we don't necessarily feel them at the moment.

Self-reflect with compassion: When you're exasperated, acting from a place of personal self-belief, self-love, and self-compassion will lead you to being open for self-exploration, insight, learning, and changing habits and behaviors. Whether or not you're fully connected to them, you can make a concerted effort to carry out these actions that align with your values. If you continue to practice from this valued place, your self-compassion will grow. You'll learn the satisfaction of feeling self-love.

In a workshop I attended, Pema Chödrön, a beloved American Tibetan Buddhist nun, eloquently said, "The more we get to know our mind, the more we foster a connection to it. We begin to soften, open up, and become curious about ourselves and others."

If only we would relate to our minds as we do to a child who is having a tantrum. We are just as deserving of being attended and attuned to, treated compassionately and given nurturance. We have the inherent capacity to provide these to ourselves if we make the effort to be mindful.

Self-compassion comes from noticing, being with, and accepting your human physical sensations, feelings, and emotional states. Whenever you learn something new about yourself and use that information to improve your quality of life, you enhance your personal development.

When we ignore, hide, or discount our needs and wants, we may become irritable, resentful, and dissatisfied. When we lean away from our values or act in ways contrary to them, we undermine our self-worth and our desire to be compassionate. Conversely, value-based actions raise our self-confidence and desire to be self-compassionate. We're able to validate that we can initiate, follow through, and maintain behavior which strengthens our belief that the more effort we put into something, the better chances we'll attain positive results because of our determination.

WEROC: 5 Steps to Practicing Self-Compassion

WEROC are the steps you can take toward building and practicing compassion.

These will help you enhance your compassion toward yourself.

What we practice gets stronger. What we commit to, we achieve and we believe.

If you increase your self-awareness, and proactively and consistently engage in compassion laden behaviors, your actions inevitably become more a part of who you are and how you are. Take time to practice these steps so you can reap the incredible benefits *compassion* offers you.

Work WITH (not against) Your Self-Critic. Think of a constructive action, and then plan for it. Do things differently, otherwise you'll have similar results. If your inner critic starts to tell you that you don't have what it takes to succeed, thank your mind for trying to protect you and ensure your comfortability. Acknowledge you are not your thoughts or feelings, and that you can choose to take action based on your core values and what's truly meaningful to you. Know you have a fundamental right to live a purposeful and meaningful life.

Engage Your Friend Voice. If you find yourself being overly self-critical, listen carefully to what your self-critic is saying. Ask yourself if you would say half those things to a good friend going through a similar situation. Or even to someone you don't like? What would you actually say? Engage your "friend" voice and act on behalf of that kindness and care. Say the things you most need to hear to be validated, comforted, and nurtured. Watch the brief video *How to Be a Friend to Yourself*[25] by The School of Life to help you with this practice.

Redirect. Redirect your inner critic's focus to specific situations and behavior, rather than broad labels or personal attributes. Instead of labeling who you are as a person, call yourself out on the behavior. Reframe expressing and identifying what value it's rubbing against (e.g., work ethic vs pleasure-seeking). Consider whether the response helps you lean toward or away from your values and being your best self.

Observe and Acknowledge. Notice your feelings and emotions in different circumstances throughout the day. Next time your self-critic pipes up, recognize that your mind may have good but misguided intentions. Recognize that your mind will attempt to ensure you're safe and comfortable. To do this, it may be overprotective or convince you to do whatever's necessary to achieve or maintain comfortability. Name it and acknowledge it, rather than trying to suppress it.

Comfort. Identify your emotions and where in your body you are feeling them. Tightness in your chest? Heaviness in your shoulders? Remind yourself that flaws and imperfections are integral to our humanness and the essence of our shared humanity. Our body reacts to our distress and alerts us when we need to make a shift. Assess your propensity to do what is most familiar and comfortable. Just notice it. Make concerted efforts to reserve self-judgment and self-criticism (Review skills on thinking mind vs observing mind in Chapter Three on "Accepting Ourselves"). Ask yourself continually what you need to feel validated and supported during moments of pain or challenge. Follow through on giving yourself the attention, words of encouragement, touch, or whatever else you may need.

WEROC - 5 STEPS TO PRACTICING
SELF-COMPASSION

R
REDIRECT

E
ENGAGE your friend voice

O
OBSERVE and acknowledge

W
WORK with your inner critic

SELF COMPASSION

C
COMFORT

My patient Sam, a college junior, came to see me a year after he'd been in a major car accident while high and drunk. Although inches from death, he and his friend miraculously escaped physically unscathed. His healthy appearance was both positive and negative, because it gave him reason to minimize and rationalize his behavior.

He had seen several other therapists but had never completed the process. "Never found it helpful," he said. It was his mother's last attempt at getting him the help she thought he needed, despite his apathy toward therapy. Since coming to me over two years ago, Sam now understands and is benefitting from ongoing treatment.

I paced myself in engaging and getting to know him as we gravitated toward discussing his values and how he saw himself. He lacked awareness of who he was, what he connected to, and what he strived for, as those were things typically dictated by his parents. He had yet to reach a matured sense of self. He saw his behavior and position in this world based on his privileged life, rather than the real world outside of himself and his community.

In one session, he discussed interactions with a friend he admitted was not the healthiest person to spend time with. We talked through it and collaboratively came up with three alternatives to consider based on internally processing where he was and where he wanted to be.

While we worked together, Sam learned to identify his values and be more vulnerable. He made so much progress that he now connects with, and genuinely expresses his feelings and practices being compassionate toward himself and others. I'm thrilled to say he's graduated, lives independently, has an impressive full-time job, and is planning on applying for graduate school in the near future.

Over time, Sam recognized that his lack of awareness of who he was and what was truly important to him, and his lack of compassion for himself and others led to his self-destructive behavior. He's naturally caring and compassionate, but he was so used to chasing the next exciting adventure and high, that he never had the chance to consider healthier, kinder ways to care for himself or others.

Throughout our work together, I introduced him to alternate ways to encounter satisfaction and contentment, in which he slows down, is with all of his experience on a deeper physical and emotional level, and sees first-hand the benefits in his personal and professional life. I used the WEROC steps to illustrate the direction we're always following to get him where he wants to go.

SELF-COMPASSION ENABLES YOU TO GET WHAT YOU NEED

You learned how compassion produces positive benefits and can personally transform your relationship with yourself and others. It develops as you become more open, curious, fully noticing, and being with all that shows up for you.

Concluding with *"What do I need?"* and *"How will I be kind to myself when I'm in pain?"* leads you to procure the warmth and nurturance you need in any given moment. When you get what you need from yourself, you're more available, present, and grounded in who you are and how you behave toward yourself and others. All most of us want is acceptance, validation, and to be attended to and nurtured. When you can secure these for yourself, you realize that everything you need lies within you.

CURIOSITY-BASED QUESTIONS AROUND SELF-COMPASSION

1. What negative core beliefs resonate with you?
2. Why do you think that is?
3. When do they most get triggered?
4. What do you need right now?
5. What do you need to feel loved by a family member, a partner, or a friend?
6. Do you have people in your life who show you compassion when you need it the most? Who are they? How do they show it?
7. Do you communicate your needs directly, or do you generally assume that others will inherently know what they are? If the latter, how willing are you to work on being more open and direct?
8. What is stopping you from being kind to yourself?

9. What is one step you can take today, and will continue to take, to chip away at this obstacle?

10. How can you be a nurturing parent to yourself?

11. How could you integrate an act of self-compassion into your everyday schedule? What would that look like? (e.g., when I make a mistake, I'll say "I'm a human and make mistakes," rather than, "I'm so useless.")

12. What's one thing in your routine that displays self-compassion? Can you be better at enacting a routine that includes self-care, rest, and mindfulness?

13. When going through the Five Steps to Practicing Self-Compassion (WEROC), which one, if any, would be most challenging for you?

14. Why would that be the case? What might come up for you?

15. How will you effectively work through the challenges that keep you from effectively practicing self-compassion?

SELF-GUIDED GROWTH EXERCISE: REFLECTING IN THE MIRROR

First, compile a list of attributes (i.e., include anything from talents, accomplishments, values, roles, etc.) that you appreciate about yourself. While looking in the mirror:

A. Look directly into your eyes for 3-5 minutes. While exercising non-judgment, recognize your rising thoughts, feelings, and sensations. If judgment comes up, as it may, notice it and return to gazing at yourself.

B. Read aloud while looking in a mirror: *I love and am proud of* _____. Express why you love and are proud of each attribute.

C. Next, recite words/affirmations of encouragement and admiration. Select as many as most resonate with you.[126]

- It's okay to think and feel however I think and feel.
- How I think and feel does not reflect who I am.
- I continually grow through my experiences.
- I can get through whatever comes my way.
- I am only human, therefore I'm imperfect.

- All I can do is my best.
- Life can be challenging, and it's okay for me to have hard moments.
- I'm not alone. I have the ability to cultivate friendship and love.
- It's okay to take a step back and recalibrate.
- I can always see things from a different perspective.
- My emotions don't define me.
- I get to choose how I respond to any situation.
- I can choose to set boundaries in my relationships that no longer serve or support me.
- I choose to listen to my mind and body about what I need.
- I choose to be mindful and present, so that I can notice all the beauty and joy that I am grateful for.
- I choose to give of myself fully and authentically, even if it requires me to be vulnerable and challenge myself.
- I will give up my attachments to old ideas and beliefs and expectations to commit to further personal growth.
- I will compare myself to me, rather than comparing myself to others.
- I deserve to be heard, validated, respected, and supported.
- If I want and need it, I will ask for help and/or support.
- I release my regrets of the past. I forgive myself for what I did not know. I am grateful that I now know better.
- I will commit to being my best self, even if I do not feel like it.
- I will intentionally create moments of joy.
- I will treat myself with kindness, patience, and understanding.

Take a moment to reflect on the exercise and evaluate how it felt to go through that process. Was there anything that came up that was unexpected? Did you learn anything new about yourself, that you'll take away with you? What impact did it have toward your self-compassion, and what commitment will you make right here, right now? Feel free to engage in this exercise once or repeat it to internalize the self-affirmations.

Please Listen to Self-Love and Mirror Guided Meditation:

Find all the ACE Your Life Guided Meditations at
www.michellemaidenberg.com/ACEYourLife

SCAN HERE FOR
SELF-LOVE & MIRROR
GUIDED MEDITATION

Congratulate yourself for taking another
step toward ACE'ing Your Life.

Unleash your best self and live the life you want.

Part IV

Empowerment
(The Third Step in the ACE Method)

Changing the way we look at ourselves and continually shifting our narrative helps us transition and unleash all the goodness already within us. We have the task of accepting, showing compassion to, and empowering ourselves. This work is an ongoing process of development that we will continue to engage in throughout our lives, so we should view it as a journey with no final destination. Our quest to be our best self and live the life we want to be living is continual and everlasting. Next you'll learn what self-empowerment is, what gets in the way of acquiring it, and how to attain it.

CHAPTER 7

What Is Empowerment & What Barriers Get in the Way of Cultivating It?

If you can't fly then run, if you can't run then walk, if you can't walk then crawl, but whatever you do you have to keep moving forward.
−Dr. Martin Luther King Jr.

Empowerment is:
- Asserting intentional effort towards one's goals and observing and reflecting on the impact of those actions.
- It's also an individual drawing on their evolving self-efficacy, knowledge, and competence related to their goals.[127]

Self-Empowerment is:
- The acquisition of knowledge and skills for coping with problems and stress.[128]
- It's also an individual's ability to have emotional knowledge, and to harness their personal qualities and apply it to effective decision making in order to take ownership over one's life.[129]

All these definitions emphasize that self-empowerment is intentionality directed toward self-awareness, the ability for one to recognize they are in control of their own decisions, and ultimately their own life, and are taking direct action toward their values and goals.

Those who want to accomplish self-empowerment must not only embody the feeling, but also take steps towards change and influence.[130] For example, we may *feel* empowered after listening to an inspiring Ted Talk, but we need to ask how we're going to apply those concepts which inspired and empowered us to strive towards our own goals, thus improving our own lives.

WHY IS SELF-EMPOWERMENT IMPORTANT?

Now that we have defined empowerment and self-empowerment, it's important to recognize why self-empowerment is so valuable. Although support networks are extremely important for our well-being, and even for us to rely upon occasionally, at the end of the day, the one person we must truly rely on and support is ourselves. As Zig Ziglar states, "You are the most influential person you will talk to today."

Empowerment is linked to greater health and well-being.[131] It can also help with the promotion of an individual's healthy lifestyle.[132] Many theorists agree that empowerment is connected to power, which is the ability to have influence in our social interactions.[133] It is also known to have a positive effect on our self-confidence.

The Empowerment Process Model,[134] developed by Lauren Bennett Cattaneo and Aliya R. Chapman, is defined as an iterative process. Individuals who begin to feel self-empowered may experience *self-efficacy* (the ability to exert control over one's own behavior, motivation, and social environment), *knowledge, and competence.* As indicated in Chapter Four on self-acceptance, throughout their life, an individual with self-acceptance and self-efficacy will strive toward self-empowerment and making meaningful change.

When we take responsibility for things we can control in our life and when we *challenge* negative thought processes by recognizing that they may limit or prevent us from achieving our goals in various areas of our lives, we have a greater trust in our capacity, abilities, and judgment. Taking responsibility to grow toward mastery ensures we live aligned with our values, contributing to our mental and physical health.

WHAT GETS IN THE WAY OF ACQUIRING SELF-EMPOWERMENT?

In order to overcome barriers to self-empowerment, it is important to recognize what they are. Somatic symptoms, such as fatigue, sometimes inhibit our self-empowerment. We can also get in our own way. Denis Waitley states, "The greatest limitations you will ever face will be those you place on yourself." Limiting beliefs, how we communicate to ourselves, compensatory strategies, and negative behaviors keep us from effectively enhancing our self-empowerment.

SOMATIC AND PSYCHOLOGICAL BARRIERS IMPACTING SELF-EMPOWERMENT

The Impact of Fatigue

Patients often report feeling fatigued, which impacts their ability to focus, stay motivated, and complete tasks. Fatigue and other somatic reactions to psychological phenomenon must also be considered when we're thinking about acquiring and sustaining an empowerment practice.

Fatigue can be experienced as a somatic reaction evoked by depression, disassociating, suppressing, etc. New research into the neural mechanisms of perseverance suggests two types of effort-based fatigue can reduce someone's willingness to exert effort for reward. Short-term fatigue is *recoverable* after a break, whereas the-longer-term type is *unrecoverable*.[135] It was deemed that the value of the reward can be discounted by the amount of effort it requires to obtain it. That makes sense. Why would someone want to persevere, and accept the trade-offs of exerting effort, if they didn't think it worth the reward they'd receive.

In the study, fMRI brain scans show that distinct portions of the frontal cortex are activated separately during the "hidden states" of recoverable fatigue and unrecoverable fatigue. According to the researchers, those with recoverable fatigue made efforts to persist after taking a short break. Conversely, those with unrecoverable fatigue had stifling motivation, which completely stopped them from wanting to persist. Willingness to exert effort fluctuates, and generally declines over time, therefore, to persist, we must consider:

- the type of fatigue
- the amount of effort being exerted
- whether the reward has perceived value

According to the latest research on unrecoverable fatigue, using your imagination to visualize that a mundane reward has usefulness, can trick the brain into persevering during goal-directed behavior.[136]

Limiting Beliefs

Our beliefs are formed by many factors including how we were raised, the society we live in, our experiences, etc. Limiting beliefs are often untrue or conjured by external stimuli we've internalized. These can inhibit our movement toward acquiring self-empowerment. Much of these internalizations occur during childhood.[137] As we develop, the opinions and perceptions of others is paramount. We're likely to be influenced by our parents, extended family, teachers, coaches, peers, and others.

During our formative years, we seek approval and acceptance as we navigate our social environment. Because our brain isn't fully developed until around the age of twenty-five, it's often challenging to process our thoughts and feelings and make mindful decisions. Throwing physical, emotional, social, and/or socio-cultural challenges into the mix complicates everything.

When we fixate on beliefs that could be limiting and repeat them mentally, they can become self-fulfilling prophecies, holding us back from progress and self-improvement. They can also prevent us from seeing opportunities or utilizing our talents. Other people's beliefs and expectations of us can typecast us in a role we think we should fulfill. While many of our limiting beliefs arise from formative years of development, we can choose whether to rely on them throughout our adult life.

For example, my second eldest son was heading off to college in California. I had recently visited the campus with him, so I decided I didn't need to fly cross country again for his drop off. I rationalized that my patients needed me; I was immersed in writing this book; my family didn't need the added expense; my husband was accompanying him, and FaceTime calls would be tantamount to being there.

As I worked on these self-empowerment chapters, it occurred to me that I wasn't empowering myself to take action on behalf of my parenting and personal growth values. I realized my limiting beliefs, based on fixed beliefs developed during my childhood, were spilling over into my current circumstance.

My parents divorced when I was three. For most of my childhood, I was raised by a single mother anxious about finances and surrounded by broken and unhealthy relationships. I had few opportunities to see intact, healthy family units.

My thoughts dictated my conclusion:
- If I went, I would not be doing everything I could to keep others from suffering.
- I needed to be more conscious and considerate of finances.
- My limiting belief was that I wasn't needed, and I wouldn't lend any value to the experience.

Fortunately, I recognized I was reacting from a skewed and narrow perspective, as well as from my anxiety. I underestimated the value of being there to support my son through his transition. I was also deflecting responsibility in order not to face my faults and imperfections.

Of course, once I made the decision to go, some self-critical and disappointing thoughts surfaced, too.
- That's so sad that I automatically thought that way.

- I perceived that being with my patients was more important than being with my son. What does that say about me as a mother?
- What if I hadn't come to that decision and stayed home?
- I wish my husband had said something and alerted me.

Surely, my skills came in handy. I accepted that these thoughts, feelings, and reactions came up, given my past and what triggers me. I chose to be self-compassionate and feel empathy for my anxious inner child and adult self. I decided to be forgiving. My thoughts and feelings sometimes slip into a regressed, repressed place: a comfortable and familiar default position that served me well and protected me throughout my childhood. Despite how anxious or uncomfortable I feel, as an adult, I'm choosing to make decisions based on being an attuned, loving, and supportive parent. I'm empowered by this decision and am proud that I continue to evolve.

Some common limiting beliefs (which can also be rationalizations!) that we may say to ourselves include:

- I'm too old/too young.
- I'm not _____ enough.
- I don't have enough time.
- I'm powerless.
- I'm going to feel miserable no matter what.
- Change is too difficult.
- I don't have enough experience.
- I can't do _____.
- I can't change.
- I need to feel _____.
- I'm okay if I feel okay.
- When _____ happens, I'll be happy.
- When _____ happens, everything will be perfect.
- It's too hard.
- If I let people too close, I will be hurt.
- I know I am going to fail, so why should I bother trying at all?
- How could I compete with _____?

- I'm not ready yet.
- I'm too far gone.
- I don't want to be hopeful and then disappointed.
- I don't have enough wherewithal/energy.
- I don't deserve _____.
- _____ is impossible to find.
- Life is hard for me.
- I have bad luck.
- Other's approval of me is critical.
- Other's needs and happiness are more important than mine.
- I'm not self-disciplined/motivated.
- My history and past define me.

We encounter many more limiting beliefs based on who we are and the experiences we've faced. These limiting beliefs can be automatic. As if on autopilot, we naturally default to them because they house our negative core beliefs, our fears, worries, and insecurities. They may have substantively helped us to cope and function in the past. They served the purpose of keeping us protected from emotional pain and discomfort, and what may result from experiencing the pain and discomfort, and we feel justified. We sometimes dig in our heels and insist they're true *all* the time and will *never* change, which may:

- help make sense or justify our or someone else's behavior,
- validate that we're right,
- allow us to feel a sense of control,
- justify our feelings,
- minimize or suppress uncomfortable memories, thoughts, feelings or sensations,
- explain our memories, thoughts, feelings or sensations.

Gaining insight into our limiting beliefs will bring them into our consciousness so we have present-moment awareness to act and react from a mindful place indicative of our best self and who we want to be.

Language and Self-Perception Impacts Self-Empowerment

The way in which we communicate to ourselves has a substantial impact on our mindset, motivation, and actions, thereby affecting our ability to feel empowered and to continue to stay invested. For example, as I was restless, fidgety, and distracted this morning riding my Peloton bike, instead of muttering, "I've had it, I'm getting off this thing," I recalibrated. "I'm finding myself disinterested and distracted, I'm going to regroup. The instructor is inspiring and engaging. Paying attention contributes to my personal strength and power." I felt proud I took the time to validate where I was, note my worthiness, and act on behalf of my best self, a better experience than if I'd chosen to get off the bike and give up.

The way we express ourselves shifts our mindset and perception. It can make or break whether we take direct action or resist and avoid. Consider these terms as examples of going from being disempowered to empowered.

EMPOWERED LANGUAGE

DISEMPOWERED	EMPOWERED
Have to	Get to/Choose to
Can't	Am willing to
Must	Desire to
I will try	I will do
But	And
Failure	Feedback
Pain	Power
Victim	Survivor/Warrior
Anger	Energy
What do I want?	What do I want to do?
Challenges	Growth opportunities
Difficult day	Difficult moment in a day
Intense emotion	Human experience

In general, language that connotes a lack of freedom or being unduly forced will generally be disempowering. This includes have to, I can't, I won't, etc. Attempt to use language that signifies self-confidence and strength such as I will, I could, I choose to, etc. I typically do an exercise with patients when they respond to me "I'll try to." I ask them to try to stand up. Their instinct is to stand up. I stop them and say, no, I asked you to try to stand up. After we go through a few iterations of this, they stop trying as they come to understand that they will get nowhere by trying, only by doing.

For one day (and hopefully more!), consider how you communicate with yourself and its impact on your mindset and perceptions. Reframe by using more empowering language and notice the personal transformation.

Cognitive Fusion

Cognitive fusion can also prevent us from attaining self-empowerment. The term *cognitive fusion* is utilized in Acceptance & Commitment Therapy (ACT) to describe entanglement in our internal dialogue and thus falling prey to believing our internal dialogue as absolute truth.[138] A state of cognitive fusion may feel like thoughts are rules or commands we must obey. We fuse with thoughts and act on behalf of them. Falling prey to cognitive fusion can disempower us and prevent us from pursuing our values or engaging in other meaningful activities.

We may give *reasons* why we can't change, such as "I'm not smart enough." We may also make judgments about ourselves and believe them to be true. "I'm ineffective." We may even determine our inability to change based on past events. "The last time I did this I failed." Detrimental thoughts like these act as self-fulfilling prophecies. It's not hard to see that self-fulfilling prophecies can lead to cycles of negative thoughts and behaviors. When we buy into beliefs about ourselves, we are more likely to act in ways that correspond to those beliefs, thus reinforcing and encouraging the same behavior. It's a vicious cycle.

For example, thirty-nine-year-old Max's constant doubt about his ability to be warm and affectionate caused him to sabotage himself. Since he believed he was "emotionally inept," he overworked and avoided dating and intimacy. Despite wanting desperately to connect with someone, he rarely, if ever, put effort into improving his circumstances. His lack of practice and experience made him feel even worse about himself, which led to greater self-doubt and even lower self-confidence. Feeling disempowered, individuals like Max often avoid challenging situations and fail to pursue their values fully.

Conceptualized self is a type of cognitive fusion. An individual identifies with their thoughts and embodies them as part of their identity.

Attachment to the conceptualized self occurs when an individual fuses with the thoughts that they are a person who is depressed, worried, has significant problems, or anything else that negatively impacts their identity. According to Russ Harris, internationally acclaimed ACT trainer and author of the ACT book, *The Happiness Trap*, "When we fuse with our self-description, it seems as if we are that description, that all those thoughts are the very essence of who we are."[139]

When we envelop positive thoughts such as "I always attempt to do my best" or "I'm skilled," self-conceptualization plays a beneficial role in creating greater self-confidence. However, negative self-talk or giving into negative or unproductive thoughts can be harmful to one's sense of self-worth and therefore gets in the way of their self-empowerment.

In Max's case, it was impossible for him to feel empowered when his behavior kept him from being proud, rubbed up against his integrity, and hobbled the way he wants to see himself. Gaining awareness allowed Max to identify when he was prompted to behave in a manner counterintuitive and remote from his self-growth.

Compensatory Strategies

Keep in mind some behaviors may be compensatory strategies. These techniques or modifications to our behavior or environment are used to compensate for a deficit, weakness, injury, or perceived inadequacy in a specific area or skill.[140] They help us cope with what we think of as a personal weakness. Cover up our deficits, and we reduce the negative or unwanted feelings or consequences associated with them. These strategies may have been needed and worked well during childhood and adolescence, but can be counterproductive or limiting during adulthood. For example, overworking seemed advantageous to Max. During adolescence when he wanted to avoid his feelings of social insecurity, he overworked academically. Currently, it provides benefits/secondary gains such as a higher bonus at work, increased knowledge, and an elevated self-confidence regarding his career. But it comes at a grave cost to his health, as well as familial and interpersonal relationships.

Note behaviors that keep you from being your best self:
- Overworking
- Shutting down/cutting off physically or emotionally
- Manipulating others
- Lashing out at others
- Procrastinating
- People pleasing
- Distancing
- Avoiding others
- Avoiding being alone
- Avoiding uncomfortable memories, thoughts, feeling and/or sensations
- Worrying, overthinking, ruminating
- Blaming
- Constantly seeking reassurance
- Giving up
- Denying
- Ignoring
- Distracting
- Becoming defensive
- Engaging in self-destructive behaviors
- Always needing an explanation
- Deflecting
- Other _____
- Other _____

Self-Defeating Behaviors Exercise

Assess this for yourself:

Which counterproductive/compensatory behaviors do you periodically or consistently engage in? When and how often do they typically show up?

_____

_____

_____

_____

How did it feel to identify and admit to these behaviors?

_____

_____

_____

_____

How do they conflict with the way in which you want to see yourself?

_____

_____

_____

_____

What value(s) do you compromise by engaging in these behaviors?

_____

_____

_____

_____

What are they helping you cope with? At what cost?

_____

_____

_____

_____

How would you prefer to see yourself? What will you do to initiate this?

_____

_____

_____

_____

Lack of Concrete Values

We also struggle with self-empowerment due to an inability to define our own personal values or when we behave remotely from them. Carl Rogers, the father of Client-Centered Therapy, was one of the first psychologists to focus on the concept of values. He stated that challenges and discontentment arise when one's conceived values (verbal expressions of what is preferred) and operative values (one's actual behavior) are not aligned.[141]

As emphasized in Chapter Two, core values inform your thoughts, decisions, and actions. They help inform what's important and meaningful to you. They're an essential foundation in finding your life's purpose. They remind you of who you are and who you strive to be. When you're remote from your values, you can easily become confused and lack a sense of direction and commitment. You can also lose sight of how to create a future you're personally proud of. Awareness of your core values guides you to act intentionally to live a more engaging and fulfilling life.

COUNTERING BARRIERS TO SELF-EMPOWERMENT

Fixed Mindset Versus a Growth Mindset

In order to counter barriers to self-empowerment, it is important that one has a *growth-mindset*. Carol Dweck, known for her research on achievement, success, and mindset, coined the term *growth mindset* in her book *Mindset* and stressed the importance of an individual's ability to recognize that their skills can develop through dedication and hard work.[142] Dweck asserted that the opposite is true of a *fixed mindset*, believing someone may not be born with the talent or ability to achieve something, and there is a cap on their learning. She proposes that effort and hard work are not the only factors in a growth mindset. Individuals must also be able to recognize when other strategies are not working as intended and take the opportunity to expand their repertoire.

Dweck provided examples on how to cultivate a growth mindset. Instead of saying, "That's OK, maybe patience is not one of your strengths," which reflects a fixed mindset, reframe it to reflect a growth mindset. "I'm not a patient person *yet.*" Just add *yet* to the end of the sentence. She spoke of the importance of using language that suggests what's expected of us as humans, that we're always learning, growing, and evolving.

Self-Efficacy and Psychological Flexibility

Martin Meadows, a bestselling personal development author, writes about self-discipline and its transformative power. He shares that self-efficacy is highly influenced by one's sense of self-mastery.[143] With increased success in task completion, one may become more confident in their own abilities, and thus increase their self-efficacy. Self-efficacy, discussed at length in Chapter Four, is a key ingredient to empowerment. Meadows and Dweck concur that strong self-efficacy correlates with a growth mindset. They believe individuals who possess strong self-efficacy can recognize that they can accomplish challenging tasks and understand that setbacks don't mean failure, but rather, an opportunity for learning and growth.

Psychological flexibility, an ACT term, explains the ability to stay in contact with the present moment regardless of the previously mentioned barriers to self-empowerment, to be with unpleasant thoughts, feelings, and bodily sensations, and to choose one's behaviors based on the situation and their personal values.[144] However, in order to increase psychological flexibility and our growth mindset, we must be aware of and be able to recognize these barriers in order to work through them, accomplish what we want, and acquire self-empowerment.

CHARACTERISTICS OF INDIVIDUALS WHO LEAD EMPOWERING LIVES

Research recognizes six characteristics of resilient individuals: (a) They accept adversity in their lives and face it; (b) They have a mission and purpose that gives them a sense of courage and strength; (c) They find meaning in challenging times; (d) They have a social support network and support others; (e) They can self-regulate and control their impulses, and (f) They are able to improvise.[145]

If you're resilient, you proactively:

- Accept your situation, no matter how challenging.
- Learn and find meaning from experiences so there's opportunity for growth and an improved future.
- Remain flexible, open, and aware.
- Have a mission and purpose led by your values.
- Open yourself to deeper, more connected relationships for getting and giving comfort and support.

When you're open to connecting with your resilience, you may seek out and discover resources and means of support you haven't thought of, reframe circumstances so there's room for hopefulness, and forge a stronger connection with values you may have been remote from.

Resilience, the personal attribute or ability to bounce back, is the process of enduring amid a personal life crisis. Posttraumatic growth comes when a traumatic event challenges an individual's core beliefs, and when positive changes occur during or after the crisis has passed. Researchers tap into the five domains of posttraumatic growth:

- Appreciation of life
- Relating to others
- Personal strength
- New possibilities
- And spiritual growth[146]

Posttraumatic growth, including the increased ability to tap into personal strength and being open to new possibilities, are also significant as means to increasing self-empowerment and living life fully.

A newer concept conveying personal growth and characteristics of those en route to living a meaningful life refers to being *psychologically rich*. These individuals seek out novel experiences that enrich their lives. They facilitate this through inner and outer experiences finding beauty and perceptive altering experiences.[147] This could be through taking a trip, venturing on to a new career path, or changing roles within the family.

Among difficult life events like death, divorce, or infertility—psychological richness abounds.

These psychologically rich individuals tend to be open, curious, and willing to experience a full range of intense emotions. They don't require meaning-making or personal growth as motivation or outcome. Rather, the focus is on how they'll make their life more interesting, which comes with profound changes in perspective.[148]

Those who are resilient, experience post-traumatic growth, and are psychologically rich, have positive characteristics which embody being self-empowered; are expansive and open to new experiences and ideas; and are proactive at doing things which make their lives more fulfilling despite their circumstances.

PEOPLE WHO LIVE EMPOWERED LIVES

- Accept and face adversity, no matter how challenging
- Have a mission and purpose led by their values
- Find meaning and opportunity for growth in challenging times
- Have a social support network and support others
- Can self-regulate and control their impulses
- Are able to improvise
- Remain flexible, open, and aware
- Are open to deeper, more connected relationships
- Seek out new experiences that enrich their lives

ATTAINING SELF-EMPOWERMENT

Mindfulness & Self-Compassion

It's essential that we counter negative self-talk with mindfulness and self-compassion in order to shift our narrative.[149] Mindfulness also may allow us to be aware of the origins of these thoughts and how they were cultivated over time. For example, fifty-four-year-old Layla functioned with the limiting belief, *If I let people get too close, they will hurt me.* This originated in her childhood with neglectful, verbally and emotionally abusive parents, and friends who hurt her repeatedly. After exploring the resulting impact and instituting a consistent mindful practice, Layla was able to challenge her current thoughts and recognize where she may have misassigned meaning or applied unproductive generalizations to other areas of her life.

Layla focused on her misconceptions, which shifted her internal dialogue and debunked her limiting beliefs. Instead of, "If I let people get close to me, they will hurt me," she grasped onto, " I have some friends that are close, and they haven't intentionally hurt me. Not every relationship will work out. Sometimes people in my life will hurt me, but I know it's the price I'll sometimes pay for being vulnerable. I can learn to assert my needs and establish better boundaries to help."

By recognizing why we have these limiting beliefs and assessing whether they're factual or are based on our history, fears and/or expectations, we can begin challenging them and flipping the script for a better future.

Engaging in Cognitive Defusion

In Layla's example, she was fusing with the belief that relationships are unsafe and she should stay clear of them. I helped her defuse from the thoughts by helping her to realize that her perspective was linear and generalized, thus not serving her well in her interpersonal relationships. In ACT, the process of cognitive defusion provides the ability to recognize these thoughts as they occur in the present moment.[150] When Layla recognized she was having these thoughts in real time, she was able to create space to take appropriate actions aligned with her values. For example, instead of engaging in her automatic thoughts which inhibited her current behavior, she recognized she was having these thoughts in the present moment and observed them for what they were, merely thoughts trying to protect her from hurt and prompt her toward familiar, comfortable behaviors that didn't serve her well.

By creating this space and by viewing the thoughts objectively, Layla diffused their power by reassigning different thoughts and feelings to them. It took the punch and power out of them. Rather than engaging in the same ineffective behavior that kept her out of sync with her values and who she wanted to be, Layla made different choices through diffusion. Diffusion empowered her to recognize that the thoughts she had about herself due to her past did not need to dictate her present identity or reality. Being able to recognize her experiences when they occur, without allowing them to define her or have them encapsulate her identity, allowed her to align committed action with her values.

Getting Clear About Values & Engaging in Committed Action

One of the most important steps necessary to strive towards self-empowerment is to become thoroughly acquainted with your values, as elaborated on in Chapter Two. In ACT, values are what we believe to be important, how we execute our daily lives, what we stand for, what guides our priorities, and what gives life deeper meaning.[151] It is when we do not live aligned with our values, that discontentment and disempowerment occurs.

Once you have a better sense of your underlying values, you can begin engaging in committed action. Committed action is being able to take steps and engage in action, behavior and patterns associated with your core values.[152] It is important that when taking committed action, that you invest in the *doing*, and that you still maintain flexibility and set realistic expectations. Being flexible and setting realistic expectations allows you to be consistent in your behaviors while also being prepared for life's inevitable challenges and obstacles.

Brooke, a fifty-two-year-old mother of three, was having challenges in her marriage. She came to me concerned about her frequent mood swings, anger, and anxiety. A recent incident involved a preplanned mother-daughter day with her sixteen-year-old. Her husband felt guilty about upsetting Brooke the night before. To make it up to her and assuage his guilt, he insisted he'd come along. Brooke consented, as she wanted to avoid adding to his distress if she restricted him. She didn't feel worthy enough to exert her own needs.

Brooke ended up feeling regretful and shamed that she didn't stick to her original plan and frustrated at herself for not asserting her needs. She also felt resentment toward her husband for putting her in that position, and sad that her daughter was disappointed that they didn't get their alone time together.

When we explored which thoughts she was fusing with, she stacked them up. "Others' needs are more important than mine. I'm responsible for making everyone happy," and "My needs don't count, so there's no point in expressing or asserting them." When we clarified which values may have been conflicting for her, she recognized that she wanted to spend alone time with her daughter predicated on her parenting values, and she wanted to appease her husband because of her compassion and kindness values.

Based on her decision, it was clear she was fused with older self-defeating beliefs influencing her current decision making. Being fused with these thoughts made it challenging for her to identify her values and act on behalf of them. When parceled out, Brooke recognized she was being triggered, which resulted in her being remote from her needs and values, and that if she were able to identify her *operating* values, she could have opted to take her daughter out as they originally planned.

That solution would also enable Brooke to give credence to her compassion and kindness by telling her husband she recognizes his regrets and efforts and could understand his sadness and disappointment about not being included that day. With this approach, she would be cognizant of her needs in the moment and take direct action on all the values which were meaningful to her.

Brooke realized it would have been in her best interest to act on behalf of her core values despite how her husband might react. She also recognized that being remote from them, including her self-worth and independence, resulted in negative consequences for her, her husband, and her daughter, which was what she had tried to avoid.

When an individual such as Brooke feels misaligned or disempowered, we review how their emotional state may impact their current decision making, invariably affecting their self-empowerment. For example, I explain that anger and/or anxiety can activate their brain and nervous system and can push them into fight-or-flight mode. Some of the rational parts of their brain shut down, decreasing ability to think and reason, or even to consider the long-term consequences of their actions. This impedes conscious and mindful decision-making, and prompts them to react impulsively rather than mindfully. With Brooke, we also revisited her core values, and I assisted her with taking the necessary steps to re-engage with committed action aligned with her values. This helped to facilitate her increased feelings of self-empowerment.

CURIOSITY-BASED QUESTIONS AROUND EMPOWERMENT

1. What substantive effort do you use to acquire greater self-awareness?
2. What concrete effort do you put toward formulating your goals?
3. How satisfied are you with your level of self-confidence? What gets in the way of you being more satisfied?
4. What limiting beliefs come up for you?
5. How do these limiting beliefs make you feel? How do they impact your behavior?
6. Do you find yourself using disempowering language? Provide examples how you do this.
7. How could you reframe it so that it's more empowering?
8. What judgments about yourself do you fuse with?
9. How do they impact your behavior?
10. Do you utilize compensatory strategies?
11. What deficit, weakness, injury, or perceived inadequacy might they be compensating for?
12. What benefits/secondary gains do you get from these behaviors? How did it help you cope? What were you rewarded with? What might you have been avoiding?
13. Would you describe yourself as having more of a fixed mindset or a growth mindset? How will you work on developing more of a growth mindset?
14. When reviewing characteristics of those who are resilient, experience posttraumatic growth, or are psychologically rich, which

characteristics do you embody? Which do you need to work on cultivating? How will you do that?

15. What was the most challenging circumstance you've had to experience that profoundly impacted and changed your life? In what way did it affect you? What did you learn from it?

16. Working on self-empowerment requires present moment awareness, giving space for psychological flexibility, defusing thoughts, and taking committed action on behalf of your values and goals. What part of this process do you expect will be most challenging? Why? What will you do to continually work on it?

SELF-GUIDED GROWTH EXERCISE: YOUR FUTURE SELF

Think from an empowered mindset. Imagine where you would ideally like to be in the future, five, ten, and fifteen years from now. Think about and/or write the story of how you got there. **Consider**:

1. What have you currently learned about yourself that's informing where you would like to be?

2. What mistakes or failures did you experience that helped you learn about your needs and reconnected you to your values?

3. What were you thinking and feeling during those events that led to your decision making?

4. What strengths or opportunities do you want to see yourself having?

5. What are you committed to doing and being in the future?

6. If you were eulogized, what would you want people to say about you? How do you want to be remembered? Are these attributes/character traits included in your vision for your future?

Please Listen to the Cultivating Ourselves Guided Meditation:

Find all the ACE Your Life Guided Meditations at www.michellemaidenberg.com/ACEYourLife

**SCAN HERE FOR
CULTIVATING OURSELVES
GUIDED MEDITATION**

Congratulate yourself for taking another step toward ACE'ing Your Life.

Unleash your best self and live the life you want.

CHAPTER 8

Discovering and Practicing Empowerment

Do the one thing you think you cannot do.
Fail at it. Try again. Do better the second time.
The only people who never tumble are those who
never mount the high wire. This is your moment.
Own it.

–Oprah Winfrey

When working on enhancing your self-empowerment, it's critical to consider your general behavior, habits, motivation, willingness, and resilience. The power is in *the doing* and having concrete examples and experiences of achievement you can point to. The goal is to feel empowered *no matter what*. With non-relenting confidence and self-belief, you'll stop at nothing to live your best life and the life you want to be living. You'll learn tangible ways to acquire self-empowerment and focus on *the doing*.

HABIT FORMATION

Our Brain and How Habits Get Formed

According to cognitive neuroscientists, we are conscious of only about five percent of our cognitive activity, so most of our decisions, actions, emotions, and behavior depend on the ninety-five percent of brain activity that goes beyond our conscious awareness.[153] From our eyes blinking to driving from our grocery store to home, we rely on *the adaptive unconscious;* that is the way our brain understands the world the mind and body must negotiate. It's the everyday functioning and decisions we make without consciously thinking about them. Our brain functions on an unconscious level relatively easily, because it requires less work and brain capacity. However, when we seek to enhance ourselves, we want to act with *conscious awareness* so we can mindfully process and strategize to ensure our behaviors align with our values and who we strive to be.

We form positive and negative habits throughout our lives. And once a habit is formed, it's hard to break free of it. It's as if our brain stops fully participating in decision making and relies on our automatic routines. Our brains form neural pathways that get stronger the more often we perform a task. When we perform a task enough times, we no longer must think about how it's done. It becomes an automatic habit, like when we drive a car, order popcorn at the movie theater, or brush our teeth before bed.

When we continue a habit, we change the mechanisms and structure of our brain. Neurons start to connect when a habit begins, then the connections strengthen, and when the behavior is continued, they get myelinated. The brain views all repetitive behavior and habits as important and does not differentiate between what is helpful for us versus what is not. It just functions to maintain the habit that's been created and it's familiar with.

Every habit starts with a psychological pattern called a "habit loop," a three-part process which includes a *cue, routine,* and *reward.* According to Charles Duhigg, Pulitzer-prize winning reporter and author of two books on habits and productivity, when we break it down into these fundamental parts, we can understand what a habit is, how it works, and how to improve it. In his book *The Power of Habit: Why We Do What We Do in Life and Business,*[154] he explains:

> What we know from lab studies is that it's never too late to break
> a habit. Habits are malleable throughout your entire life. But we

also know that the best way to change a habit is to understand its structure—that once you tell people about the cue and the reward and you force them to recognize what those factors are in a behavior, it becomes much, much easier to change.

In James Clear's book, *Atomic Habits: An Easy & Proven Way to Build Good Habits & Break Bad Ones*,[155] he sees it as a four-step habit loop: *cue, craving, response,* and *reward.* The cue is the trigger that kicks off the habitual behavior; our brain takes in data through our five senses or a thought. The craving is about wanting the reward. The response is about obtaining the reward. Rewards take on many forms: money, power, praise, approval, satisfaction, etc. They are the end goal of every habit.[156] James Clear suggests the three laws of behavior change that we ask ourselves: *How can I make it obvious? How can I make it attractive? How can I make it easy? How can I make it satisfying?*

Dopamine is a neurotransmitter produced by the hypothalamus, a small region of your brain that helps you feel pleasurable sensations. It's an important part in your reward system and plays a large role in habit formation.[157] The brain releases dopamine when you do things that feel good or pleasurable or when you complete a task. If the behavior is done repeatedly, dopamine is released, and it strengthens the habit even more. When we're not doing those things, dopamine creates the craving to want to do the behavior continually to experience the pleasurable sensations. Dopamine strengthens incentive motivation, allows for quicker and stronger pleasurable and positive associations, and maintains reinforcement.

When trying to rid ourselves of habits, we tend to gravitate toward a quick fix solution to expedite the process and avoid as much discomfort as possible. For example, despite research deeming that diets don't work, and ninety-five percent of all dieters regain their lost weight in one to five years, individuals still diet.[158]

Most people look for a quick weight loss fix through some magical diet or gimmick. A 2019 market data report stated that the US weight loss market is a staggering $78 billion industry.[159] The weight loss from extreme diets is often temporary, with weight gain to inevitably follow. By some estimates, as many as 80 percent of overweight people who manage to slim down noticeably after a diet, gain some or all of the weight back within one year.[160] *The secret to lifelong healthful behaviors is found in our daily decision making and consistent practice. It's not with quick fixes. We can't will ourselves to change without sustainable practice.*

Just as skilled and seasoned professional athletes continually practice, we need to practice if we want to sharpen our skills and effectively maintain behaviors. Just as we commit to our vehicles' routine maintenance via oil changes and tune ups, the same goes for our bodies or whatever else we're working on.

18 WAYS TO WORK ON HABITS TO FOSTER THE EMPOWERMENT PROCESS

Learning about habits is an integral part of the empowerment process. It's important to know ways to integrate good habits or extinguish bad habits:[161]

1. Do something simple and achievable every day until it becomes automatic. Repetition of an action causes habits to form. Even after conscious motivation decreases, once a habit is formed, less focus, conscious motivation, and effort is needed, which makes the habit far more likely to continue. This is why habits are useful—we're able to use less mental energy because they become automatic.

2. Start out small, so you won't be discouraged. Gradually build up to bigger tasks and goals. For example, if your goal were to run a marathon, you wouldn't start out of the gate running 15 miles. You would gradually and incrementally increase your milage to avoid injury, exhaustion, and discouragement.

3. When looking to create a habit, choose an easy context cue (e.g., after breakfast, when you finish reading a book, etc.).

4. You must determine your own goals, so you have more agency and investment in them.

5. A behavior can reach a peak and plateau if you don't set a new goal to strive for. For example, if you're running up and down the same street every day for a prolonged period, you're likely to get bored, disinterested, and unmotivated. To re-engage your motivation, you can move on to other routes where you could appreciate other more challenging terrains and new sights, or set a longer distance goal.

6. When considering habits, you need to assess and consider intrinsic and external motivators. Intrinsic motivation comes purely from within; it's not due to any anticipated reward, deadline, or outside pressure.[162] For example, people intrinsically motivated to run, do so because they love the feeling of running itself and take pride in their bodily strength. They see it as an important part of their identity which serves as a continuous source of motivation. Extrinsic motivation can increase motivation in the short term, but over time, it can wear you down or even backfire. It's also generally non-sustaining (e.g., deciding to lose weight because your daughter's wedding is slowly approaching).

7. Especially until your behavior reaches automaticity, forming habits requires you to have awareness, a willingness to be uncomfortable, and self-control.

8. Understand that more complex behaviors (this is individually evaluated and varies from person to person) take longer to form automaticity than easier behaviors.

9. For all tasks, especially harder ones, it's possible to achieve a great degree of automaticity. However, circumstances will require more of your willingness for discomfort, self-control, self-regulation, and effort. Times when you need to step it up include when you're feeling particularly emotionally vulnerable, you don't feel grounded or physically well, and/or you're directly triggered in some way. It's important to remember that if it were an easy task, everyone would be doing it. It's challenging, and it will probably require more from you.

10. The purpose of rewards is to satisfy our craving and to teach us which actions are worth remembering. As we go through life, our sensory nervous system is continuously monitoring which actions satisfy our desires and deliver pleasure. For good habits, this substantiates the need to consistently return and reinforce the rewards, which help you to create and sustain the habit. For bad habits, understanding your habit loop and the pleasurable sensations it evokes helps you extinguish habits that don't serve you well.

11. Evidence has shown that as the strength of a habit grows, intention becomes decreasingly predictive of the behavior.[163] That's why even when you intend to change behavior, because of all the ongoing processes related to your brain (i.e., production of dopamine, memory and consolidated learning, associations it makes, etc.), it's not enough to do so. This reinforces that intention to change behavior won't cut it; there's a need to consciously and proactively commit to incrementally doing things differently than you had before.

12. For behaviors involving repetition, habits are crucial. In Wendy Wood's research in *Good Habits, Bad Habits: The Science of Making Positive Changes That Stick*,[164] she found that our actions are habitual 43 percent of the time. She substantiates that willpower or self-control are not enough to change or sustain your behaviors. *You have to devote time and effort to behaving differently whether or not you feel like it in the moment.*

13. To change or break a habit, reconstruct the environment around you to prompt good behaviors and increase friction so that bad habits are inconvenient.[165]

14. For accountability and to sustain interest and motivation, it's often helpful to create habits alongside a buddy who's committed or to enlist support from family members, friends, or someone else who's encouraging.

15. To help break unproductive habits, instead of struggling mentally, tap into mindfulness training in order to turn toward experiences,

rather than away from them. Learn to gradually sit with the discomfort in service of doing what you want to be doing.

16. Cultivate mindful awareness and an interminable state of curiosity. Mindful awareness helps facilitate curiosity and personal insight. It forges an openness to new habits and decisions and will help to break habit loops leading you to more mindful actions.[166]

17. To create continual motivation and fuel creation and sustain habit, you must find your purpose or personal meaning in completing certain behaviors connected directly to your values.

18. Find intentional and meaningful ways to encourage your positive habits and growth through self-compassion and self-love. Surround yourself with people who encourage you, believe in you, and support you.

FOSTER THE EMPOWERMENT PROCESS &
WORK ON HABITS

SIMPLE
Do something simple and achievable every day.

SMALL
Start out small so you won't be discouraged. Build up to bigger tasks.

EASY CUE
Choose an easy context cue to kick off habit (ie: after breakfast).

OWN GOALS
Determine your own goals so you have more investment in them.

STEP IT UP
Behavior can reach a peak, so step it up to maintain interest & avoid boredom.

MOTIVATORS
Consider intrinsic & external motivators. Internal may work better.

SELF-CONTROL
You need awareness, okay being uncomfortable, and self-control.

TIME COMMITMENT
More complex behaviors take longer to form habits than easier behaviors.

COMMITMENT
It can be done, but harder tasks will require more commitment from you.

REWARDS
Understand rewards satisfy our cravings and reinforce behavior.

INTENTION
Consciously commit to incrementally do things differently than before.

TIME & EFFORT
Devote time & effort to act differently whether you feel like it in the moment.

RECONSTRUCT
To change a habit, change the environment and make them harder to do.

ENCOURAGEMENT
Form a habit with a buddy or get help from others who are encouraging.

MINDFULNESS
Tap into mindfulness training to turn toward new experiences.

OPENNESS
Cultivate curiosity to be open to new habits and to break habit loops.

VALUES
Find your purpose or personal meaning as tied to your values.

SELF-COMPASSION
Encourage your positive habits and growth through self-compassion, self-love.

Many people think it takes just twenty-one days to change a habit, but one recent study suggests that the average might be closer to sixty-six days or even longer—especially if a habit is particularly hard to pick up.[167] Habits never completely disappear; they become encoded into the structure of our brain which is advantageous as we can often pick up creating a habit where we left off. You can grab that neglected three-speed in the garage, get back on the saddle, and you're good to go because of memory recall and your childhood habit of bike riding.

The challenge? Our brain can't tell the difference between good and bad habits, so if you have a bad one, it's always lurking, waiting for the right cues and rewards to get reactivated.[168] Therefore, it's important to remember that changing any habit requires intentional awareness, repetition, and persistence.

Let's look at habits that Clay, age seventeen, formed around vaping nicotine. It started with social and academic stress (cue/trigger). From that, it moved to a classmate offering to get together with him after school to vape e-cigarettes (response/behavior). For a brief time that initial stress is reduced (reward). His brain recognizes a particular behavior—in this case, vaping—alleviates, however briefly, the feeling that the initial trigger sparks in him. With that reward of lowered stress, the brain says *go do that behavior again* when the urge gets evoked. This emotional dependence develops into a physical dependence to nicotine, and he has the additional urge connected to getting his fix.

Obviously, vaping nicotine doesn't work directly on the stress related to the social and academic pressures, nor does it give him the social, stress management, and coping skills he needs. Instead, it reinforces avoidance. All it takes is a bit of stress to keep him going back to feed his vaping habit.

We can increase awareness of our habit loops by learning their mechanics. Then we understand why, when we're looped in, we're on autopilot, immediately reacting without consciously thinking.

The first step is to observe ourselves and gain self-awareness about our own habit loops.

Understanding Your Habits Exercise

Identify a habit you've been working on, or want to work on. (e.g., speaking more kindly and compassionately to your kids, cutting down on alcohol consumption, asserting yourself at work, eating healthfully and exercising, etc.).

_____

_____

_____

_____

How has the habit developed? What's the habit loop (cue, craving, response, reward)?

_____

_____

_____

_____

How have you tried to work on the habit? What's worked? What hasn't?

_____

_____

_____

_____

Were you intrinsically or externally motivated? How has that contributed to or taken away from your goals?

_____

_____

_____

_____

How willing are you to put in concerted effort, even if it's difficult and challenging? What can get in your way?

_____

_____

_____

_____

How willing are you to be uncomfortable? Assert self-control? What can get in your way?

_____

_____

_____

_____

How will you reconstruct the environment around you to support your positive behaviors?

_____

_____

_____

_____

How will these positive behaviors connect to your values? How can they help you find personal meaning and purpose?

_____

_____

_____

_____

How will you encourage yourself to stick to these habits (e.g., mindfulness practice, social support, practicing self-compassion, etc.)?

_____

_____

_____

_____

PAYING ATTENTION TO THE DIFFERENT SYSTEMS IN OUR BRAIN

It's difficult to say no when our impulsive primitive brain wants what it wants when it wants it, and it gravitates toward instant gratification and pleasurable sensations. Luckily, our sophisticated rational brain engages in complex problem solving and helps us question and logically think through our decisions. Flipping back and forth between the cognitive and impulsive systems can make us feel as if we have two people living inside our mind.

To truly empower ourselves, we need to behave consciously and rationally. In Kelly McGonigal's book *The Willpower Instinct,* she refers to the *I will power* and *I won't power* in regard to self-control and why it matters.[169] She asserts that saying, "I will," and "I won't," are two distinct parts of what willpower is. It's important to understand both the part that leads us closer to our goals and the part that leads us away from them. We need true understanding of what gets in our way of what we need to do—even if we don't feel like it. It's also important to have awareness about the part of us that doesn't want to follow through.

Research on habits, motivation, and willpower consistently confirms that paying attention is one of our greatest allies.[170] Studies make clear the essence of training our brain is to pause before we act. We build on our self-confidence and self-empowerment by keeping our rational, conscious mind formative. Thus, we behave in line with our core values. Setbacks will occur. Occasionally, we'll have a hard time. But acting mindfully, gaining awareness, learning from those experiences, and building your self-confidence will empower you to move onward and upward.

SETBACKS, SLIPS AND FALLS

Gaining Perspective on Setbacks

You'll continually evaluate whether you're doing "right" or "wrong." Your mind will further loop to suggest that when you're doing it "wrong," you're ineffective and you'll never get it right. This may convince you that you need to get the behavior right all the time. This reflects all-or-nothing, black-and-white thinking (see Chapter Five "The Most Common Types of Self-Limiting Thinking"). You may fear that you'll forget what you learned about yourself, be frustrated that you can't follow through all the time or feel concerned that you'll return to behaviors that make you feel like a failure and remote from your values.

Our humanness dictates our imperfections. There is always room for slips, refocusing, and recalibrating. Inevitably, you'll have days when behaviors are effortless or it's more difficult to sustain them. *It's the overall picture that matters most.* Over time, are you generally consistent and committed? Consider the adversity you face daily. You will always be exposed to triggers and challenging situations.

Your brain's reward center still wants the dopamine release that some behaviors provide. It may not stop "wanting," even if you make a philosophical change to how you approach yourself and your behaviors. You'll still have ongoing responses to your behaviors, as well as self-defeating thoughts and feelings. Your continuing need to work through them requires acceptance and understanding. At times, these vulnerabilities will make it harder to be your best self.

The practice of living the life you want to be living comes with what may feel like setbacks. Slips are expected and inevitable. They need to be put into perspective and worked through so that a challenging day or week does not become challenging weeks and months. Typically, the longer the slip lasts, the greater the chance you'll feel hopeless and decide to give up all together.

Like any good practice, skills and habits build one day at a time. Even if you had a particularly challenging day, you can rebound and focus on getting back on track with commitment and effort.

Gaining Perspective on Slip Ups

- Slips are inevitable. Expect them to happen.

- To diminish the potential for avoidance, procrastination, and self-defeating thoughts, it is best to get back on track as soon as you possibly can after a slip.
- We all slip, a characteristic of our being human. A slip is not a sign of failure, it's a temporary setback amidst a difficult challenge.
- No slip can erase all of your healthful progress.
- You can always rebound from a slip.
- You can always learn something valuable about yourself from a slip. Think about it as a growth opportunity.
- Use a slip as a signal that you're in need of support—seek and be accepting of it.
- You may get discouraged and frustrated, especially during a slip. These are typical feelings. Accept whatever comes up. They're only thoughts and feelings. They do not dictate what you do with them. You can feel discouraged and still get back on track.
- The best thing you can do is understand the slips so they can be avoided or worked through effectively as they occur.

What to Do During and After Slips

When you slip, you may be tempted to throw in the towel because of your mistaken perception that you may not succeed. But if you think rationally, you'll realize your progress won't be thwarted by your momentary slip into old behaviors and habits. When you stick to your goals despite a setback, you give yourself the opportunity to repair the notion that you are "not good at it" so "why bother trying?" All is not lost. There is always the ability to get back on track.

If and when you slip, self-criticism is likely to surface. Acceptance and compassion may be nowhere to be found. Beating yourself up won't help you regain the control you feel you lost. It erodes your self-confidence when you need it most. These thoughts can be reframed. "*I'm having the thought that I'm not good at it,*" as opposed to "*I'm buying into the belief that I'm not good at it,*" or "*I have the thought that I'm not good at it, but I'm choosing to still try my best and accept that I won't be perfect. All is not lost, and I can be proud of my accomplishments."*

When you have particularly negative thoughts regarding yourself, challenge them by asking these two questions:

1. What is a more useful or helpful way of looking at this?
2. If a friend described the same situation and reaction, what advice would you give to them? How would you treat them? You would probably be calm, supportive, and kind. So apply those loving kindness sentiments to yourself.

Reframe the situation for yourself. Was the slip due to any of the challenges or cues below? Or some others?

1. an emotional response, whether positive or negative, to a situation
2. a break in daily routine
3. a heightened physiological state
4. confronting an intense urge

Taking an inventory of the negative thinking and what was challenging about a given situation helps you gain awareness about what causes your slips. It enables you to continue to make progress so slips are less frequent and you're less inclined to feel discouraged, ashamed, and hopeless. You'll have a better sense of how to handle them effectively.

Identifying the Triggers

Here's a step-by-step way for you to identify what caused a slip up. Analyze a recent one of yours:

1. What circumstance led to the slip?
2. What were you thinking before? During? After the slip? How were you feeling?
3. How did you act?
4. What else could you have done?
5. What resources/supports need to be in place for you to react differently?

6. Do you notice a habit loop or pattern(s) with your slips?

Every circumstance is a learning moment. Each enhances your self-awareness and ability to problem solve. You are learning to track your patterns of thoughts, feelings, and behaviors before, during, and after a slip. You are practicing working through challenging situations to reconnect to your values.

THE SLIP-FALL CYCLE

You want to recover quickly from a slip to avoid a full-fledged fall—a prolonged period of successive engagement in the bad habit or behavior(s)—which is far more challenging to rebound from. For example, if you're running and you feel a pain in your heel, it's often better to sit out the race than struggle and worsen your injury.

The initial injury (grade 1) can result in approximately a one-week rest period.

Whereas a significant injury (grade 3) can require a month or longer rest period.

The longer and more significant the fall, the more difficult the rebound, so it's best to avoid that pattern and learn to quickly get back on track.

Gain awareness of the slip-fall pattern to break the cycle:

SLIP-FALL PATTERN

01 CUE

02 CRAVING

03 SLIP *(response & reward)*

04 NEGATIVE THINKING

05 SHAME & HOPELESSNESS

06 CONTINUE TO SLIP

07 MORE INTENSE NEGATIVE THINKING

08 FALL

8 Steps to Break the Slip-Fall Cycle

Step 1: Recognize that no matter how you may feel after the slip, it's not unusual to slip. Be open to seizing the learning opportunity.

Step 2: Identify the negative thoughts and uncomfortable feelings that lead you to a fall rather than getting you back on track toward your goals after a slip. For example, you may be engaging in all-or-nothing thinking, *I'm never going to be able to do this* or *What's the point? This will always be a problem.* You may think, *I might as well give up,* and end up intensely discouraged. You may rationalize your behavior to avoid facing your vulnerabilities (see Chapter Five "Common Rationalizations/Excuses"). These are sabotaging, exaggerated thoughts that lead you to spiral, prolong the slip, or prompt you towards a fall. Put these thoughts into perspective. Realize that you are generally successful at this. Slipping is *sometimes* a problem, but is not a problem *all* the time. Actually, over time, behavioral changes become less strenuous and more habitual and manageable. *Decide that instead of making an excuse, you'll make a plan.*

Step 3: Despite the temptation to give up, allow room for those thoughts and feelings. Even if you aren't feeling successful, keep moving toward your values and goals and avoid putting yourself down.

- Encourage yourself.
- Point out moments of success and notable progress.
- Take action toward more positive behaviors.

Step 4: Evaluate the situation. Reconsider the plan you had in place and whether you need to make adjustments. For example, was acting out on your anger triggered by a cluster of events such as a misunderstanding with a friend, work stress, an argument with your partner? Consider:

- What was challenging about the situation?
- Is it likely to happen again?
- What would you consider doing differently the next time?

Step 5: Reconnect with your values and goals (review Chapter Two). Remind yourself of your specific values and why connecting to them is so important to you, the cost of unhealthy behaviors, and how you'll recommit to your goals.

Step 6: Problem solve through the challenge. Commit to making at least two small changes in the moment. To build your confidence and show you can and will do something toward your self-belief and self-worth, do something proactive right away.

Step 7: Develop a concrete plan for handling "slippery" situations. For example, write down:

- I find myself in slippery situations when _____ _____.

- The plan I will put into place includes _____ _____.

Step 8: Seek support and check in with yourself on a daily and weekly basis to acknowledge your accomplishments and assess your values.

BREAK THE SLIP-FALL CYCLE

RECOGNIZE THAT IT'S NOT UNUSUAL TO SLIP. BE OPEN TO LEARNING. ▼ **IT'S OK** 1

2 **IDENTIFY CAUSE** ▼ IDENTIFY THE NEGATIVE THOUGHTS & FEELINGS THAT LED TO THE SLIP.

KEEP MOVING TOWARDS YOUR VALUES AND GOALS. ▼ **DON'T GIVE UP** 3

4 **EVALUATE** ▼ RECONSIDER THE PLAN YOU HAD AND IF YOU NEED TO MAKE ADJUSTMENTS.

RECONNECT WITH YOUR VALUES AND GOALS. REMEMBER THE IMPORTANCE. ▼ **RECONNECT** 5

6 **PROBLEM SOLVE** ▼ COMMIT TO MAKING AT LEAST TWO SMALL CHANGES IN THE MOMENT.

MAKE A CONCRETE PLAN FOR HANDLING "SLIPPERY" SITUATIONS. ▼ **DEVELOP PLAN** 7

8 **GET SUPPORT** ▼ SEEK SUPPORT AND CHECK IN WITH YOURSELF DAILY AND WEEKLY.

Reconnect With Your Best Self Following a Slip

It's critical to gain awareness about the psychological barriers that impact your behaviors. After a slip, write a guided journal entry. This helps to integrate the information and lessons, and adopt more positive behaviors. Included in the guided entry you will:

- Look at what triggered the behavior.
- Assess and accept what happened, including negative, uncomfortable thoughts and feelings.
- Identify what you could learn for future circumstances.

- Encourage yourself to do it differently next time, so that you can be your best self.

Journal Recovering From a Slip

The challenging situation: _____
_____ .

I am vulnerable to slips with my _____
behavior when _____
_____ .

I'm prompted toward a fall when _____
_____ .

At this moment, I also want to remember my past
successes, which include: _____
_____ .

I'll notice my negative thoughts and feelings about myself
and about the situation. Instead of giving up and letting
it affect me even more, I choose to take control. I'll get
back on track by doing the following things: _____
_____ .

I'm going to do these things despite thinking and feeling
_____. I know this is a typical part of the process.

I'm going to take the moment to learn about my behaviors.
What I've learned from this experience includes: _____
_____ .

I'm going to reconnect to my values which are: _____
_____ .

Tell yourself, "These points are going to help me, so I slip less often. I care about being my best self, and I am committed to continuing to work on and enhancing my life. *Anything I want to be successful at, I need to continually commit to working on.* I will embrace and be mindful of this mantra."

YOUR UNRELENTING CONFIDENCE

As you continue to put effort into your habits and behavior, they become a natural part of who you are and how you live your life. You end up with the added benefit of feeling more confident in yourself and your abilities. It's important you realize that if you're sidetracked, you can't change the past, but there's always an opportunity to get back on track and create your own present and future. It is never too late to improve. At any age, any time, now and throughout your life, there's room for growth. We can always want to find ways we can work on our self-empowerment by resetting and increasing our confidence and personal power.

Mark Manson, bestselling author of *The Subtle Art of Not Giving a F*ck: A Counterintuitive Approach to Living a Good Life*,[171] asserts that confidence is rooted in our perception of ourselves. Additionally, he says confidence is in "the perception that you *lack nothing*, that you are equipped with everything you need, both now and for the future." Lastly, he notes, "The charade with confidence is that it has nothing to do with being comfortable in what we achieve and everything to do with being comfortable in what we *don't* achieve."

He sees that those who are confident are so because they're comfortable with uncomfortable experiences tied to failure, rejection, vulnerability, etc. He elaborates that people often worry that if they fail, they'll become a failure, when the opposite is the case. They become failures because they're afraid to fail. "Comfort in our failures allows us to act without fear, to engage without judgment, to love without conditions. It's the dog that lets the tail go, realizing that it's already a part of himself."

18 Things Empowered People Do

Empowered people embody similar traits. To understand empowerment and how to cultivate it, thereby increasing your confidence, understand that empowered people:

1. **Are perpetually in the present moment.** Instead of focusing on what was and what will be, focus on what is, right here, right now. The past already happened, and the future awaits you. Through our regrets and worries, we spend much of our time gravitating toward the past and future. Unfortunately, you then lose sight of what's right here before you. You miss out on living life.

2. **Invest in discomfort by leaning into challenging or uncomfortable thoughts, feelings, and sensations.** Do this incrementally, remaining aware, curious, and self-compassionate. Despite the discomfort that arises, note what gets evoked, and what you're prompted to do based on what arises and how you select to behave. Be driven by your values, never by your thoughts, feelings, or sensations. They're unreliable barometers.

3. **Waste little time beating themselves up.** Those who see setbacks, disappointments, and failures as an indication of who they are, are likely to undermine themselves and be self-disparaging. If you have an internal locus of control and believe you have control over what happens to you, you'll see those occurrences as opportunities for feedback and growth.

4. **Don't get caught up in the comparison trap.** Many people get caught up measuring their worth by comparing themselves to others. There's no comparison. You're your own person. Use your own measuring stick. Attempt to do better with each passing day.

5. **Realize that not all feelings need to be reacted to.** We give too much credence to our emotions and are under the impression we must always react to them. They're helpful in letting you know what's meaningful to you, but that doesn't mean you have to react to them. Take time to observe, contemplate, and become more familiar with all aspects of yourself, including your feelings.

6. **Don't automatically react to thoughts and feelings.** Thoughts and feelings ebb and flow, contingent on experiences, acculturated socio-cultural factors based on your race, religion, how you identify, etc. Take pauses, study your thoughts and feelings. Have

curiosity about them, rather than reacting to them immediately and at face value.

7. **Don't believe everything that's thought or felt.**[172] Question the quality of your thoughts and feelings. How do they show up? Why do they show up that way? What does it mean to you? Recognize they're not an evaluation of who you are, or a sign of your progress. They're not set in stone and are often not factual but rather associations we make and can be disruptive because our mind is trying to protect us. Thoughts and feelings can be reframed and shift.

8. **Recognize that confidence is an emotional state of mind.**[173] Self-confidence is the way you approach and take action on your life overall. If you believe you have self-worth and self-respect, then everything you *do* will reflect it. *The way you do anything is the way you do everything.* If you approach life that way, you'll put concerted effort into all circumstances, decisions, and opportunities for progress.

9. **Understand that success and failure are synonymous.** We realize life is not linear. Twists and turns along the way can derail us at times. We recalibrate and pivot when we need to. Obstacles are needed for us to grow, and they occur *for* us not *to* us. Experiencing failure doesn't mean you are a failure. It just means that you're engaging in a life well-lived where you're learning and growing.

10. **Challenge their fears.** Our fears are often layered with predictions about the way things are or will be, and they keep us perpetually stuck. As the inspirational Peloton instructor, Robin Arzon says in her cycling classes, "Your fears don't know your strengths. Do you want it more than you fear it?" and "Fear kills more dreams than failure does." Fearing something is an indication of what you should be doing. The only way to work through fears is by doing, otherwise you limit yourself from accomplishing, re-writing your narrative, and discovering your resilience and strength.

11. **Take personal responsibility and accountability.** Being human is messy. We're imperfect, make mistakes, and sometimes mis-

judge ourselves and others. Fess up and face it. You need to be able to see yourself for who and what you are, even when you'd rather not. Accepting and working with our vulnerabilities makes us approachable, authentic, and human.

12. **Have daily practices.** Consistently practice and challenge yourself for change. As Alex Toussaint, another Peloton instructor raves, "What you commit to, you achieve, and you believe!" When you're creating habits by committing to a daily practice, to fortify your plan, make sure to include a routine of relatively easy and enjoyable things.

13. **Consistently check in and realign with their core values.** On a daily basis, assess if you're leaning into or away from your values. Rather than getting down on yourself for what you didn't do, consider what you could do more of going forward. Rather than seeing yourself as deficient, see yourself as capable of doing more. In that process, continue to reevaluate. Edit, add, or omit goals and values as you evolve.

14. **Create personal SMART goals (Specific, Measurable, Achievable, Relevant, and Time-based) directly linked to their values.** Take this Goal Setting Skills Test[174] sponsored by *Psychology Today* to find out whether your goal-setting attitude and behavior are conducive to success. Keep in mind that parts of you are open to progress, and for various reasons, other parts may resist. Often it's because of the discomfort that may ensue and the tradeoff of giving up something (e.g., when moving, familiarity of your setting) in order to get something (e.g., adventure of re-locating to a new city). Openly and compassionately seek to understand the barriers keeping you from achieving your goals. Don't give up on finding ways to make change. If Plan A doesn't work, go with Plan B. Go through the whole alphabet if you need to, but commit to not giving up no matter what. You're worth not giving up on.

15. **Pay attention to *all* their accomplishments.** Every action that increases your self-belief and self-confidence is worth acknowledg-

ing. You deserve that validation, and it builds your confidence, thereby increasing your ability to be self-accepting, self-compassionate, and attain self-empowerment. We don't do enough to notice every action taken on behalf of leaning into our values and our best self. We're quick to notice what's not right, but not as quick to notice all that's right with us. Christopher Bergland suggested cultivating an underdog mindset to celebrate smaller wins, as it fortifies motivation and resilience and may trigger the feel-good dopamine neurotransmitter.[175]

16. **Act on behalf of values, rather than on how they're responded or reacted to.** We don't have control over other's behavior, only our own. Rather than reacting to another person based on how they spoke or treated you, act from a place that clearly communicates your values, who you are, and what you want to stand for. It helps you not rely on your thoughts and feelings to dictate how you behave and values grounds you in your decision making.

17. **Have the ability to be self-compassionate and self-soothe.** Without the ability to be self-compassionate and comfort ourselves when we need it most, we can't feel empowered. Because setbacks, disappointments, and failures are inevitable, you must be able to comfort yourself and move on in the direction of who you deserve and strive to be.

18. **Commit to continually building on their confidence and best self.** Get into the habit of asking, "Does this support my being my best self and the life I'm trying to create?" *What you continually practice grows stronger. Change is inevitable, progress is not.* We get to decide each day whether we want to continue filling the ACE bucket and make consistent movement toward a life that we're personally proud of.

EMPOWERMENT TRAITS

Empowered people embody these similar traits
Are perpetually in the present moment.
Invest in discomfort by leaning into challenging or uncomfortable thoughts, feelings, and sensations.
Waste little time beating themselves up.
Don't get caught up in the comparison trap.
Realize that not all feelings need to be reacted to.
Don't automatically react to thoughts and feelings.
Don't believe everything that's thought or felt.
Recognize that confidence is an emotional state of mind.
Understand that success and failure are synonymous.
Challenge their fears.
Take personal responsibility and accountability.
Have daily practices.
Consistently check in and realign with their core values.
Create personal SMART goals (Specific, Measurable, Achievable, Relevant, and Time-based) directly linked to their values.
Pay attention to all their accomplishments.
Act on behalf of values, rather than how they're responded or reacted to.
Have the ability to be self-compassionate and self-soothe.
Commit to continually building on their confidence and best self.

COMMITTING TO THE 3RS—RESET, RECONNECT & REINVEST

Even as fully empowered people, we will all have moments where we need to reconnect, awaken, and unleash the power within us. You can do that by committing to the 3Rs. By reciting *reset, reconnect* and *reinvest*, you empower yourself to flip your script when you need it most. It's also a grounding technique to return to the present moment and gain conscious awareness of where you are regarding your thoughts, feelings, sensations, and behaviors. It helps you move in the direction of your values, best self, and the life you want to be living.

- **Reset**: Intentionally reset and come back to yourself in the present. Stand, sit, or lie down. Take at least two minutes to gain full awareness of your thoughts, feelings, bodily sensations, and behavior. Repeat *"reset"* at least three times. Slow yourself down by imaging your mind and body moving at the pace of a second hand on a clock, an inchworm, a turtle, or any helpful imagery. You could also think of it as if you're rebooting, as you would your PC if it froze. You would go back to your task only after your PC restarted and the programs fully loaded. You want to give yourself the time that's needed to slow down and recenter.

- **Reconnect**: Intentionally reconnect by going from an unconscious space driven by your amygdala to a conscious space driven by your prefrontal cortex. Notice every nuance about yourself without judgment or expectation. If those appear, that's perfectly okay, just label them *judgment(s)*, *expectation(s)*, *negativity*, or whatever else is showing up, and return to noticing yourself in the here and now. Also notice the part that may be resisting reconnecting. You can put your two hands out in front of you and create a weighted scale with the part that wants to reconnect and the part that doesn't. Observe the disparity and recognize all the more effort you need to put in toward compassionately helping the resistant part (e.g., with anxiety, you may have to face something fear evoking, which can be incredibly frightening and will require you to encourage and support yourself). Reconnect with the value(s) that may be rubbed up against, threatened, or needs attention. Acknowledge why that value is meaningful to you and why, based on its importance, you might react and behave now. Thank your mind for trying to alert you, protect you (from discomfort, shame, etc.), and let you know there's a need to understand yourself better.

- **Reinvest:** Intentionally reinvest and *do* what's in line with directly connecting to your value and what's meaningful to you. *Remind yourself that progress and change take time and effort, that you're worth investing in, whether you feel like it or not, and that you deserve to be treated as the most important person you know.* Also, that when you *do*, you're never regretful, but always proud of your accomplishments. No one ever said "I regret that I worked out," "I regret that I was mindful of my anger" or "I regret that I paid better attention to my child." It's always the first step that's the hardest. You're endlessly deserving of validation, care, and nurturance from yourself.

3Rs
RESET, RECONNECT & REINVEST

RESET
*Come back
to yourself
in the present*

RECONNECT
*Notice every nuance
of yourself
without judgment
or expectation*

REINVEST
*Intentionally DO
what's in line with
connecting to
your values*

I am so proud of my dear friend who I previously spoke about. Time steadily passes since her death. I still feel moments of deep pain and a longing to speak to her. I imagine that this pang will be enduring. As I've shared, when she couldn't get out of bed and function at her full capacity, she didn't want anyone to visit with her, including her children. She wanted to be remembered as she had been.

Our deep talks included her wrestling over her values of dignity and connection. I found out from one of her children that the day before she died, she invited each of them to say goodbye. I knew how hard that was for her. I felt so proud of her for deciding that connection was ultimately vital for her. It helped give her the peace of mind to completely let go.

She realized that if she compromised her connection to her children, whom she loved, but avoided getting the love she deserved from them, then her dignity would be compromised as well. Giving them and herself this gift enabled her to die fully aligned with her values and her best self. I especially wish I could share with her how much I admire her strength.

The moments we are fully accepting of ourselves, have self-compassion, and act from a place of self-empowerment are priceless. We must always remember that we have a time-limited, fast-moving precious life to live fully and meaningfully.

Seize the opportunity and narrate a new story for yourself—one you're personally proud of and feel empowered by. I appreciate you going on this journey with me. I believe in you wholeheartedly and unconditionally. Go proudly and ACE your life!

CURIOSITY-BASED QUESTIONS AROUND EMPOWERMENT

1. What meaningful thing(s) have you learned about yourself recently?
2. What part of the slip-fall cycle gets you stuck?
3. What steps in the slip-fall cycle might be the most challenging? Why do you think that is?
4. In what way will you work on it?
5. How did you previously define confidence for yourself? How do you see it now?
6. Are you settling for less than what you are worth? In what arena of your life? Why?
7. Out of the 18 things empowered people do, which ones do you accomplish?

8. Which of those things don't you do, and what keeps you from carrying them out?

9. What part of the 3Rs challenge you the most? Why?

10. How willing are you to continue practicing them until they get habituated?

11. Can you think of additional ways that will help you reset?

12. Can you think of additional ways that will help you reconnect?

13. Can you think of additional ways that will help you reinvest?

14. If your current life were a movie, what would the title be? What would you want it to be?

15. How can you make your life more meaningful, starting in this moment?

SELF-GUIDED GROWTH EXERCISES: JOURNALING AND EMPOWERING YOURSELF WITH MUSIC

A. My Future Self

Journaling is a great way to boost your mood, manage stress, and enhance your well-being.[176] It also enhances your self-awareness.[177] First, write using the prompts on page 209, which you could review monthly. Concurrently, use the journal template on page 210 to empower yourself daily. Following the daily writing, you'll participate in a brief self-love activity with reward for putting effort into being your best self and living the life you want to be living.

Use these 10 prompts to write about yourself:

Prompts for Writing About Yourself

My best attributes are...

I feel gratitude for...

I feel thankful when...

I have always wanted to...

I get my strength from...

Something I deeply desire is...

I flourish when...

I feel most proud of myself for...

I feel most confident when...

What I want the future to hold for me is...

Use this journal template to write daily:

Daily Journal

I showed myself acceptance and compassion today by...

Examples throughout the day when
I leaned into my values...

Examples throughout the day when I leaned
outside my values...

Values I will pay more attention to
and lean into tomorrow are...

I will specifically do ...
to lean into my values tomorrow.

I took opportunities to build on my confidence
today by doing...

After completing the journal prompt, show yourself a gesture of self-love. You can recite an empowering loving kindness mantra ("I care about myself and my well-being"), show yourself a physical gesture (give yourself a hug by crossing your hands on your chest, cupping your hands on your heart, or cradling your hands on your cheeks), or elicit a memory whereby you overcame a challenge and felt personally proud. Sit with those satisfying thoughts and feelings, or anything else that signifies self-love to you.

B. Empowering Yourself with Music

Music or other creative arts are wonderful tools to help ground you or assist you in tapping into your confidence and personal power. With the following empowering tunes: *Fight Song*[178] by Rachel Platten, *Rise Up*[179] by Andra Day, *This Is Me*[180] on the Greatest Showman soundtrack, *I Won't Back Down*[181] by Tom Petty, *Love Myself*[182] by Hailee Steinfeld, or (Girl) *Power*[183] by Little Mix, or a favorite of your choosing, sit or lie down and close your eyes.

As you listen and pay attention to the lyrics, note how you're thinking, feeling, and what sensations come up in your body. Imagine yourself embodying the words you hear. Fully open yourself up and absorb your greatness. Imagine giving yourself a fist bump or high five for all that you are and strive to be. *Declare that being your best self and living the life you want is non-negotiable.*

Please Listen to the Empowerment Guided Meditation:

Find all the ACE Your Life Guided Meditations at www.michellemaidenberg.com/ACEYourLife

SCAN HERE FOR
EMPOWERMENT
GUIDED MEDITATION

Congratulate yourself for taking another step toward ACE'ing Your Life.

Unleash your best self and live the life you want.

CONCLUSION

As we mature and as we develop and age, as our life circumstances change, and as society evolves, we have daily opportunities to either show up as our best selves or to sink into past patterns that no longer serve us. The work is harder on some days than others. It takes effort to change. But always, it's rewarding and worth choosing to live the life you want to be living.

As I've learned from my work and personal experience, there's much we can't control, but also much we can. Your mind consistently tries to protect you, and it is sometimes so overprotective it blinds and numbs you from what's best. *What if fear and discomfort are the very feelings you need in order to lean into being in the moment, to challenge yourself, and to connect with your values? What if you reframed the discomfort as healing rather than hurting, because it gets you closer to being your authentic self?*

The battle is constant within your mind to rid yourself of these uncomfortable feelings or stay with them to propel you toward personal growth. It is a tussle we all have with ourselves every day, and it profoundly impacts decision making. You have to question what's bigger, your fears or your sense of purpose toward choosing and living your worthwhile life.

There's often no way to predict or prepare for what lies ahead, so it's in our best interest to contemplate how we want to live each and every day, no matter what may happen. Sometimes it's a straight path, and sometimes we need to pivot. Life is an ongoing journey.

How are sculptures made? The beautiful image is already there. It's embedded. The excess material must be chiseled away for the incredible image/sculpture to appear. Many barriers get in the way of us embodying acceptance, compassion, and empowerment to ACE our lives. You must chisel away those barriers and "stuckness" to reveal and unleash your personal power. You have to ask, "How do I want to show up for me to be my best self and live the life that I want?"

We can't live our lives avoiding facing our fears and uncomfortable emotions. You must walk through life proactively with curiosity and flexibility, exercising acceptance and compassion to cultivate self-worth, self-belief, self-love and self-efficacy. Your growing confidence, grounded in your values, will lead you to *do* what you need in order to live your best life.

Self-acceptance and self-compassion do not imply accepting mediocrity and rationalizing your negative or unhelpful behavior, but rather, empathizing and supporting your experiences in order to curiously and willingly venture into your journey of personal growth. It requires looking at yourself internally and externally, facing all parts of yourself, which are *wonderful, worthy, and enough.*

We are the sky. Even when it rains, thunders, and hails, we don't question whether the sky is okay. We know foundationally that it can withstand harsh weather and that the sun will eventually rise. We can rely on the sky persevering. We can experience an array of challenging circumstances and uncomfortable emotions, as well, because at our core, we're resilient and whole. We'll come through whatever stands in our way. We learn to embrace and understand that *our emotions warn us, tell us about our needs, and connect us with meaning. We can appreciate our emotions and align our actions with our values.*

Living your best life comes with concerted effort and commitment. The willingness and desire to live life more meaningfully can drive you to do more, sometimes over and beyond what you think you're capable of.

Your biggest chance for living a better life lies in what holds you back or scares you. What you most fear is what you need to be doing. It's the part of you that needs to grow the most. There will always be parts of you that want you to act and parts that don't. You inevitably get to decide what you want to do. Do you want to die longing? Wondering? Or regretful? *The only thing constant in life is change. You will evolve whether you want to or not. It becomes your choice as to what direction you take.*

You came into this world crying. Leave this world smiling because you're personally proud. Empower yourself to do what you don't want to do. Discomfort is temporary. Despite how it feels, you'll build self-belief, and you'll be ready when future challenges erupt. You'll also build your willingness and mindset to face and tackle adversity.

Life is bound to be precarious with challenges along the way. How you choose to approach these moments is inevitably up to you. If you're hiking up a mountain and become tired and feel discouraged, do you descend downhill? No, you take a rest and reset, reconnect, and reinvest and forge ahead uphill toward the summit. This will be an ongoing process throughout your life.

Like a wound that heals with stronger scar tissue able to withstand more than your regular skin, you'll emerge stronger and more empowered to further improve your life.

You have not come this far to come this far. Keep moving forward. In Ryan Holiday's article, "Believing in yourself is overrated: There's a better way," he writes, "Believe in yourself! Fake it until you make it! The problem is that it's bulls*it. Great people don't have to believe in themselves. They don't have to fake anything. They have evidence."[184]

Perpetually fill that ACE bucket with things you do and opportunities you take to enhance your life. Those moments can be plentiful. Now, the choice is yours to ACE your life and unleash your best self and live the life you want.

ACKNOWLEDGMENTS

Deep gratitude goes to my loving family, Eric, Addison, Foster, Wyatt, and Cora. This book is a product of their everlasting devotion, care, and support.

Thank you to David Hancock, the Founder and CEO at Morgan James Publishing. You recognized the value in my work and appreciated the impact it has on helping others. I want to acknowledge Shannon Peters, Author Relations Manager, at Morgan James Publishing for answering my numerous questions happily and expeditiously.

Appreciation to Leslie Guccione for your continual editorial support and for your helpful suggestions. To Randee Paraskevopoulos, I appreciate your incredible talent in creating the graphics and for additionally helping with editing.

Thank you to Michael Ebeling, my literary agent. I appreciate your vision and for believing in me and the work that I do.

Much appreciation goes to my readers who offered their expertise, support, and guidance: Dr. Mark Banschick, Dr. Heather Maguire, Steven Farkas, Lori Ginsberg, Terry Klotz, and Kathy Brodmerkel. I'm grateful to my former student Sheri Mei and my former intern Maayan Aizenberg for their research input. Much thanks to Jack Nathan Richards for your social media and marketing expertise.

I especially want to acknowledge and thank Dr. Steven C. Hayes, Dr. Aaron T. Beck, Dr. Judith S. Beck, Dr. Marci G. Fox, Dr. Francine Shapiro, Dr. Lisa Salvi and Pema Chödrön who have greatly influenced my clinical practice.

Finally, I want to express gratitude to my patients, students, friends, and colleagues who continue to feed my passions and inspiration. You profoundly influence my writing, my practice, and my life.

I have the benefit of having a career that I truly love. Every day I get to learn something new, get deeply emotionally moved, and witness incredible transformations. I consider these gifts which I'm eternally grateful for.

Mindfulness Resources

- *Radical Acceptance: Embracing Your Life with the Heart of a Buddha*, by Tara Brach
- *Radical Compassion: Learning to Love Yourself and Your World with the Practice of RAIN*, by Tara Brach
- *How to Meditate: A Practical Guide to Making Friends with Your Mind*, by Pema Chödrön
- *When Things Fall Apart: Heart Advice for Difficult Times*, by Pema Chödrön
- *Mindfulness in Plain English*, by Bhante Henepola Gunaratana
- *The Miracle of Mindfulness: The Classic Guide to Meditation by The World's Most Revered Master*, by Thich Nhat Hanh
- *10% Happier: How I Tamed the Voice in My Head, Reduced Stress Without Losing My Edge and Found Self-Help That Actually Works. A True Story*, by Dan Harris
- *Peak Mind: Find Your Focus, Own Your Attention, Invest 12 Minutes a Day*, by Amishi P. Jha
- *Self-Compassion: The Proven Power of Being Kind to Yourself*, by Kristin Neff
- *Real Change: Mindfulness to Heal Ourselves and the World*, by Sharon Salzberg
- *Think Like a Monk: The Secret of How to Harness the Power of Positivity and Be Happy Now*, by Jay Shetty
- *Aware: The Science and Practice of Presence, The Groundbreaking Meditation*, by Daniel Siegel

- *Practicing Mindfulness: 75 Essential Meditations to Reduce Stress, Improve Mental Health, and Find Peace in the Everyday*, by Matthew Sockolov
- *The Power of Now: A Guide to Spiritual Enlightenment*, by Eckhart Tolle
- *Book Of Joy*, by Desmond Tutu and the Dalai Lama
- *Mindfulness: An Eight-Week Plan for Finding Peace in a Frantic World*, by Mark Williams and Danny Penman
- *Full Catastrophe Living: Using the Wisdom of Your Body and Mind to Face Stress, Pain and Illness*, by Jon Kabat-Zinn
- *Mindfulness for Beginners: Reclaiming the Present Moment—and Your Life*, by Jon Kabat-Zinn

ABOUT THE AUTHOR

Michelle P. Maidenberg, Ph.D., MPH, LCSW-R maintains a private practice in Harrison, NY. She is the Co-Founder and Clinical Director of "Thru My Eyes", a non-profit 501c3 organization that offers free clinically guided videotaping to chronically medically ill individuals who want to leave video legacies for their children and loved ones. She is also adjunct faculty at New York University teaching a graduate course in Mindfulness Practice.

Dr. Maidenberg is a Board of Directors member at The Boys & Girls in Mount Vernon. She is a member of the American Red Cross Crisis Team and serves on the Board of Directors of the Westchester Trauma Network (WTN) in Westchester NY.

She is a Certified Group Therapist through the American Group Psychotherapy Association and a Diplomate and certified member of the Academy of Cognitive Therapy. She has advanced training in Cognitive-Behavioral Therapy (CBT), Acceptance and Commitment Therapy (ACT), Structural Family Therapy, Mindfulness, and is a Level II trained Eye Movement Desensitization Reprocessing (EMDR) therapist.

Dr. Maidenberg is the author of the book *Free Your Child from Overeating: 53 Mind-Body Strategies for Lifelong Health*. She is a blogger for *Psychology Today* and is a contributing editor of GROUP, the journal of the Eastern Group Psychotherapy Society. She is dedicated and invested in health and mental health advocacy. She lives in Southern Westchester, NY with her husband, four children and four dogs. www.michellemaidenberg.com

NOTES

Introduction:

1   Thru My Eyes Foundation. www.thrumyeyes.org.

2   Maidenberg, M. (2016). *Free your child from overeating: A handbook for helping kids and teens. 53 mind-body strategies for lifelong health.* NY: The Experiment.

3   Seltzer, L. F. (2008). The path to unconditional self-acceptance. *Psychology Today.* Retrieved from https://www.psychologytoday.com/us/blog/evolution-the-self/200809/the-path-unconditional-self-acceptance.

4   Neff, K. (2021). Definition of self-compassion. Retrieved from: https://self-compassion.org/the-three-elements-of-self-compassion-2/.

Chapter 1:

5   Hayes, S.C. (2014). Get out of your mind: Transforming your life through acceptance, mindfulness, and values. *Psychology Today*, February 19, 2012.

6   Tseng, J., and Poppenk, J. (2020). Brain meta-state transitions demarcate thoughts across task contexts exposing the mental noise of trait neuroticism. *Nat Commun*, 11, 3480. https://doi.org/10.1038/s41467-020-17255-9.

7   Lewis, R. (2019). What actually is a thought? And how is information physical? Thoughts are physical representations or maps. They have shape and weight. *Psychology Today.* https://www.psychologytoday.com/us/blog/finding-purpose/201902/what-actually-is-thought-and-how-is-information-physical. February 24, 2019.

8   Brewin C. R. (2011). The nature and significance of memory disturbance in posttraumatic stress disorder. *Annual Review of Clinical Psychology.* 7, 203–227.

9   Vytal K, and Hamann S. (2010). Neuroimaging support for discrete neural correlates of basic emotions: A voxel-based meta-analysis. *J Cogn Neurosci,* 22(12), 2864-85. doi: 10.1162/jocn.2009.21366. PMID: 19929758.

10   Leahy, R. L. (2006). *The worry cure: Seven steps to stop worry from stopping you.* Harmony Books: New York, NY.

11   Brown, K.W., and Ryan, R.M. (2003). The benefits of being present: Mindfulness and its role in psychological well-being. *Journal of Personality and Social Psychology*, 84(4), 822–48.

Hölzel, B. K, Carmody, J., Vangel, M., et al. (2011). Mindfulness practice leads to increases in regional brain gray matter density. *Psychiatry Research,* 191(1), 36–43.

Hutcherson, C., Seppala, E. M., and Gross, J. J., et al. (2008). Loving-kindness meditation increases social connectedness. *Emotion*, 8(5), 720–24.

Greeson, J. M. (2008). Mindfulness research update: 2008. *Complementary Health Practice Review*, 14(1), 10–18.

Grossman, P., Tiefenthaler-Gilmer, U., Raysz, A., and Kesper, U. (2007). Mindfulness training as an intervention for Fibromyalgia: Evidence of postintervention and 3-year follow-up benefits in well-being. *Psychotherapy and Psychosomatics*, 76, 226–33.

Grossman, P., Niemann, L., Schmidt, S., and Walach, H. (2004). Mindfulness-Based Stress Reduction and health benefits: A meta-analysis. *Journal of Psychosomatic Research*, 57(1), 35–43.

Kabat-Zinn, J. (1990). *Full catastrophe living: Using the wisdom of your body and mind to face stress, pain, and illness.* New York: Delacorte.

Kabat-Zinn, J., Lipworth, L., and Burney, R. (1985). The clinical use of mindfulness meditation for the self-regulation of chronic pain. *Journal of Behavioral Medicine*, 8(2), 163–90.

Kristeller, J. L., and Hallett, C. B. (1999). An exploratory study of a meditation-based intervention for Binge Eating Disorder. *Journal of Health Psychology*, 4(3), 357–63.

Keng, S. L., Smoski, M. J., & Robins, C. J. (2011). Effects of mindfulness on psychological health: a review of empirical studies. *Clinical Psychology Review*, *31*(6), 1041–1056. https://doi.org/10.1016/j.cpr.2011.04.006.

Lazar, S. W., Kerr, C. E., Wasserman, R. H., et al. (2005). Meditation experience is associated with increased Cortical thickness. *NeuroReport*,

16(17), 1893–97.

Miller, J. J., Fletcher, K., and Kabat-Zinn, J. (1995). Three-year follow-up and clinical implications of a Mindfulness-Based Stress Reduction intervention in the treatment of Anxiety Disorders. *General Hospital Psychiatry*, 17(3), 192–200.

Schreiner, I., and Malcolm, J. P. (2008). The benefits of mindfulness meditation: Changes in emotional states of depression, anxiety, and stress. *Behaviour Change*, 25(3), 156–68.

Shapiro, D., Cook, I. A., Davydov, D. M., et al. (2007). Yoga as a complementary treatment of depression: Effects of raits and moods on treatment outcome. *Evidence-Based Complementary and Alternative Medicine*, 4(4), 493–502.

Teasdale, J., Segal, Z. V., Williams, J. M., et al. (2000). Prevention of relapse/recurrence in Major Depression by Mindfulness-Based Cognitive Therapy. *Journal of Counseling and Clinical Psychology*, 68(4), 615–23.

Zeidan, F., Johnson, S. K., Diamond, B. J., et al. (2010). Mindfulness meditation improves cognition: Evidence of brief mental training. *Consciousness and Cognition*, 19(2), 597–605.

12   Brach, T. (2018). Tara Talks: Pain x Resistance = Suffering. https://youtu.be/3JywTh5O8ys.

13   Maidenberg, M. (2021). 6 tips for making difficult decisions: Challenging decisions often pit our core values against each other. *Psychology Today*. March 16, 2021. https://www.psychologytoday.com/us/blog/being-your-best-self/202103/6-tips-making-difficult-decisions.

14   Burns, D. D. (2020). *Feeling great: The revolutionary new treatment for depression and anxiety*. Eau Claire, WI: PESI Publishing & Media.

15   Forsyth, J. P. and Eifert, G. H. (2007). *The Mindfulness and Acceptance workbook for anxiety: A guide to breaking free from anxiety, phobias & worry using Acceptance & Commitment Therapy*. New Harbinger: Oakland, CA.

16   Delistraty, C. You'll be happier if you let yourself feel bad. *The Uncut*. August 28, 2017. https://www.thecut.com/2017/08/youll-be-happier-if-you-let-yourself-feel-bad.html.

17   Ciesla J. A., Reilly L. C., Dickson K.S., Emanuel A.S., and Updegraff J. A. (2012). Dispositional mindfulness moderates the effects of stress

among adolescents: Rumination as a mediator. *J Clin Child Adolesc Psychol.* 2012;41(6):760-70. doi: 10.1080/15374416.2012.698724.

18   Masedo A. I., and Rosa Esteve M. (2007). Effects of suppression, acceptance and spontaneous coping on pain tolerance, pain intensity and distress. *Behav Res Ther.* Feb;45(2):199-209. doi: 10.1016/j.brat.2006.02.006.

19   Mitmansgruber, H., Beck, T., Höfer, S. & Schüßler, G. (2009). When you don't like what you feel: Experiential avoidance, mindfulness and meta-emotion in emotion regulation. *Personality and Individual Differences.* .46. 448-453. 10.1016/j.paid.2008.11.013.

20   Kabat-Zinn, J. (1994). *Wherever you go, there you are: Mindfulness meditation in everyday life.* New York: Hyperion. p. 4.

21   Davis, D. M., and Hayes, J. A. (2011). What are the benefits of mindfulness? A practice review of psychotherapy-related research." *Psychotherapy,* 48(2), 198–208.

22   Pickert, K. (2014). The art of being mindful: Finding peace in a stressed-out, digitally dependent culture may just be a matter of thinking differently. *Time,* February 3, 2014.

23   Ackerman, C. E. (2021). 23 amazing health benefits of mindfulness for body and brain. PositivePsychology.com. https://positivepsychology.com/benefits-of-mindfulness/#:~:text=%20To%20recap%2C%20 this%20article%20included%20numerous%20potential,and%20rumination%3B%205%20Enhanced%20job%20performance%3B%20 More%20.

24   Stoddard, J. A., and Afari, N. (2014). *The Big Book of ACT Metaphors: A Practitioner's Guide to Experiential Exercises and Metaphors in Acceptance and Commitment Therapy.* Oakland, CA: New Harbinger Publications.

25   Mayo Clinic (2013). Mindfulness: Learning to live in the moment. Special Report, Supplement to *Mayo Clinic Health Letter,* October 2013.

26   Winona University. (2021). Grounding: Create personal calm. Retrieved from: https://www.winona.edu/resilience/Media/Grounding-Worksheet.pdf.

27   Healthline. (2021). 10 breathing techniques for stress relief and more. Retrieved from: https://www.healthline.com/health/breathing-exercise.

28   Maidenberg, M. (2021, November 20). Michelle Maidenberg: Circum-
      venting Emotional Avoidance. Retrieved from: https://www.ted.com/
      talks/michelle_maidenberg_circumventing_emotional_avoidance.

Chapter 2:

29   Selig, M. (2018). 9 surprising superpowers of knowing your core values:
      Values help you live your truth as well as provide 9 other magical ben-
      efits. *Psychology Today*. Retrieved from: https://www.psychologytoday.
      com/us/blog/changepower/201811/9-surprising-superpowers-know-
      ing-your-core-values.

30   Harris, R. (2008). *The happiness trap: How to stop struggling and start liv-
      ing*. Boston, MA: Shambhala Publications.

31   Hayes, S. C. (2018). 10 signs you know what matters. Values are what
      bring distinction to your life. You don't find them, you choose them. And
      when you do, you're on the path to fulfillment. *Psychology Today*. Re-
      trieved from: https://www.psychologytoday.com/us/articles/201809/10-
      signs-you-know-what-matters.

32   Hayes, S. C., 2018.

33   Creswell J. D., Welch W. T., Taylor S. E., Sherman D. K., Gruenewald T.
      L., & Mann T. (2005). Affirmation of personal values buffers neuroendo-
      crine and psychological stress responses. Psychol Sci., 16(11), 846-851.
      doi:10.1111/j.1467-9280.2005.01624.x.

34   Allicock, M., Sandelowski, M., DeVellis, B., & Campbell, M. (2008).
      Variations in meanings of the personal core value "health". *Patient
      Education and Counseling*, 73(2), 347–353. https://doi.org/10.1016/j.
      pec.2008.07.029.

35   Creswell, D. J., Dutcher, J. M., Klein, W. M. P., Harris, P. R., & Levine,
      J. M. Self-affirmation improves problem-solving under stress. *PLoS ONE*,
      8(5): e62593 doi: 10.1371/journal.pone.0062593.

36   Parks, L. and Guay, R. P. (2009). Personality, values, and motivation.
      Personality and Individual Differences. 47, 675–684.

37   Iguisi, O. (2009). Motivation-related values across cultures. *African Jour-
      nal of Business Management*. 3(4), 141-150. http://www.academicjournals.
      org/AJBM.

38   Newberg, A. and Waldman, M. R. (2014). Words can change your brain. The Penguin Group: New York, NY. https://www.amazon.com/Words-Can-Change-Your- Brain/dp/1491512652.

39   Newberg, A. and Waldman, M. R. (2012). What is your deepest communication value? Reflect on this question before speaking and you'll build greater empathy. *Psychology Today*. Retrieved from: https://www.psychologytoday.com/us/blog/words-can-change-your-brain/201206/what-is-your-deepest-communication-value.

40   Fukuyama, M. A., & Greenfield, T. K. (1983). Dimensions of assertiveness in an Asian-American student population. *Journal of Counseling Psychology*, 30(3), 429– 432. https://doi.org/10.1037/0022-0167.30.3.429.

41   Boyer, L.O. (2018). Build your confidence by understanding your personal values. Retrieved from: https://medium.com/@LarryBoyer/build-your-confidence-by-understanding-your-personal-values-e5ee456eb7d5.

42   Hayes, S., 2018.

43   Hayes, S., 2018.

44   Harris, R. (2011). *The confidence gap: A guide to overcoming fear and self-doubt*. Durban, South Africa: Trumpeter Publishing.

45   Clear, J. (2021). Retrieved from: https://jamesclear.com/core-values.

46   Jeffrey, S. (2021). Core values list over 200 personal values to discover what's most important to you. Retrieved from: https://scottjeffrey.com/core-values-list/.

47   Life Values Inventory. Retrieved from: https://www.lifevaluesinventory.org/.

48   Harris, R. (2021). Acceptance and Commitment Therapy values card sort. Retrieved from: http://meetingpointcounseling.com/tools/ACT-card-sort/.

49   Stoddard, J. A., and Niloofar, A. (2014). *The big book of ACT metaphors: A practitioner's guide to experiential exercises and metaphors in Acceptance and Commitment Therapy*. Oakland, CA: New Harbinger Publications.

50   Pearson, A. N., Heffner, M., & Follette, V. M. (2010). *Acceptance and Commitment Therapy for body image dissatisfaction: A practitioner's guide to using mindfulness, acceptance, and values-based behavior change strategies.*

Oakland, CA: New Harbinger Publications.

51   LeJeune, J and Luoma, J. B. (2019). *Values in therapy: A clinician's guide to helping clients explore values, increase psychological flexibility & live a more meaningful life.* Context Press: Oakland, CA.

52   Stoddard, J. A. and Niloofar, A. (2014). *The big book of ACT metaphors: A practitioner's guide to experiential exercises and metaphors in Acceptance and Commitment Therapy.* Oakland, CA: New Harbinger Publishing.

53   Hayes, S. C., Strosahl, K. D, & Wilson, K. G. (2012). *Acceptance and Commitment Therapy: The process and practice of mindful change* (2nd ed.). New York: Guilford Press.

54   Cohen G. L., Garcia J., Apfel N., & Master A. (2006). Reducing the racial achievement gap: a social-psychological intervention. *Science,* 313(5791), 1307-1310. doi:10.1126/science.1128317.

55   Chase, J. A., Houmanfar, R., Steven C.Hayes, S. C., Ward, T. A., Plumb Vilardaga, J., & Follette, V. (2013). Values are not just goals: Online ACT-based values training adds to goal setting in improving undergraduate college student performance. *Journal of Contextual Behavioral Science,* 2(3-4), 79-84.

Chapter 3:

56   Seltzer, L. F. (2008). The path to unconditional self-acceptance. *Psychology Today.* Retrieved from https://www.psychologytoday.com/us/blog/evolution-the-self/200809/the-path-unconditional-self-acceptance.

57   Kabat-Zinn, J. (1994). *Wherever you go, there you are: Mindfulness meditation in everyday life.* New York: Hyperion. p. 4.

58   Fletcher, L., & Hayes, S. C. (2005). Relational frame theory, acceptance and commitment therapy, and a functional analytic definition of mindfulness. *J Rat-Emo Cognitive-Behav Ther*, 23, 315–336. https://doi.org/10.1007/s10942-005-0017-7.

59   Salzberg, S. (2017). *Real love: The art of mindful connection.* NY: Flatiron Books.

60   Angelou, M. (2009). *Letter to my daughter.* NY: Random House. https://www.amazon.com/Letter-My-Daughter-Maya-Angelou/dp/0812980034.

61   Linehan, M. (2014). *DBT skills training manual*, Second Edition. NY: The Guilford Press. https://www.amazon.com/DBT%C2%AE-Skills-Training-Manual-Second/dp/1462516998.

62   Brach, T. (2004). *Radical acceptance: Embracing your life with the heart of a Buddha*. NY: Random House Publishing Group. https://www.amazon.com/Radical-Acceptance-Embracing-Heart-Buddha/dp/0553380990/ref=sr_1_1?dchild=1&keywords=radical+accepting+tara+brach&qid=1626554485&sr=8-1.

63   Rogers, C. (2021). *Client-Centered Therapy: Its current practice, implications, and theory*. London, United Kingdom: Robinson Publishing. https://www.amazon.com/Client-Centered-Therapy-Current-Practice-Implications/dp/1841198404/ref=sr_1_4?dchild=1&keywords=carl+rogers&qid=1626554866&sr=8-4.

64   Jung, C. G. (2006). *The undiscovered self: The dilemma of the individual in modern society*. NY: Berkley Publishing. https://www.amazon.com/Undiscovered-Self-Dilemma-Individual-Society/dp/0451217322/ref=sr_1_1?dchild=1&keywords=carl+jung+undiscovered+self+dilemma&qid=1626555220&sr=8-1.

65   Hall, K. (2013). Three blocks to radical acceptance: Accepting reality means less emotional suffering in the long run. *Psychology Today*. Retrieved from https://www.psychologytoday.com/us/blog/pieces-mind/201312/three-blocks-radical-acceptance.

66   Rollin, J. The importance of practicing 'Radical Acceptance': Fighting against pain leads to suffering. *Psychology Today*. Retrieved from https://www.huffpost.com/entry/the-importance-of-practicing-radical-acceptance_b_592da801e4b0a7b7b469cd99.

67   Seltzer, L. F. (2008). The path to unconditional self-acceptance. *Psychology Today*. Retrieved from https://www.psychologytoday.com/us/blog/evolution-the-self/200809/the-path-unconditional-self-acceptance.

68   Chamberlain, J. M., & Haaga, D. A. F. (2001). Unconditional self-acceptance and psychological health. *Journal of Rational-Emotive & Cognitive-Behavior Therapy*, 19(3), 163–176. https://doi.org/10.1023/A:1011189416600.

69   Harris, R. (2008). *The happiness trap: How to stop struggling and start liv-*

ing. Boston: Trumpeter.

    Manson, M. (2012). Your two minds. markmanson.net, December 7, 2012.

70   Ramirez, D. (2021). Exploring the mind-body connection through research. *Positive Psychology*, 1-30-21. https://positivepsychology.com/mind-body-connection/.

71   Neff, K. D. (2016). The Self-Compassion Scale is a valid and theoretically coherent measure of self-compassion: Erratum. *Mindfulness, 7*(4), 1009. https://doi.org/10.1007/s12671-016-0560-6.

72   Perry, B. D., and Winfrey, O. (2021). What happened to you? Conversations on trauma, resilience, and healing. Flatiron Books: New York, NY.

73   Salzberg, S. (2017). *Real love: The art of mindful connection*. NY: Flatiron Books.

74   Davis, D. E., Ho, M. Y., Griffin, B. J., Bell, C., Hook, J. N., Van Tongeren, D. R., DeBlaere, C., Worthington, E. L., Jr., & Westbrook, C. J. (2015). Forgiving the self and physical and mental health correlates: A meta-analytic review. *Journal of Counseling Psychology, 62*(2), 329–335. https://doi.org/10.1037/cou0000063.

75   Sirois, F. M. (2014) Procrastination and stress: Exploring the role of self-compassion, *Self and Identity*, 13:2, 128-145, DOI: 10.1080/15298868.2013.763404.

76   McCroskey, J. C., Richmond, V. P., Daly, J. A., Falcione, R. L. (1977). Studies of the relationship between communication apprehension and self-esteem, *Human Communication Research*, 3(3), 269–277. https://doi.org/10.1111/j.1468-2958.1977.tb00525.x

    Neff, K. D., and Beretvas, S. N. (2013). The role of self-compassion in romantic relationships, *Self and Identity*, 12(1), 78-98, DOI: 10.1080/15298868.2011.639548.

77   Mackintosh, K., Power, K., Schwannauer, M., & Chan, S. (2018). The relationships between self-compassion, attachment and interpersonal problems in clinical patients with mixed anxiety and depression and emotional distress. *Mindfulness, 9*(3), 961–971. https://doi.org/10.1007/s12671-017-0835-6.

    Neff, K. D., and Beretvas, S. N. (2013). The role of self-compassion in romantic relationships, *Self and Identity*, 12(1), 78-98, DOI: 10.1080/15298868.2011.639548.

78   Pillay, S. (2016). Greater self-acceptance improves emotional well-being. *Harvard Health Blog*. Retrieved from https://www.health.harvard.edu/ blog/greater-self-acceptance-improves-emotional-well-201605169546.

79   Agroskin, D., Klackl, J., & Jonas, E. (2014). The self-liking brain: A VBM study on the structural substrate of self-esteem. *PloS one*, 9(1), e86430. Doi:10.1371/journal.pone.0086430.

80   University of Hertfordshire. (2014). Self-acceptance could be the key to a happier life, yet it's the happy habit many people practice the least. *ScienceDaily*. www.sciencedaily.com/releases/2014/03/140307111016.htm.

81   Clay, R. A. (2016). Don't cry over spilled milk: The research on why it's important to give yourself a break. *American Psychological Association*, 47(8), 70. Retrieved from https://www.apa.org/monitor/2016/09/ce-corner.

82   Neff, K. D., Kirkpatrick, K. L., & Rude, S. S. (2007). Self-compassion and adaptive psychological functioning, *Journal of Research in Personality*, 41(1), 139-154.
https://doi.org/10.1016/j.jrp.2006.03.004. https://self-compassion.org/ wp-content/uploads/publications/JRP.pdf.

83   Kuehner C, Huffziger S, & Liebsch K. (2009). Rumination, distraction and mindful self-focus: Effects on mood, dysfunctional attitudes and cortisol stress response. *Psychol Med*. 39(2), 219-28. doi: 10.1017/ S0033291708003553. Epub 2008 May 19. PMID: 18485265.

84   Chamberlain, J. M., and Haaga, D. A. F. (2001). Unconditional self-acceptance and psychological health. *Journal of Rational-Emotive & Cognitive-Behavior Therapy*, 19, 163–176. https://doi. org/10.1023/A:1011189416600.

85   Fadaee S. B., Beetham K. S., Howden E. J., Stanton T., Isbel N. M., & Coombes J. S. (2017). Oxidative stress is associated with decreased heart rate variability in patients with chronic kidney disease. *Redox Rep*, 22(5):197-204. doi: 10.1080/13510002.2016.1173326. Epub 2016 Apr 19. PMID: 27090392; PMCID: PMC6837656.

86   Jaworski, M. (2019). The negativity bias: Why the bad stuff sticks and

how to overcome it. Retrieved from: https://www.psycom.net/negativity-bias.

87   YouTube Video – Choose Beautiful. https://www.youtube.com/watch?v=W07P3i5Yaak.

88   YouTube Video – Dove Real Beauty Sketches – Extended Version. https://www.youtube.com/watch?v=Qxk0Xs69ioA.

89   YouTube Video – Our Common Fate. https://www.youtube.com/watch?v=s50wMyVjiXY.

90   Nass, C. and Yen, C. (2012). *The man who lied to his laptop: What we can learn about ourselves from our machines.* Carmel, IN: Current Publishing.

91   Tugend, A. (2012). Praise is fleeting, but brickbats we recall. Retrieved from: *New York Times.* https://www.nytimes.com/2012/03/24/your-money/why-people-remember-negative-events-more-than-positive-ones.html?_r=1.

92   David, S. (2016). *Emotional agility: Get unstuck, embrace change, and thrive in work and life.* NY: Avery Publishing.

93   Firestone, R. W. (2016). *Overcoming the destructive inner voice: True stories of therapy and transformation.* NY: Prometheus.

Chapter 4:

94   Chamberlain, J. and Haaga, D. (2001). Unconditional self-acceptance and psychological health. *Journal of Rational-Emotive and Cognitive-Behavior Therapy.* 19, 163-176. doi: 10.1023/A:1011189416600.

95   Chamberlain, J and Haaga, D. (2001). Unconditional self-acceptance questionnaire. Retrieved from: https://scales.arabpsychology.com/s/unconditional-self-acceptance-questionnaire-usaq/.

96   Grohol, J. (2016). 15 common defense mechanisms. *PsychCentral.* Retrieved from: https://psychcentral.com/lib/15-common-defense-mechanisms.

      Robbins, T. (2021). The top 10 defense mechanisms: How to spot self-defeating habits that are holding you back. Retrieved from: https://www.tonyrobbins.com/mind-meaning/10-common-defense-mechanisms/.

97   Bandura, A. (Ed.). (1995). *Self-efficacy in changing societies.* Cambridge:

UK: Cambridge University Press.

98 Cherry, K. (2020). Self-efficacy and why believing in yourself matters. *Very Well Mind*. Retrieved from: https://www.verywellmind.com/what-is-self-efficacy-2795954.

99 Head, R. (2019). Self-Efficacy and sports performance. *Sports Psychology Today*. Retrieved from: https://www.sportpsychologytoday.com/youth-sports-psychology/self-efficacy-and-sports-performance/.

100 Kim, J. (2019). 3 steps to worry less and overcome your negativity bias. Retrieved from: https://positivepsychology.com/3-steps-negativity-bias/.

Chapter 5:

101 Neff, K. (2021). Definition of self-compassion. Retrieved from: https://self-compassion.org/the-three-elements-of-self-compassion-2/.

102 Tirch, D. D. (2012). Compassionate-mind guide to overcoming anxiety: Using Compassion-Focused Therapy to calm worry, panic and fear. New Harbinger: Oakland, CA.

103 Neff, K. (2105). Self-Compassion Scale (SCS). Retrieved from: https://self-compassion.org/wp-content/uploads/2021/03/SCS-information.pdf.

104 Neff, K. Test how self-compassionate you are. Retrieved from: https://self-compassion.org/self-compassion.test/

105 Germer, C. K. and Neff, K. D. (2013). Self-compassion in clinical practice. *Journal of Clinical Psychology*. 69(8), 856–867. DOI: 10.1002/jclp.22021. https://self-compassion.org/wp-content/uploads/publications/germer.neff.pdf.

106 Neff, K. D. (2015). *Self-compassion: The proven power of being kind to yourself*. NY: William Morrow Paperbacks, HarperCollins Publishers. https://www.amazon.com/Self-Compassion-Proven-Power-Being-Yourself/dp/0061733520/ref=sr_1_3?crid=Y1DVE0NWKYMR&dchild=1&keywords=kristen+neff+compassion&qid=1628441766&sprefix=kristen+neff%2Caps%2C165&sr=8-3.

107 Neff, K. D. and Germer, C. (2018). *The mindful self-compassion workbook: A proven way to accept yourself, build inner strength, and thrive*. NY: Guilford Press. https://www.amazon.com/Mindful-Self-Compassion-Workbook-Yourself-Strength/dp/1462526780/

ref=sr_1_1?dchild=1&keywords=The+mindful+self-compassion+work-book%3A+A+proven+way+to+accept+yourself%2C+build+inner+strengt
h%2C+and+thrive.&qid=1628466097&sr=8-1.

108   Breines, J. G. and Chen, S. (2012). Self-compassion increases self-improvement motivation. *Personality and Social Psychology Bulletin.* 38, 9, 1133-1143. doi:10.1177/0146167212445599. https://journals.sagepub.com/doi/abs/10.1177/0146167212445599.

109   Neff, K. D., Rude, S. S., & Kirkpatrick, K. L. (2007). An examination of self-compassion in relation to positive psychological functioning and personality traits. *Journal of Research in Personality,* 41, 4, 908-916. https://doi.org/10.1016/j.jrp.2006.08.002.. https://www.sciencedirect.com/science/article/pii/S009265660600095X.

110   Neff, K. D. and Vonk, R. (2008). Self-compassion versus global self-esteem: Two different ways of relating to oneself. *Journal of Personality.* 77, 1, 23-50. https://doi.org/10.1111/j.1467-6494.2008.00537.x. https://onlinelibrary.wiley.com/doi/full/10.1111/j.1467-6494.2008.00537.x.

111   MacBeth, A. and Gumley, A. (2012). Exploring compassion: A meta-analysis of the association between self-compassion and psychopathology. *Clinical Psychology Review.* 32, 6, 545-552. https://doi.org/10.1016/j.cpr.2012.06.003. https://www.sciencedirect.com/science/article/pii/S027273581200092X.

112   Sirois, F. M. (2013). Procrastination and stress: Exploring the role of self-compassion. *Self and Identity.* 13, 2, 128-145. DOI: 10.1080/15298868.2013.763404. http://dx.doi.org/10.1080/15298868.2013.763404.

113   Neff, K. D. (2011). Self-compassion, self-esteem, and well-being. *Social and Personality Psychology Compass.* 5/1, 1–12, 10.1111/j.1751-9004.2010.00330.x. https://self-compassion.org/wp-content/uploads/2015/12/SC.SE_.Well-being.pdf

114   Mantelou, A. and Karakasidou, E. (2017). The effectiveness of a brief self-compassion intervention program on self-compassion, positive and negative affect, and life satisfaction. *Psychology.* 8, 4, 590-610. DOI: 10.4236/psych.2017.84038. https://www.scirp.org/journal/paperinformation.aspx?paperid=74938.

115   Neff, K. D. (2003). Development and validation of a scale to measure self-compassion. *Self and Identity*, 2, 223-250.

      Neff, K. D. Self-Compassion Scale. Retrieved from: https://self-compassion.org/wp-content/uploads/2015/06/Self_Compassion_Scale_for_researchers.pdf.

116   Tartakovsky, M. (2015). Nurture yourself: Accept yourself. Retrieved from: www.UrbanBalance.com, https://urbanbalance.com/nurture-yourself-accept-yourself/; https://deborahserani.com.

117   Ibid.

118   Neff, K. D. (2021). Why we need to have compassion for our inner critic. Retrieved from: https://self-compassion.org/why-we-need-to-have-compassion-for-our-inner-critic/.

119   Neff, K. D. and Davidson, O. (2016). Self-compassion: Embracing suffering with kindness. In I. Ivtzan & T. Lomas (Eds.), *Mindfulness in Positive Psychology* (pp. 37- 50). Rutledge. https://self-compassion.org/wp-content/uploads/2016/07/Neff-and- Davidson.2016.pdf.

120   Beck, A. T. (1963). Thinking and depression: Idiosyncratic content and cognitive distortions. *Archives of General Psychiatry*, 9, 324–33.

      Beck, A. T. (1964). Thinking and depression: Theory and therapy. *Archives of General Psychiatry*, 10, 561–71.

121   Adapted from Beck, J.S. (2008). *The Beck Diet Solution: Train your brain to think like a thin person.* Birmingham, AL: Oxmoor House.

Chapter 6:

122   Osmo, F., Duran, V., Wenzel, A., et al. (2018). The negative core beliefs inventory (NCBI): Development and psychometric properties. *Journal of Cognitive Psychotherapy*, 32, 1, 1-18. http://eprints.lincoln.ac.uk/id/eprint/31173/2/31173%20accepted%20JCP-32-1-00005_print.pdf.

123   Jung, C. (1975). *Psychology and religion: West and East* (The Collected Works of C. G. Jung, Volume 11) (Collected Works of C.G. Jung (50)). Princeton, NJ: Princeton University Press. p. 131. https://www.amazon.com/Psychology-Religion-West-Collected-Works/dp/0691097720/ref=sr_1_1?dchild=1&keywords=jung+carl+west+and+east&qid=1628445531&sr=8-1.

124   Jung, C. (1939). *The integration of personality*. NY: Farrar & Rinehart, Inc. https://www.amazon.com/Integration-Personality-Carl-G-Jung/dp/B0008569ZC.

125   The School of Life. (2017). How to be a friend to yourself. Retrieved from: https://www.youtube.com/watch?v=wFUxiIjp-Nk.

126   Maidenberg, M. (2020). 26 positive affirmations to empower you now: You always have choices. *Psychology Today* Blog. https://www.psychologytoday.com/us/blog/being-your-best-self/202011/26-positive-affirmations-empower-you-now.

Chapter 7:

127   Cattaneo, L. B. and Chapman, A. R. (2010). The process of empowerment: A model for use in research and practice. *American Psychologist*, 65,7, 646–659. https://www.researchgate.net/profile/Lauren-Cattaneo/publication/46576624_The_Process_of_Empowerment_A_Model_for_Use_in_Research_and_Practice/links/0912f50892f9a7090a000000/The-Process-of-Empowerment-A-Model-for-Use-in-Research-and-Practice.pdf.

128   Cheung, Y. W., Mok, B. H., & Cheung, T. S. (2005). Personal empowerment and life satisfaction among self-help group members in Hong Kong. *Small Group Research*, 36, 3, 354–377.

       Lawson, T. and Garrod, J. (2001). *Dictionary of sociology*. London: Fitzroy Dearborn.

       Lyons, M., Smots, C., & Stephens, A. (2001). Participation, empowerment and sustainability: (How) do the links work? *Urban Studies*, 38, 1233-1251.

       Simon, B. L. (1994). *The empowerment tradition in American social work: A history*. NY: Columbia University Press.

       Solomon, B. B. (1976). *Black empowerment: Social work in oppressed communities*. NY: Columbia University Press.

       Somerville, P. (1998). Empowerment through residence. *Housing Studies*, 13, 233-257.

129   Cheung, Y. W., Mok, B. H., & Cheung, T. S. (2005). Personal empowerment and life satisfaction among self-help group members in Hong Kong. *Small Group Research*, 36, 3, 354–377.

130 Winch, G. (2011). How to attain real personal empowerment. Retrieved from: https://www.psychologytoday.com/us/blog/the-squeaky-wheel/201101/how-attain-real-personal-empowerment.

131 Cattaneo, L. B. and Chapman, A. R. (2010). The process of empowerment: A model for use in research and practice. *American Psychologist*, 65,7, 646–659. https://www.researchgate.net/profile/Lauren-Cattaneo/publication/46576624_The_Process_of_Empowerment_A_Model_for_Use_in_Research_and_Practice/links/0912f50892f9a7090a000000/The-Process-of-Empowerment-A-Model-for-Use-in-Research-and-Practice.pdf.

Chandola, T., Kuper, H., Singh-Manoux, A., Bartley, M., & Marmot, M. (2004). The effect of control at home on CHD events in the White-hall II study: Gender differences in psychosocial domestic pathways to social inequalities in CHD. *Social Science & Medicine*, 58, 1501–1509.

Griffin, J. M., Fuhrer, R., Stansfeld, S. A., & Marmot, M. (2002). The importance of low control at work and home on depression and anxiety: Do these effects vary by gender and social class? *Social Science & Medicine*, 54(5), 783-98. DOI: 10.1016/s0277-9536(01)00109-5. PMID: 11999493.

Rodin, J. and Langer, E. J. (1977). Long-term effects of a control-relevant intervention with the institutionalized aged. *Journal of Personality and Social Psychology*, 35, 897–902.

Sue, D. W. (1978). Eliminating cultural oppression in counseling: Toward a general theory. *Journal of Counseling Psychology*, 25, 419–428.

132 Bakhshi, F., Shojaeizadeh, D., Sadeghi, R., Taghdisi, M. H., & Nedjat, S. (2017). The relationship between individual empowerment and health-promoting lifestyle among women NGOs in northern Iran. *Electronic physician*. 9(2), 3690–3698. https://doi.org/10.19082/3690.

133 Cattaneo, L. B. and Chapman, A. R. (2010). The process of empowerment: A model for use in research and practice. *American Psychologist*, 65(7), 646–659. https://www.researchgate.net/profile/Lauren-Cattaneo/publication/46576624_The_Process_of_Empowerment_A_Model_for_Use_in_Research_and_Practice/links/0912f50892f9a7090a000000/The-Process-of-Empowerment-A-Model-for-Use-in-Research-and-Practice.pdf.

134 Ibid.

135 Müller, T., Klein-Flügge, M.C., Manohar, S.G., et al. (2021). Neural and computational mechanisms of momentary fatigue and persistence in effort-based choice. *Nature Communications,* 12, 4593. https://doi.org/10.1038/s41467-021-24927-7.

136 G. Castegnetti, Zurita, M., & De Martino, B. (2021). How usefulness shapes neural representations during goal-directed behavior. *Science Advances,* 7(15), 1-13. DOI: 10.1126/sciadv.abd5363. https://advances.sciencemag.org/content/7/15/eabd5363.full.

137 Novak, J. M. (2019). 62 Self-limiting beliefs that block happiness and success believe and create. Retrieved from https://believeandcreate.com/62-beliefs-that-limit-your-happiness-and-success/.

138 Harris, R. (2009). *ACT made simple: An easy-to-read primer on Acceptance and Commitment Therapy.* Oakland, CA: New Harbinger Publications.

139 Ibid.

140 Williams, Y. (2016). Compensatory strategies: Definition & examples. *Study.com.* Retrieved from https://study.com/academy/lesson/compensatory-strategies-definition-examples.html.

141 Rogers C. R. (1964). Toward a modern approach to values: The valuing process in the mature person. *Journal of Abnormal and Social Psychology.* 68(2), 160–167.
     Rogers C. R. (1989). *On becoming a person: A therapist's view of psychotherapy.* NY: Houghton Mifflin. (Original work published 1961)

142 Dweck, C. (2006). *Mindset: The new psychology of success: How we can learn to fulfill our potential.* NY: Random House.
     Dweck, C. (2015). Carol Dweck Revisits the 'Growth Mindset'. [online] Education Week. Retrieved from: https://www.edweek.org/leadership/opinion-carol-dweck-revisits-the-growth-mindset/2015/09.

143 Meadows, M. (2015). *Confidence: how to overcome your limiting beliefs and achieve your goals.* Meadows Publishing.

144 Hoffman, D., Rask, C. U., & Frostholm, L. (2019). Chapter 7: Acceptance and Commitment Therapy for health anxiety. Erik Hedman-Lagerlöf (Eds.), *The Clinician's Guide to Treating Health Anxiety: Diagnosis, Mechanisms, and Effective Treatment (pp. 123 - 142).* Stockholm, Sweden. Academic Press.

145   Coutu, D. L. (2002). How resilience works: Confronted with life's hardships, some people snap, and others snap back. *Harvard Business Review.*
May 2002. https://static1.squarespace.com/static/5d1536ab4e50d-
c0001a5f6e6/t/5ed49a11d1fbb47d97587bbf/1590991378838/HBR.
Resilience03Couto.pdf.

Frankl, V. E. (2006). *Man's Search for Meaning.* Boston, MA: Beacon
Press.

Luthar, S., Crossman, E., & Small, P. (2015). Resilience and adversity.
Handbook of Child Psychology and Developmental Science, 3(7), 247-286.
doi: 10.1002/9781118963418.childpsy307. https://www.researchgate.
net/publication/286529886_Resilience_and_Adversity.

Vltelll, R. (2018). What makes us resilient? New research explores the
psychology of resilience. *Psychology Today.* Retrieved from: https://www.
psychologytoday.com/us/blog/media-spotlight/201804/what-makes-us-
resilient.

Zimmerman, E. (2020). What makes some people more resilient than
others: The very earliest days of our lives, and our closest relationships,
can offer clues about how we cope with adversity. *New York Times*, June
21, 2020.

146   Tedeschi, R. G. and Calhoun, L. G. (2004). Posttraumatic growth: Con-
ceptual foundations and empirical evidence. *Psychological Inquiry*, 15(1),
1-18. doi: 10.1207/s15327965pli1501_01.

Taku, K., Cann, A., Calhoun, L. G., & Tedeschi, R. G. (2008). The
factor structure of the posttraumatic growth inventory: A comparison of
five models using confirmatory factor analysis. *Journal of Traumatic Stress*,
21(2), 158-164. https://doi.org/10.1002/jts.20305.

147   Neo, P. (2020). What does it mean to have a "psychologically rich" life?
Mindbodygreen. Retrieved from: http://www.mindbodygreen.com/articles/
what-does-it-mean-to-have-psychologically-rich-life.

148   Oishi, S., and Westgate, E. C. (2021). A psychologically rich life: Beyond
happiness and meaning. Advance online publication. *Psychological Review.*
https://doi.org/10.1037/rev0000317.

149   Brady, A. (2019). 6 ways meditation can transcend limiting beliefs.
Chopra. Retrieved from: https://chopra.com/articles/6-ways-medita-

tion-can-transcend-limiting-beliefs.

150 Luoma, J. and Hayes, S. C. (2009). Cognitive defusion. In W. T.O Donohue & J. E. Fisher (Eds.), *Empirically supported techniques of cognitive behavioral therapy: A step-by-step guide for clinicians* (2nd ed., pp. 181 – 188). NY: Wiley & Sons.

151 Collis, R. (2011). Getting Clear About Values. Retrieved from: https://workingwithact.com/2011/03/26/getting-clear-about-values/.

   LeJeune, J. and Luoma, J. B. (2019). *Values in therapy: A clinician's guide to helping clients explore values, increase psychological flexibility, and live a more meaningful life.* Oakland, CA: Context Press.

152 Schenck, L. K. (2012). How to translate values into committed action. Retrieved from: https://www.mindfulnessmuse.com/acceptance-and-commitment-therapy/how-to-translate-values-into-committed-action.

Chapter 8:

153 Ayan, S. (2018). The brain's autopilot mechanism steers consciousness. *Scientific American*. Retrieved from: https://www.scientificamerican.com/article/the-brains-autopilot-mechanism-steers-consciousness/.

   Szegedy-Maszak, M. (2005). Mysteries of the mind: Is your unconscious making your everyday decisions? *US News*. Retrieved from: http://faculty.fortlewis.edu/burke_b/personality/Readings/AdaptiveUnconscious.pdf.

154 Duhigg, C. (2014). *The Power of Habit: Why We Do What We Do in Life and Business*. NY: Random House Trade Publishing.

155 Clear, J. (2018). *Atomic Habits: An Easy & Proven Way to Build Good Habits & Break Bad Ones*. NY: Avery Publishing.

156 Clear, J. (2021). How to start new habits that actually stick. Retrieved from: https://jamesclear.com/three-steps-habit-change.

157 Wise, R. (2004). Dopamine, learning and motivation. *Nat Rev Neurosci*, 5, 483–494. https://doi.org/10.1038/nrn1406.

158 Grodsten, F., Levine, R., Troy, L., et al. (1996). "Three-Year Follow-up of Participants in a Commercial Weight Loss Program: Can You Keep It Off?" *Archives of Internal Medicine*, 156(12), 1302.

   Neumark-Sztainer, D., Haines, J., Wall, M., & Eisenberg, M. E.

(2007). "Why Does Dieting Predict Weight Gain in Adolescents? Findings from Project EAT-II: A 5-Year Longitudinal Study." *Journal of the American Dietetic Association*, 107(3), 448–55.

159 LaRosa, J. (2020). $71 billion U.S. weight loss industry pivots to survive pandemic. *Marketdata Enterprises*. Retrieved from: https://blog.market-research.com/71-billion-u.s.-weight-loss-market-pivots-to-survive-pandemic.

160 MacMillian, A. (2011). After dieting, hormone changes may fuel weight regain. *CNN*. Retrieved from: https://www.cnn.com/2011/10/26/health/post-diet-weight-regain/index.html.

161 Gardner, B., et al. (2012). Making health habitual: the psychology of 'habit-formation' and general practice. *The British Journal of General Practice: The Journal of the Royal College of General Practitioners*, 62(605), 664-6. doi:10.3399/bjgp12X659466.

162 Psychology Today Staff. What is intrinsic motivation? *Psychology Today*. Retrieved from: https://www.psychologytoday.com/us/basics/motivation#-sources-of-motivation.

163 Gardner, B. (2015). A review and analysis of the use of 'habit' in understanding, predicting and influencing health-related behaviour. *Health Psychol Rev*, (3): 277–295. doi: 10.1080/17437199.2013.876238. https://www.ncbi.nlm.nih.gov/pmc/articles/PMC4566897/.

164 Wood, W. (2019). *Good habits, bad habits: The science of making positive changes that stick*. NY: Farrar, Straus and Giroux Publishing Company.

165 Groopman, J. (2019). Can brain science help us break bad habits? Studies suggest that relying on will power is hopeless. Instead, we must find strategies that don't require us to be strong. *The New Yorker*. October 28 Issue.

166 Brewer, J. (2015). A simple way to break a habit. YouTube. Retrieved from: https://www.ted.com/talks/judson_brewer_a_simple_way_to_break_a_bad_habit?referrer=playlist-talks_to_form_better_habits.

167 Phillippa, L., van Jaarsveld, C.H.M., Potts, H.W.W., & Wardle, J. (2010). How are habits formed: Modelling habit formation in the real world. *European Journal of Social Psychology*, 40(6), 998–1009.

168 Farnam Street. The science of habit formation and change. Retrieved from: https://fs.blog/2012/03/everything-you-need-to-know-about-hab-

its-the-science-of-habit-formation-and-change/.

169 McGonigal, K. (2013). *The willpower instinct: How self-control works, why it matters, and what you can do to get more of it.* NY: Avery Publishing.

170 Lino, C. (2021). The psychology of willpower: Training the brain for better decisions. Positive Psychology. Retrieved from: https://positivepsychology.com/psychology-of-willpower/.

171 Manson, M. (2016). *The subtle art of not giving a f*ck: A counterintuitive approach to living a good life.* NY: HarperCollins Publishers.
     Manson, M. (2021). The only way to be truly confident in yourself: Mark Manson explains how to break free from the 'confidence conundrum.' *Forge Medium.* Retrieved from: https://forge.medium.com/the-only-way-to-be-truly-confident-in-yourself-c5ddbfc6cf44.

172 Leahy, R. L. (2020). *Don't believe everything you feel: A CBT workbook to identify your emotional schemas and find freedom from anxiety and depression.* Oakland, CA: New Harbinger Publications.

173 Manson, M. (2021). The only way to be truly confident in yourself: Learning how to be confident presents a conundrum: How are you supposed to be confident when you have nothing to feel confident about? Retrieved from: https://markmanson.net/how-to-be-confident.

174 Psychology Today. (2021). Goal-setting skills test. Retrieved from: https://www.psychologytoday.com/us/tests/career/goal-setting-skills-test.

175 Bergland, C. (2021). The motivational perks of cultivating an underdog mindset: Conquering everyday molehills can feel like summiting Everest with this mindset. *Psychology Today.* Retrieved from: https://www.psychologytoday.com/us/blog/the-athletes-way/202104/the-motivational-perks-cultivating-underdog-mindset.

176 Baikie, K. and Wilhelm, K. (2005). Emotional and physical benefits of expressive writing. *Advances in Psychiatric Treatment.* 11(5), 338-346. doi:10.1192/apt.11.5.338.

177 Kaczmarek, L., Kashdan, T., Drążkowski, D., Enko, J. et al. (2015). Why do people prefer gratitude journaling over gratitude letters? The influence of individual differences in motivation and personality on web-based interventions. *Personality and Individual Differences.* 75, 1-6. doi: 10.1016/j.paid.2014.11.004.

178 Fight Song by Rachel Platten. Retrieved from YouTube: https://www.youtube.com/watch?v=xo1VInw-SKc.

179 Rise Up by Andra Day. Retrieved from YouTube: https://www.youtube.com/watch?v=lwgr_IMeEgA.

180 This Is Me on the Greatest Showman soundtrack. Retrieved from YouTube: https://www.youtube.com/watch?v=wEJd2RyGm8Q.

181 I Won't Back Down by Tom Petty. Retrieved from YouTube: https://www.youtube.com/watch?v=nvlTJrNJ5lA.

182 Love Myself by Hailee Steinfeld. Retrieved from YouTube: https://www.youtube.com/watch?v=bMpFmHSgC4Q.

183 (Girl) Power by Little Mix. Retrieved from YouTube: https://www.youtube.com/watch?v=Dw8B1q1tKgs.

Conclusion:

184 Holiday, R. (2021). Believing in yourself is overrated: There's a better way. *Forge Medium*. Retrieved from: https://forge.medium.com/believing-in-yourself-is-overrated-acf1d9bbc21b.

A free ebook edition is available with the purchase of this book.

To claim your free ebook edition:

1. Visit MorganJamesBOGO.com
2. Sign your name CLEARLY in the space
3. Complete the form and submit a photo of the entire copyright page
4. You or your friend can download the ebook to your preferred device

Print & Digital Together Forever.

Snap a photo   Free ebook   Read anywhere

CPSIA information can be obtained
at www.ICGtesting.com
Printed in the USA
JSHW022216090123
36001JS00001B/33